T5-AFO-360

Employment and Unemployment in the United States

Employment and Unemployment

IN THE UNITED STATES

A Study of the American Labor Force

SEYMOUR L. WOLFBEIN
Deputy Manpower Administrator, U.S. Department of Labor,
Office of Manpower, Automation, and Training;
and Adjunct Professor of Economics,
The American University, Washington, D.C.

SCIENCE RESEARCH ASSOCIATES, INC., Chicago

Library of Congress Catalog Card Number: 64-12588

To Mae

TABLE OF CONTENTS

Employment and Unemployment in the United States

INTRODUCTION

THIS VOLUME IS BASED ON THE AUTHOR'S EXPERIENCE IN SEVERAL FIELDS. FOR THE past fifteen years I have taught courses on the labor force at the American University in Washington, D.C., and the present book stems from the series of lectures and accompanying discussions which took place in a classroom situation. For many years I have also worked with vocational guidance and counseling personnel, especially at the secondary school level. This book reflects my experiences in this arena and what I think represents some of the major dimensions of information that ought to be part of the endowment of such personnel in advising young people on their career choices. I have also had the opportunity to meet with thousands of people in the trade union and management fields who work with these materials and I have tried to orient the presentation in this book to their needs and interests, too.

While these may seem to be disparate groups and interests, there is a very important and strong common denominator which ties them together. It is the need to appreciate and to understand the conceptual and technical ground rules that form the basis for information in this field, and the need to assess the substantive facts and forces that shape the current and future manpower picture. No matter from what point the student or practitioner moves, these are essential for operating effectively in this field.

This is why we begin, in Part I, with an intensive review of the development and current status of the definitions, concepts, and technical structure of the basic sources of information in the labor force field which, together, provide us with the facts and figures used in program and policy design.

With this kind of background, we move, in Part II, to a discussion of what these data show about the length and pattern of our working lives, the major trends, demographic and socioeconomic, that have operated in this country to affect labor force activity, and a look ahead to what is in store for us by 1970. Part III turns specifically to the events that have upended the job picture in the United States of America, and analyzes current and expected trends in the occupational and industrial deployment of the working population.

Since the beginning of its history this country has been on the move in response to the changing geography of job opportunities, and Part IV reviews the patterns of moving and migration that have prevailed in the recent past. Also included is a discussion of the responsiveness of the American labor force, in terms of turnover and occupational and job mobility, to variations in economic activity and the changing demands of business and industry.

We conclude, in Part V, with a consideration of a problem which was in the forefront of discussion at the genesis of modern labor force analysis in the 1930s and remains a ranking problem in our field—unemployment. In the context of announced government policy to maintain maximum employment, we review what are considered the basic causes of unemployment in the United States, our record in this respect during the period following World War II, a detailed examination of who and where the unemployed are, and how we fare in comparison with other countries of the world.

Since I have been part of the development of the labor force field and have been helped immeasurably by workers in that field for the past twenty years, I cannot possibly list individually all of those who had a determining influence on this book. Some are mentioned in the text, particularly in citations to their work. I will, however, take this occasion to note those who have seen me run the gauntlet of discussion and questions and anwers: the press corps before whom I performed for some years, my colleagues in the Labor Department, and my students at the American University and the University of Michigan.

SEYMOUR L. WOLFBEIN

PART ONE

Concepts and Measurements

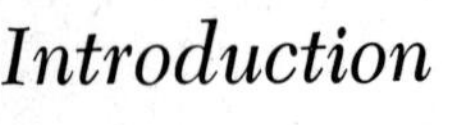

SUPPOSE THAT A QUARTER OF A CENTURY AGO—DURING THE LATE 1930s—SOMEone had said, "I would like to see the government collect some really reliable and meaningful information on employment and unemployment in the United States." What definitions should be used? What concepts should be employed? How should the government go about getting the information?

Actually, there would have been very little we could have done to help our inquirer. Despite almost a decade of very serious depression, with many millions of persons unemployed, we did not at that time have an organized, current, systematic governmental collection of this kind of information.

The result was inevitable: Many organizations made their own estimates of the numbers of unemployed and, as might be expected, their figures frequently differed from one another's by millions (see Table 1).

Since 1940 the U.S. government has had, in the *Monthly Report on the Labor Force* and allied programs, current statistics on the labor force, employment, and unemployment in our country. These figures are reported in the press monthly.

Employment and unemployment figures, since the depression of the 1930s, the Employment Act of 1946, and the different turns of the business cycle in the period after World War II, are news.

TABLE 1
Selected Estimates of Unemployment in the United States 1929–39 (In Thousands)

Year	Alexander Hamilton Institute	AFL	CIO	National Industrial Conference Board	Robert Nathan
1929	3,456	1,864	1,831	429	1,752
1930	6,929	4,734	4,710	2,896	4,646
1931	10,939	8,568	8,322	7,037	8,118
1932	14,728	12,870	12,120	11,385	11,639
1933	14,394	13,271	12,643	11,842	11,942
1934	12,419	11,424	10,845	9,761	9,998
1935	11,629	10,652	10,050	9,092	9,102
1936	10,008	9,395	8,756	7,386	7,723
1937	8,366	8,282	8,109	6,403	6,856
1938	11,934	10,836	11,030	9,796	9,865
1939	10,696	9,979	10,813	8,786	9,835

Source: "Labor Force Employment and Unemployment, 1929–39: Estimating Methods," *Monthly Labor Review,* July 1948.

At the same time the labor force itself has changed enormously in numbers, proportions of youth, older people, and married women. Concurrently there have been vast changes in the places where people work and what they do on the job under the impact of automation and technological advance, changing levels of living and patterns of consumption, population increases, and migration.

Part I of this study, consisting of Chapters 1 through 6, explains the concepts and procedures behind current labor force statistics. While a good deal of the subject is technical, it is essential, for intelligent discussion of employment, unemployment, and manpower policies, to understand the basis of the labor force statistics used today.

On an overall basis, the statistics most in use are those resulting from household enumeration, coming from responses to questions put by U.S. government interviewers to a carefully selected sample of the U.S. population.

The conceptual basis of the questions, the wording and sequence of the questions, the skill of the interviewer, and the soundness of the sampling method all enter into the results obtained. By changing the wording of one or two questions or by changing the time period involved, one could introduce large differences in the resulting statistics.

The U.S. Bureau of the Census, which conducts the enumerations, does an outstanding job. The concepts and questions have evolved after long and careful discussion by public officials and by experts in the labor force field, over a period of years. In general, these directly reflect a publicly felt response to the particular needs of the times. They are undoubtedly more accurate today than they were twenty-five years ago, and the outlook is for more improvements as we make advances in the art and science of gathering and analyzing this kind of information.

In the United States, as in most nations, there are three major sources of information on the labor force, employment, and unemployment. Each has its own methodology and techniques, advantages and limitations. Our assessment of what is happening in this field at any given time is based on information produced by these three sources: household enumeration, establishment reporting, and social-insurance statistics.

The first information source, *household enumeration,* is the most familiar. For example, every ten years the Census Bureau counts us all by sending a corps of enumerators to our places of residence—the classic example of household enumeration. The bureau also uses this procedure in collecting current monthly reports on the labor force, employment, and unemployment. Every month, Census Bureau enumerators sample respondents to classify the population as to labor force status (employed, unemployed, in the labor force, not in the labor force) in the *Monthly Report on the Labor Force* (MRLF).

The second procedure, *establishment reporting,* is the oldest source of information on employment. Here a schedule or form specially designed for this purpose is sent to the respondent, who returns the schedule with the requested information to the statistical agency for processing.

The employing entity—store, factory, mine, building construction project, bank, government agency—reports the number of people on its payroll, hours worked, and pay earned. Since passage of the

Fair Labor Standards Act of 1938, which regulates wages and hours, payrolls have improved enormously in accuracy and they represent an excellent source of important information.

The third source of labor force information, *social-insurance statistics,* is a by-product of social legislation. The U.S. unemployment insurance system provides benefits to eligible unemployed workers. The process of operating this system supplies such key figures as a weekly count of persons receiving unemployment insurance. Similar data are available on those making their initial claims for unemployment compensation—a good indication of new, developing unemployment. These data are also available in considerable geographic detail. This is not a sample count but a full-universe total.

Following is a description of these types of information, the government agencies collecting them and publishing the tabulations resulting therefrom, and the chapters of Part I of this book in which the resulting publications are discussed. Detailed references will be found in the list of readings following each chapter.

Labor Force Statistics

Household Enumeration

Decennial census information on employment. Conducted by U.S. Bureau of the Census and published with other decennial census information. Current labor force concepts used beginning with 1940 census. Since these figures report only on labor force status in April of the decennial years (1940-50-60), they do not provide current information. Data prior to 1940 have been adjusted to make them as comparable as possible with current concepts, and they provide the essential materials for analyzing the long-term changes in the American labor force. For each of the decennial years the census also provides a storehouse of invaluable information, not available elsewhere, on states, cities, even neighborhoods within cities, as well as detailed data on the occupational distribution of workers. (Chapters 1 and 4)

Monthly report on the labor force. Conducted monthly on a sample basis by Census Bureau; available 1940 to date; analyzed and published by the U.S. Department of Labor, Bureau of Labor Statistics, in the *Monthly Report on the Labor*

Force (MRLF), containing detailed current data on labor force, employment, and unemployment, by age, sex, color, marital status, duration of unemployment. (Chapters 1 and 3)

ESTABLISHMENT REPORTING

Employment and earnings reports of nonagricultural employment, dating mostly from 1919. Information collected from employers by cooperating state agencies, in most cases by employment security agencies. Issued monthly by the Bureau of Labor Statistics in *Employment and Earnings,* containing data on employment, hours of work, and earnings in considerable industrial detail, nationally and by states and areas. (Chapter 4)

Farm employment reports. Conducted by U.S. Department of Agriculture through its system of crop reporters, available from 1909. Published monthly by Statistical Reporting Service, Crop Reporting Board, as *Farm Labor,* containing information on family and hired farm employment, earnings, and some geographic detail. (Chapter 5)

SOCIAL-INSURANCE PROGRAMS

Complete current count of insured unemployment. Information collected by state employment security agencies, published weekly by the U.S. Department of Labor, Bureau of Employment Security; available from July 1945. Information provided by state, and for week ending nearest 15th of the month, for major labor market areas. *The Insured Unemployed,* issued monthly by the BES, also provides information on personal and economic characteristics of unemployment insurance claimants. (Chapter 6)

Data on covered employment under the federal unemployment insurance and old-age and survivors insurance systems. These are also available back to the beginnings of each system. Quarterly reports on OASI coverage issued by the Bureau of Old-Age and Survivors Insurance contain information on age and sex distribution of workers as well as a number of series on wages. (Chapter 6)

Area labor market trends. The Bureau of Employment Security publishes a monthly bulletin entitled *Area Labor Market Trends,* which classifies 150 major labor market areas according to their employment and unemployment status. Areas are graded on a scale, in use since May 1955, from A through D, E, and F, ranging from "areas of current overall labor shortage" to "areas of relatively substantial unemployment." Areas classified as D, E, or F may also be classified further as "areas of substantial and persistent unemployment." In addition, the BES classifies certain smaller areas as "smaller areas of substantial unemployment." Areas with substantial unemployment may qualify for certain government benefits relating to government contract awards, redevelopment-area assistance, and public-works and small-business loans. (Chapter 6)

These, then, are our main sources of information on the American labor market. We will now describe each one in turn and show how they are brought together to supply detailed information on the current status of the labor force, employment, and unemployment.

CHAPTER ONE

Toward a Labor Force Definition

THE PROBLEM INVOLVED IN GATHERING RELIABLE INFORMATION ON EMPLOYMENT and unemployment can be pointed up by asking: If you were an enumerator interviewing a household, what questions would you ask of whom in order to find out about employment and unemployment in that family?

The writer has posed the problem in this way to scores of classes and groups studying the American labor force. The answers were extremely varied, as we might expect—but in almost every instance, two recommendations were made:

1. That a question be asked concerning a person's *ability to work.*
2. That a question be asked concerning a person's *willingness to work.*

Certainly, most people say, no one should be counted as unemployed if he is unable or unwilling to work.

In proposing these two basic concepts—ability to work and willingness to work—our respondents followed precedents several hundred years old reflecting public attitudes toward the unemployed.

Criteria applied to determining who are the employed and who are the unemployed express basic social attitudes toward these groups. "Ability" and "willingness" to work have played a dominant role in the treatment of these individuals throughout history.

The English Experience

It is often useful to study another country's experience in assessing our own attitudes. Great Britain, for instance, had an unemployment problem well before our own country was first being settled. From the very beginning of her industrial development, "ability" and "willingness" to work played important roles in that country's attitudes toward the unemployed worker.

How British society's views of "ability" and "willingness" fluctuated with the times is excellently described by A.C.C. Hill, Jr., and Isador Lubin in *British Attack on Unemployment.*(1)

These authors point out how, in England, around the fifteenth century, the breakup of the feudal system and the enclosure for sheep raising of common fields squeezed large groups of men off the land and into the villages and cities. The great majority of these, propertyless and unskilled people, became what we would now label as unemployed.

Sir Thomas More in his *Utopia* described these unfortunate people, who "go aboute and worke not: whom no man wyl set a worke, though thei never so willyngly profre themselves thereto . . ." (note the word *willyngly*). In a generally unsympathetic society, they suffered increasingly severe punishment.

Hill and Lubin report that by the middle of the sixteenth century, it was not uncommon for such men to be branded on the shoulder with a *V* (for vagabond) and to be consigned to two years slavery to any who would have them. A first attempt to escape meant further branding, this time with an *S* on the cheek and slavery for life; a second attempt meant death. By 1600 the law stated that "all wandering persons and common laborers, being persons able in body that are found loitering" shall "be openly whipped" until "the body be bloody" (note the word *able*). Many of these men and their descendants were among the first settlers of the American colonies.

After 1600 and the time of the first Queen Elizabeth, British methods for dealing with persons out of work changed substantially. Every locality (parish) in England was charged with the responsibility of appointing overseers of the poor, with the power to assess and collect a levy from local residents for relief of the poor. Thousands of persons were supported with food, lodging, and allowances from these "parish rates."

Soon after a report by a Royal Commission on the Poor Laws (1832–34), this system for the subsidization of the destitute unemployed was replaced with a new policy of so-called deterrence—putting as many obstacles as possible in the way of the unemployed. One not only had to admit that he was a pauper but also suffered disenfranchisement and had to go to a workhouse in order to get relief. The assumption was that most of the people who were unemployed were idle by choice, and that these deterrents would make them prefer a job to idleness.

Unemployment Related to Business Cycle

Factors such as the consequences of the Industrial Revolution in Great Britain, the major depression in the Lancashire cotton textile industry in 1861–62, and the widespread joblessness from 1884 to 1886 indicated that fluctuations in overall economic conditions often seemed to be decisive in determining employment and unemployment. More and more public, private, and trade union practices grew up to take care of the unemployed.

By the early twentieth century this policy of deterrence was in serious question and a new Royal Commission on the Poor Laws was appointed in 1905 and made its report in 1909. Both the majority and the minority of the commission agreed that the existing approach had to be altered drastically, and that a national system of employment exchanges and unemployment insurance be inaugurated.

The minority report was prepared by Sidney and Beatrice Webb. It stressed particularly that unemployment was *not* a personal problem related to ability or willingness to work, but rather that it was a problem involved with the ebb and flow of business activity.

In 1909 there also appeared a book by William Beveridge, later

Sir William, one of England's foremost social insurance economists. The book, *Unemployment: A Problem of Industry,* also held that unemployment, rather than being a personal problem, was related to alternations in economic activity.

Beveridge pointed to the obvious example of workers in the construction industry. During the summer they work; during the winter, when building sites are shut down by bad weather, they are out of a job. Is there some seasonal variability in their ability or willingness to work? Or is it a problem substantially beyond the control of the employer and employee?

From the era preceding World War I, in England as well as in other industrialized nations, including our own, the problem of employment and unemployment has increasingly focused on economic events relating to the labor market. Since then there has been wide-scale adoption of social insurance, programs of training and retraining, public employment offices, and a whole spectrum of programs aimed at the effects of sudden downturns in the business cycle, as well as accelerations and the achievement of high levels of economic growth.

"Ability" and "Willingness" in Current Use

The principles of ability and willingness to work are still very much a part of the U.S. concept of employment and unemployment.

In the Employment Act of 1946 the Congress declared "that it is the continuing policy and responsibility of the Federal Government to use all practicable means . . . to coordinate and utilize all its plans, functions and resources for the purpose of creating and maintaining . . . conditions under which there will be afforded useful employment opportunities . . . *for those able, willing and seeking to work* [italics ours] and to promote maximum employment, production and purchasing power."

In addition, under state unemployment insurance systems, a person must be available for work in order to receive unemployment benefits. Not being able to work renders a person ineligible for these benefits. Similarly, a person unwilling to accept a job offer at his accustomed skill level and rate of pay also becomes ineligible.

These principles, however, are today seen within the context of overriding economic phenomena—trade cycle, automation, technological change, business failures and mergers, depletion of resources, and geographic variations in employment opportunities.

Against this brief background, it will come as no surprise to find that most of the unemployment surveys made in the United States before 1940 used the concepts of ability and willingness to work as devices for sorting out the unemployed. In other words, a person was enumerated as unemployed principally on the basis of the fact that he did not have a job but was able and willing to work.

Dr. John N. Webb, who pioneered in the development of the different concepts now in use, in the late 1930s examined forty surveys of unemployment conducted between 1929 and 1937. Thirty-five used the concepts of ability and willingness to work, singly or in combination. Of the remaining five, four used an allied concept of the "gainful worker."(2)

The Gainful Worker Concept

Before 1940 all figures on the U.S. labor supply, occupations, and unemployment in our decennial censuses were based on the so-called gainful worker concept.

The major purpose of the gainful worker concept was not to enumerate unemployed persons but to obtain occupational data. Census enumerators recorded the occupation of every person ten or more years of age who said that he or she followed an occupation in which money or its equivalent was earned. A gainful worker was one who reported a gainful occupation. No time reference was given and therefore the returns often included persons who considered themselves *usually* gainfully occupied. Many retired persons, for example, returned themselves as gainful workers, while some with temporary part-time jobs reported themselves as students or homemakers. A brand-new worker seeking his first job was not considered a gainful worker, not having yet had a chance to follow an occupation. What was absent, of course, was explicit reference to an *activity at some given period of time.*

The gainful worker concept had no reference to unemployment. Because of the growing importance of unemployment, the 1930 decennial census did attempt to adapt the concept by giving the following instructions to the enumerators:

> "Persons (i.e., gainful workers) will be found who have been long unemployed because of a change in industry, the

> introduction of machines, or the decline of production in certain lines. If *able and willing* to do work of any kind, these persons should be returned as usually working at a gainful occupation, without regard to the length of the period of idleness, provided *they still expect* to find employment and resume work" [italics ours]. (3)

The census then went on to sort out various unemployment groups (seven unemployment classes, to be exact), but, as can be seen from the above excerpt from the detailed instructions, the criteria were still without any time reference and the groupings were based upon the previously discussed, subjectively determined concepts of ability, willingness, and expectation.

"Ability" and "Willingness" Reconsidered

The problem with the "able" and "willing" concepts, stipulating their validity and relevance to the definition of unemployment, was found to be in their precise definition. How is one to define ability to work? How is such a definition or determination to be made by an enumerator in the field? This writer's past personal experience in enumerating hundreds of households throughout the country is that virtually every individual reports himself able to work. We have interviewed persons in the terminal stages of cancer who insisted they were *able* and *could* do some work. Under certain conditions, they might be perfectly right.

During the depression, when jobs were at a premium, thousands of persons with physical disabilities found it just about impossible to find employment. A few years later, when workers were at a premium, these handicapped workers were employed in defense industries. Ability to work turns out to be a subjective matter varying with the person or with the business cycle.

Much the same can be said for "willingness to work." Again, virtually everyone reports himself as willing to work. The writer's opinion is that these are usually perfectly honest and sincere answers. The problem is that again this is a subjective matter, almost impossible to assess by an enumerator and obviously related to such complex factors as where the job might be, work hours, and pay.

In the next chapter we shall see how current labor force surveys employ an "activity" concept.

A Labor Force Distribution of the Population

Let us now refer to Table 2-1 in Chapter 2 and examine a recent labor force enumeration.

There were, according to Table 2-1, about 187 million human beings in the United States in August 1962. Of these, about 130 million were fourteen years of age and over and were not in institutions (prisons, mental institutions, and the like). On that date there were about 70 million persons employed, nearly 4 million unemployed, and about 54 million not in the civilian labor force (nonworking students, nonworking housewives, and others).

How did we reach these figures? The next several chapters will tell some of the problems involved in this kind of operation and will describe the decisions that have been made in trying to solve these problems.

Here we might say that a few changes in our conceptual framework or in the specific questions asked respondents in the *Monthly Report on the Labor Force* could change the totals by millions. Hence it is extremely important in any discussion of employment or unemployment to understand what government statistics mean when they say that a person is

> in the labor force,
> not in the labor force,
> employed, or
> unemployed.

Reference Notes

1. Washington, D.C.: The Brookings Institution, 1934.
2. John N. Webb, "Concepts Used in Unemployment Surveys," *Journal of the American Statistical Association*, Vol. 34 (March 1939), pp. 49–59.
3. *Instructions to Enumerators, Population and Agriculture, Revised* (15th Census of the United States), p. 43.

Readings

The early evolution of U.S. labor force concepts is described by John D. Durand in

DUCOFF, LOUIS J., and HAGOOD, MARGARET J. *Labor Force Definition and Measurement.* (Social Science Research Council Bulletin No. 56.) New York: the Council, 1947.

CHAPTER TWO

The Labor Force Defined

WE HAVE DISCUSSED ATTITUDES TOWARD EMPLOYMENT AND UNEMPLOYMENT, including the definition of an unemployed person as one who is willing and able to work but has no job.

As we have seen, the "willing" and "able" doctrine continues in our thinking and legislation today—including the Employment Act of 1946.

"Willingness" and "ability" to work, however, though certainly desirable as personal attributes, are difficult to establish when one is conducting an enumeration of the labor force. How, then, shall we sort out our population into the different labor force and nonlabor force categories?

In 1939 John N. Webb, to whom reference has been made, reported on a study carried out in the Work Projects Administration, on the basis of which he proposed using the concept of "activity" in surveys of employment and unemployment. (1) He proposed that a person working be counted as employed and a person seeking work be counted as unemployed and said:

> "Like 'working,' 'seeking work' is an activity that can be reported in terms of what the individual is doing at the time of the inquiry. It does not depend on a judgment by the respondent, and it can readily be phrased in neutral terms. Moreover, it meets the test of applicability in the determination of unemployment at a particular point in time more closely than any of the other concepts.
>
> "Unemployment measured by means of 'seeking work' distinguishes the unabsorbed portion of the actual labor supply in the sense used by the economist in analyzing the supply of, and the demand for, workers.
>
> "The objectivity of this procedure arises out of the single fact that it reports what the worker is *doing* within a particular unit of time." (2)

The Activity Concept

These proposals became the basis of current labor force surveys, which utilize questions about the activity of the respondent. An individual at work during the time of reference is employed; a person actively seeking work is enumerated as unemployed.

The "activity" concept obviates the problem of whether a person is "willing" or "able." (It does not eliminate the concepts themselves; willingness and ability are demonstrated objectively by what a person is actually doing—working, or seeking or not seeking a job.) No direct inquiry is made about an individual's ability or willingness to work. Being at work classifies him as employed, seeking work as unemployed.

Actively seeking work can take place in a number of ways, such as registering at an employment office, meeting with a prospective employer, answering a want ad, going down to the factory gate. Any of these activities classifies the person as unemployed.

For most cases the activity criterion turns out to be an effective, objective sorter for judging a person's employment status. The relation of people to the labor market, however, is extraordinarily complex, and no classification system can settle each situation in an unequivocal manner. For example, at the time of enumeration many persons may be neither at work nor actively seeking work (sick, on vacation, and the like). What shall we do about them? Let us discuss some typical problems of classification, with examples that illustrate some of the decisions that have to be made.

The Economically Active

In current procedures, civilian labor force activities are conceived as involving only those which result in the production and exchange of goods and services. The labor force, thus conceived, is a group infinitely varied—including men, women, teen-age youth, the elderly, unskilled laborers, skilled craftsmen, farmers, miners, scientists, full-time workers, part-time workers, employed, and unemployed.

What differentiates this group from the rest of the population is its activities involving work or looking for work. The work, in turn, involves remuneration—pay or profit for the production of marketable goods or services. This means that the labor force excludes housewives who may also produce goods and services, but not for the market, and nonworking students who are in the process of preparing themselves for their future labor market activities.

Time Reference: The Survey Week

Our basic formula is still not completed—to measure activity, we must have in mind some definite period of time. Shall our questions concerning work or seeking work refer to a day? a week? a month? In the United States, current procedures for gathering labor force information employ a time period of one week. Specifically, it is the week in each month that contains the 12th of that month. (3) All current labor force information is based on people's activities during one specified week's time.

The choice of the one-week survey period reflects the need for a period short enough to give a person's current status; it is also short enough to be easily recalled. On the other hand, too short a time period, such as a day, might involve problems—for instance, the survey day might fall on a holiday.

In summary, the monthly data that are regularly published refer to a specific week's information for each month, and "annual average" data are similarly based upon twelve one-week observations.

We have established, then, that current labor force data have three conceptual dimensions. The factors that differentiate members of the working population are

(1) their activities (not such subjective matters as ability or willingness to work)
(2) in the labor market, where they produce goods or services for remuneration (thus not including such activities as family housework)
(3) during a specific period of time—the week of each month containing the 12th.

Basic Categories of the U.S. Population

Let us now apply our three-dimensional concept (activity—in relation to labor market—as of a given time) and see how it works.

The Active Employed

For the great majority of our working population the situation is quite unequivocal. They are found to be at work during the survey week and are classified as employed. They meet our definition squarely. It should be noted that *one hour* of work during the survey week is sufficient to classify a person as *at work*, and therefore employed. Thus part-time, full-time, temporary, and regular year-round work all count.

We have said that persons are counted as employed if they are working for pay or profit or their equivalent. There is a group of unpaid persons, however, who fall into categories such as these:

A-B is sixteen years old and goes to school. He has no paid job, but does help in his father's grocery store for about twenty hours during the week.

C-D is twenty-six years old, a housewife and mother of two. She also has no paid job, but for two eight-hour days at the beginning and end of each week (Mondays and Saturdays) she helps in her husband's new dental office.

Strictly speaking, these two do not meet one part of our definition. But both are counted as employed. They are called *unpaid family workers*. Into this category go all persons who work without pay for fifteen or more hours in an enterprise owned by a person to whom they are related by blood or marriage. (Note that here we talk of fifteen hours per week—not one hour.) The rationale here, of course, is that they definitely fill a manpower need, actually fill a slot that would involve another worker if they were not available. That this is a hard practical fact is shown by the particularly significant manpower contribution they make in agriculture and retail trade.

The Inactive Employed

How about the following cases?

E-F reports that he was neither working nor seeking work. He was on vacation during the survey week.

G-H reports that she has been working for years, but during the survey week she was out, in bed with a bad case of grippe.

I-J reports that he spent all week on the picket line. Yes, he has a job, but he, as well as the other workers, was on strike during the survey week.

K-L reports he is a carpenter on a big building project that has been under way for seven months. But heavy snows kept the project shut down during all of the survey week.

M-N also reports he has been and is a steady jobholder. During the survey week, however, he was away from the city for personal reasons involving the settling of the estate of his recently deceased father.

These five persons did no work. They produced no goods or services for pay or profit. They did have jobs, but were away from them for reasons varying from being on vacation to being on strike.

Under current procedures, all are included in the employed total.

Tabulated separately as *with a job but not at work,* they are encompassed in the employed total because they do have a definite job slot from which they are away temporarily—and they are not seeking other employment.

Thus, we move away from an ironclad application of our activity criterion and recognize that a person on vacation, for example, still has a job, and that his employer is not recruiting for anyone else. The person himself is not looking for another job. The same applies to others "with a job but not at work"—such as the person who is out temporarily because of illness or bad weather.

Who, then, are the employed?

The employed include:

1. The *active employed:* those at work (including persons working without pay in a family enterprise for at least fifteen hours a week).
2. The *inactive employed:* those with a job, but not at work, because they are
   a) on vacation (paid or unpaid);
   b) temporarily ill;
   c) engaged in a labor-management dispute;
   d) prevented from working by bad weather;
   e) taking time off for personal reasons.

Estimates for Groups 1 and 2 are published separately every month—as they are for the individual categories within Group 2—the "with a job but not at work" group. Together, they make up the employed total in the United States for any given month.

The Active Unemployed

For most of the unemployed, too, the situation is quite clear: they were actively seeking work during the survey week. Some of them are experienced workers who recently lost their jobs; others are new graduates in search of their first full-time job. Others—such as housewives whose children have grown up—are searching for employment after an absence of many years; perhaps a retired worker, faced with an expensive illness in the family, returns to the job market looking for additional income. All of them are impinging on the labor force, making an active effort to secure employment.

Thus, just as we have the *active employed,* we also have the *active unemployed* who unequivocally meet our definitions.

The Inactive Unemployed

How about the following cases?

O-P has had a job in a large store for some years and has been working regularly at it. During the survey week the store is closed down for inventory and O-P is laid off and told she will be recalled as soon as this process is completed. Knowing and expecting that she will be called back, she does not look for any other work.

Q-R has been looking for a job for quite a while. During the survey week, however, he could not go out of the house because of a severe sore throat. As soon as he is fit again, he resumes his job seeking.

S-T resides in a severely depressed area, long affected by a decline in the cotton textile industry, the area's economic mainstay. He has been actively seeking work for months and knows that a person with his skills cannot find a job. He ceases looking for work, believing none available, although he is ready to take any job offer.

U-V received her college degree in education a few months ago. When interviewed, she tells the enumerator that she has found a teaching job and is now waiting to start her new job within three weeks.

Again, these four persons' activities did *not* involve actively seeking work. Under current procedures, however, all are classified as unemployed. (The numbers in these categories are relatively small and in most months do not affect the jobless total significantly.) These "inactive" unemployed are included in the jobless total because only special circumstances obviated their active search for employment.

Again, we move away from a rigorous application of our activity criterion. The person who actually has been seeking work for a long time but fails to do so during one survey week because of temporary illness is continued in the unemployed category, as is the long-term unemployed worker who knows that employment opportunity is nil for his age and trade in his community. Similarly, persons temporarily laid off from a job or those awaiting a new job are enumerated as unemployed because experience indicates that, however sincerely felt and believed, these expectations do not always come to fruition.

Who, then, are the unemployed?

The unemployed include:

1. The *active unemployed:* those actively seeking work.
2. The *inactive unemployed:* those who, when interviewed, reported that they had no job and
   a) were waiting to be called back to a job from which they had been laid off;
   b) would have been actively looking except for temporary illness;
   c) would have been actively seeking except that there was no work in their line available in their community;
   d) were waiting to start a new job to begin within thirty days. (4)

Together, these groups make up the unemployed total in the United States.

The Labor Force

The labor force of a country equals the employed plus the unemployed. In other words, the labor force includes all those classified as employed, active and inactive, and all those classified as unemployed, active and inactive. We may state this in the form of a simple equation:

$$E + U = LF$$

For those familiar with equations, this very important point will be clear: If any one member of this equation changes, some other member will be affected too. In fact, any or all may (and often do) change during a given month.

Let us illustrate:

It is quite possible for employment and unemployment both to rise at the same time. In fact, they always do in the summertime, when many youngsters go in search of between-school-term jobs. Some get the jobs and join the ranks of the employed; some look for but don't find jobs and are classified as unemployed. With both *E* and *U* going up, the labor force also moves up substantially.

In the fall the youngsters return to school. Some leave their jobs; some stop looking—employment and unemployment (*E* and *U*) fall and so does the labor force (*LF*) in what has become the standard seasonal performance during any September. So end our illustrations of simultaneous growth and simultaneous decline in employment and unemployment.

On the other hand, it is just as possible for, say, employment to rise while total unemployment remains stable—this by the entry into the labor force of previous nonworkers who get jobs. The spring entry of women into the agricultural work force and the entry of housewives into temporary store jobs during the Christmas season are familiar examples. In this case the *E* and, consequently, the *LF* in our equation ($E + U = LF$) move up (or down) while *U* can remain unchanged.

Not in the Labor Force

By our "activity" concept, those not working or seeking work (actively or inactively) are outside the labor force.

Students are generally outside the labor force but move into it by seeking temporary summertime jobs or their first full-time job. Many workers, in turn, join the nonworker ranks by retiring, for example, or getting married and running a house, or returning to full-time school. These nonworkers—*those not in the labor force*—are an important part of our manpower picture, contributing most of the ins and outs of the labor force figures.

The Basic Priorities

There yet remain several criteria in the determination of the employed and unemployed. What about the following cases?

> W-X is a full-time student at the state university. To supplement her income, she works five hours each Saturday at the local department store.

Y-Z is a retired man receiving his old age pension. Each Monday morning he makes ten dollars for five hours in a store setting the stock in order for the rest of the week.

Full-time students and retired men are excellent examples of persons classified as not in the labor force. But they did put in a little work during the survey week. And as we have noted, just one hour of work puts an individual into the employed category.

The rule: *Labor force activities take precedence over nonlabor force activities.* W-X and Y-Z are classified as in the labor force—as employed.

A-A has a job at which he was working all of the survey week. For some time, however, he has been dissatisfied with his current situation and took an hour off to answer a want ad that gave promise of a higher-paying job.

B-B has been actively seeking work for some time, now that her two children are of school age. During the survey week she continued to make an active effort to locate a full-time job but, lacking that, worked for half a day on a typing job for a small law firm.

While both of these persons were actively seeking work during the survey week, they were also at work during the very same week. How shall we classify them, employed (at work) or unemployed (actively seeking work)?

The rule: *Being at work takes precedence over unemployment.*

Thus, partially employed or underemployed persons are included among the *employed.* Any fractions of weeks such persons spent in job hunting will not be reported as unemployment if some work was done during the survey week. (As we will see later, however, their hours of work are reported, so that we can identify persons in this status.)

In the cases of A-A and B-B, looking for work and being at work occurred simultaneously. Note the following cases:

C-C worked on Monday and Tuesday of the survey week, but then was laid off with the rest of his crew because of a lack of orders for their product. He immediately registered at his local employment office and was referred to several openings, but was still out of a job at week's end.

D-D answered a want ad on Monday for a promising job that did not develop; on Tuesday she went to an office on referral by a friend, but this job also failed to work out; on Wednesday she received a call from the local public employment office referring her to a job which she got and on which she started that very day—and which she still has.

In both instances there was actually a sharp break in status during the survey week. At the end of the given week, one person was unemployed after losing a job and the other was employed after spending some time in actual search of a job. In both instances the priority rule still holds: *being at work takes precedence over unemployment,* and both C-C and D-D will be reported as employed for that month's returns.

E-E is a teacher on paid vacation during August. After spending July at the seashore, she feels she could use some additional funds before going back to her school job and looks for work during the survey week.

F-F has been on strike for twelve weeks. He lives in a state that permits the payment of unemployment insurance benefits to strikers after a waiting period, which has now elapsed; he goes to his local employment office and registers for his benefits and is thus put in the file of active seekers for a job.

In each case the individual involved is in an inactive employed status—with a job but not at work—one on vacation, the other on strike. But both were seeking work as well. Which takes priority?

The rule: *Looking for work takes precedence over having a job but not being at work.* E-E and F-F are classified as unemployed.

Household Enumeration: Putting Our Concepts to Work

Labor force statistics are gathered by household enumeration. The information is collected by the U.S. Census Bureau in carefully chosen sample areas. The data are published by the U.S. Bureau of Labor Statistics a week to ten days after the survey period in the *Monthly Report on the Labor Force.* Under this system every person in a visited household is accounted for; and every person for whom data are enumerated is counted once and only once. Unlike other statistical systems such as establishment reporting, in which an individual may be counted twice if he appears on two payrolls, *household enumeration classifies a person under one and only one heading.* A person is either in or out of the labor force, employed or unemployed. If he does perform more than one job during the same week, he is listed in the industry and occupation in which he worked the most hours.

Given the priorities we have set down, it is evident that the size of the labor force, employment, and unemployment will vary with the length of the time period chosen for enumeration.

For example: If, instead of a survey *week,* we had a survey *month,* then just one hour of work during the month would put a person into the employed category even if he was looking for work all the rest of the month. Employment would tend to be higher and unemployment lower under this one-month time period. The same would hold for the labor force category as against the nonworker category because, again, any labor force activity during the entire month would result in a worker classification, even if the rest of the month was spent outside the labor force.

On the other hand, the choice of a *day* as the time reference would have the opposite effect, with unemployment higher and employment and the labor force both lower.

Those Not Enumerated

To what part of the population shall all of these concepts and measurements apply? In accordance with a decision made in the late 1930s after considerable discussion, three groups are *excluded from enumeration* altogether:

1. *Persons under fourteen years of age* are automatically excluded as being too young to work. Fourteen was chosen as the cutoff age because it excludes a very small number of persons. In the postwar period the trend toward more education, plus laws concerning minimum working ages, has caused a considerable decline in labor market participation by these youngsters. During 1963, for in-

stance, persons fourteen and fifteen years of age accounted for only a little over 1.5 percent of the U.S. labor force. Now there is some discussion of raising the age cutoff to sixteen.

Many countries of the world—for example, Great Britain—have upper age limits as well. Not so in the United States. For example, 1,384,000 persons seventy years of age and over were counted in the labor force in the United States in 1961.

2. *Persons in institutions,* such as jails or asylums or hospitals, are automatically excluded on the basis of the fact that they, by the nature of their position, could not be engaged in either work or seeking work for pay or profit in the labor market as we have defined it.

3. *Members of the armed forces,* of course, are not only doing extremely important work but are paid as well. The ebb and flow in their numbers, however, is related not to alternations in economic activity but to national security. They do not work (or look for work) in terms of our definitions and concepts.

While servicemen are excluded from enumeration, monthly figures on the size of the armed forces are available from the Department of Defense—except in times of war. The armed-forces figure is customarily added to the civilian labor figures to provide a total labor force estimate for those who wish it.

With these three groups excluded, the population enumerated each month therefore represents the noninstitutional civilian population fourteen years of age and over.

Summary of Concepts

Now we may proceed with a complete definition of the employed and unemployed in terms of current concepts:

The *employed* during any given month represent that part of the noninstitutional civilian population fourteen years of age and over who, during the week containing the 12th, performed at least one hour of work for pay or profit *or* did at least fifteen hours of work without pay in a family enterprise *or* were temporarily absent from their jobs because they were on vacation, ill, on strike, or prevented from working by bad weather or various personal reasons—*provided* that these latter persons who had a job but were not at work did not look for work as well.

The *unemployed* during any given month represent that part of the noninstitutional civilian population fourteen years of age and over who, during the week containing the 12th, were not at work and were actively seeking a job *or* were not at work and would have been looking for a job but for the fact they were temporarily ill, waiting to be called back to a job from which they had been laid off, believed there was no work available for them in their customary trade in the place they live, or were waiting to start on a new job within thirty days—except that students in the last category are classified as nonworkers and not as unemployed.

The *civilian labor force* represents the sum of the employed and unemployed as defined above. The *total labor force* is the civilian labor force plus an independently provided (not enumerated) figure on the armed forces.

Two Monthly Surveys Compared

We close this part of our discussion with data (Table 2-1) showing how the total population of the United States, applying these concepts, was distributed in two specific months—April and August 1962. April is a month that is about average so far as seasonal variations are concerned. August is a month when there are some sharp seasonal movements that illustrate some of our concepts.

Population

In April 1962 the Census Bureau estimated the population of the United States at 185,817,000. This figure is currently estimated independently by the Census Bureau monthly, using as a base the actually enumerated figure in April 1960, when the last decennial census was taken. Each month thereafter the Census Bureau adds births and immigration, subtracts deaths and emigration. These cumulated monthly estimates, when checked against the succeeding decennial census, have proved remarkably accurate so far (because of the excellence of U.S. vital statistics and other factors). The Census Bureau went through this procedure for ten years after the census of

TABLE 2-1
Employment Status of the Population, April 1962 and August 1962 (In Thousands)

	April 1962	August 1962
Total population	185,817	186,843
Less those under 14 years of age	54,450	54,691
Less inmates of institutions 14 years of age and over	1,780	1,791
Noninstitutional population 14 years and over	129,587	130,359
Total labor force	73,654	76,554
Less armed forces	2,885	2,859
Labor force (civilian)	70,769	73,695
Employed	66,824	69,762
At work	64,830	62,923
With a job but not at work	1,994	6,839
On strike	40	12
On vacation	428	5,132
Idle because of bad weather	104	3
Temporarily ill	949	843
Other	474	849
Unemployed	3,946	3,932
On temporary (less than 30-day) layoff	93	183
Scheduled to start new job in 30 days	111	259
Not in civilian labor force	55,933	53,805
Homemakers	35,076	35,734
Students	12,077	783
Other	8,781	17,289

Source: U.S. Department of Labor, Bureau of Labor Statistics.

1950, and its estimates were only a fraction of 1 percent off from the actually enumerated 1960 census figure.

From the total population group we now subtract 54,450,000 boys and girls under fourteen and 1,780,000 inmates of institutions in April 1962. These two groups—also estimated independently by the Census Bureau—accounted for 30 percent of the total population at that time.

The other excluded group, the armed forces, according to the Department of Defense, totaled 2,885,000 in April 1962.

Labor Force

The remainder represents the noninstitutional civilian population fourteen years and over and it is this segment of the population that is differentiated into labor force–nonlabor force, employment-unemployment status. It is for this segment of the population, as we shall see, that a virtual cornucopia of monthly demographic and economic data are made available—by age, sex, color, marital status, occupation, duration of unemployment, and the like.

Employed

As was indicated earlier, the vast majority of persons counted as employed are in the unequivocal position of actually being at work during the survey week. Among those "with a job but not at work," a few categories can be specifically mentioned. (1) Those temporarily ill are normally the biggest single numerical group, remaining relatively high both in April and in August (the winter months usually present an even higher figure). (2) There is, as might be expected, a drastic seasonal change in the numbers of persons enumerated as on vacation, the figure running above the 5-million mark in the vacation month of August 1962. (3) The total of those enumerated as being prevented from working on their job because of bad weather also fluctuates substantially with the season, usually being high in the winter and sometimes practically nonexistent in the summer.

Unemployed

Among the unemployed, the great majority are also in the active status of seeking work. We have included two of the inactive unemployed groups to illustrate the effects of how the calendar happens to fall in any given month. In May 1962 the 12th fell on Saturday and the week of reference was the 6th to the 12th—the earliest possible survey week. During August 1962, the survey week was at the latest possible time: the 12th fell on a Sunday (the survey week runs from Sunday through Saturday) and the week of reference ran from the 12th to the 18th. In August this brought many new teachers waiting to start their new jobs in the fall school term into the unemployed total, and those enumerated in this category rose to about a quarter of a million persons. This particular week also happened to coincide with the period when auto production fell to practically zero while the industry was changing models, giving a relatively high figure for persons on temporary layoff.

Not in the Labor Force

The category of those not in the labor force (not to be confused with those excluded from enumeration altogether) is made up mostly of homemakers, students, and an all-other subcategory made up of such persons as retired workers—a fast-growing group in the United States. These groups are excluded on the basis of their responses to specific "activity" questions during the enumeration process. Note the use of the term *homemaker* (not *housewife*); about 100,000 men are estimated to be in this category each month (among them men whose major activity is taking care of the house during their wives' illness). Note, too, the change in magnitudes for "students" and "others" between a month like April and one like August. During April, in the heart of a school term, the student figure is large; in August a substantial number are on between-school vacations and are classified as "other" nonworkers.

Reference Notes

1. The activity concept was used, but rarely, in the various unemployment surveys of the 1930s. It was, for example, one of the concepts used in a sample survey used to check the voluntary registration census of November 1937. See C. L. Dedrick and M. H. Hansen, *The Enumerative Check Census,* Vol. IV (Final Report of National Unemployment Census; Washington, D.C., 1938).
2. John N. Webb, "Concepts Used in Unemployment Surveys," *Journal of the American Statistical Association,* Vol. 34 (March 1939).
3. Until July 1955 it was the week containing the 8th. The change was made to effect closer correspondence to the payroll period ending nearest the 15th of the month, used in establishment reporting.
4. There is an exception to this point. Any person who is a student and responds that he is neither working nor seeking work, and then reports that he is waiting to start a new job within thirty days, is retained in his student status and classified as not in the labor force at all. (Many students may so report themselves toward the end of the school year.)

Readings

An examination of concepts used in prior unemployment surveys and a suggested proposal that first embodied the current labor force concepts were put together in the Division of Social Research, WPA, and described in a memorandum that was later published as

WEBB, JOHN N. "Concepts Used in Unemployment Surveys," *Journal of the American Statistical Association,* Vol. 34 (March 1939).

These concepts were applied in actual measurement in a number of cities in the United States and published in such works as

BROWN, MALCOLM, and WEBB, JOHN N. *Seven Stranded Coal Towns.* (Research Monograph XXIII.) Washington, D.C.: Division of Research, WPA, Federal Works Agency, 1941.

Facts About Unemployment. (WPA Social Problems Series No. 4.) Washington, D.C.: Division of Research, WPA, Federal Works Agency, 1940.

WOLFBEIN, S. L. *The Decline of a Cotton Textile City.* New York: Columbia Univ. Press, 1944.

Descriptions of current labor force concepts can be found in

Concepts and Methods Used in Current Employment and Unemploy-

ment Statistics Prepared by the Bureau of the Census. (Series P-23, No. 5.) Washington, D.C.: Department of Commerce, Bureau of the Census, May 9, 1958.

How the Government Measures Unemployment. Washington, D.C.: Department of Labor, Bureau of Labor Statistics, May 1962.

WOLFBEIN, S. L. "Counting the Employed and the Unemployed," *Michigan Business Review,* Vol. 14 (March 1962). Ann Arbor: Univ. of Michigan.

A critical review of these concepts can be found in

BANCROFT, G. *The American Labor Force.* New York: John Wiley & Sons, 1958. Appendix C, "Some Problems of Concepts and Measurement."

Special mention should be made of

Measuring Employment and Unemployment. Washington, D.C.: President's Committee to Appraise Employment and Unemployment Statistics, 1962. Chapter II, "Concepts and Definitions." The President's Committee included Professor R. A. Gordon, University of California, chairman; Professor R. Dorfman, Harvard; Professor A. E. Rees, University of Chicago; Professor F. F. Stephan, Princeton; S. H. Ruttenberg, AFL-CIO; and M. R. Gainsbrugh, National Industrial Conference Board. This outstanding report contains an appraisal of labor force concepts and a substantial amount of quantitative information, as well as recommendations for future action. It will be cited frequently in succeeding chapters as the Gordon Committee Report.

CHAPTER THREE

Enumerating the Labor Force

A SET OF CONCEPTS OR DEFINITIONS, NO MATTER HOW WELL CONCEIVED AND objectively formulated, must meet the acid test of translation into real-life situations. How this test is put and how well the concepts meet the test are the subjects of this and the following chapter.

All in all, five major operations are involved, and they attempt to answer the following questions:

1. What kind of schedule of questions shall respondents be asked in order to get the information we need?
2. How shall we select, train, and check the enumerators who will ask the questions and record the answers?
3. In what places and in which households shall the enumeration take place?
4. How shall we process the answers into a reliable, meaningful set of labor force estimates?
5. When and in what form shall the information be published?

Schedule of Questions

The first step in the movement from our agreed-upon concepts to the publication of the final results is the preparation of a schedule of specific questions that will enable us to get the information we need. Experience has proved that the choice of questions asked, the choice of wording, and the sequence of questioning all influence the answers that one will receive. They may influence the results by as much as several million persons.

The "Old" Schedule (1940–45)

Such was the experience with the original form (Fig. 3-1), which was used from 1940 to 1945.

This schedule asked persons, under the heading "activity during census week," whether they were at work or actively seeking work. In keeping with our conceptual scheme, the former were classified as employed, the latter as unemployed. A final "activity" question asked persons who had answered "no" to the first two questions *why* they were not seeking work.

It was the answers to this key question that made the final sort among those neither working nor seeking work:

> Employed: those on vacation, away from job because of bad weather or other reasons.
>
> Unemployed: those who believed no work was available in the community.
>
> Not in labor force: students, homemakers, and others.

Additional questions on the demographic characteristics of the respondents and the occupation and industry of workers rounded out the schedule.

In January 1945, after the regular enumeration, a small sample of persons who had been classified as not in the labor force were re-interviewed and asked, "In addition, did this person do any work or look for work during the census week?" About 1.25 million persons answered "yes," indicating that they should have been classified as employed or as job seekers rather than outside the labor force; another check, in April 1945, showed 2.5 million persons who met the

MONTHLY REPORT ON THE LABOR FORCE SCHEDULE USED FROM 1940 TO JULY 1945

Monthly Report on the Labor Force
SS-370c

U.S. Department of Commerce
Bureau of the Census

Budget Bureau No.
Approval Expires
Sample ______ Schedule No. ______

1. Address:
   (a) Segment No. ______
   (b) Block No. ______
   (c) E.D. No. ______
   (d) ______ (City or town)

2. Does this household live on a farm? Check:
   (a) Yes ____
   (b) No ____

3. Number of persons in household:
   (a) 14 yrs & over ______
   (b) Boys 13 yrs & under ______
   (c) Girls 13 yrs & under ______
   (d) Total (all ages) ______

County ______ State ______

4a. ______ (Interviewer) ______ (Date completed)

4b. ______ (Person interviewed)

Line No. (5)	Age last birthday (6)	Sex (M or F) (7)	Race (W, NEG, or OTH) (8)	Persons 14 years of age and over — Activity during census week: AT WORK on private or gov't job. Enter PE-W, OA, E, UP, G, or NO. (9)	(Leave blank) (10)	If NO in (9): ACTIVELY SEEKING WORK. Enter date present seeking began, or NO. (11)	If NO in (9) and (11): REASON FOR NOT SEEKING WORK. Enter Code (see below). (12)	If PE-W,OA, E,UP, or G in (9); or J in (12): HOURS WORKED during census week. (13)	OCCUPATION AND INDUSTRY — Of CURRENT job if PE-W,OA,E,UP, or G in (9); or J in (12). Of LAST full-time private or gov't job of 2 weeks or more if a date or NA in (11); or I, L, or N in (12). If never worked at such a job, enter NONE. (14)	(Leave blank) (15)	(Leave blank) (16)
1											
2											
3											
4											
5											
6											
7											

Column 12—Reason for not seeking work (print in col. 12)

Code
H. Engaged in home housework.
S. Enrolled in school.
U. Permanently unable to work or too old.
J. Has a job, business, etc.* Also indicate class of worker on this job; i.e., enter J-W, J-OA, J-E, or J-G.

Code
I. Temporary illness as reason for NOT SEEKING WORK
L. Lay-off (temporary), no specific instructions to return to work; off-season in particular trade or industry.*
N. Believes no work available.*
OTH. (Specify in footnote.)

*Note—Do not include occasional workers or unpaid family workers not working during the census week. (See detailed instructions.)

Footnotes:

FIG. 3-1

definition of a worker—but had been classified as outside the labor force.

These results, on top of similar findings from other tests made between 1940 and 1945, made it clear that the schedule was not

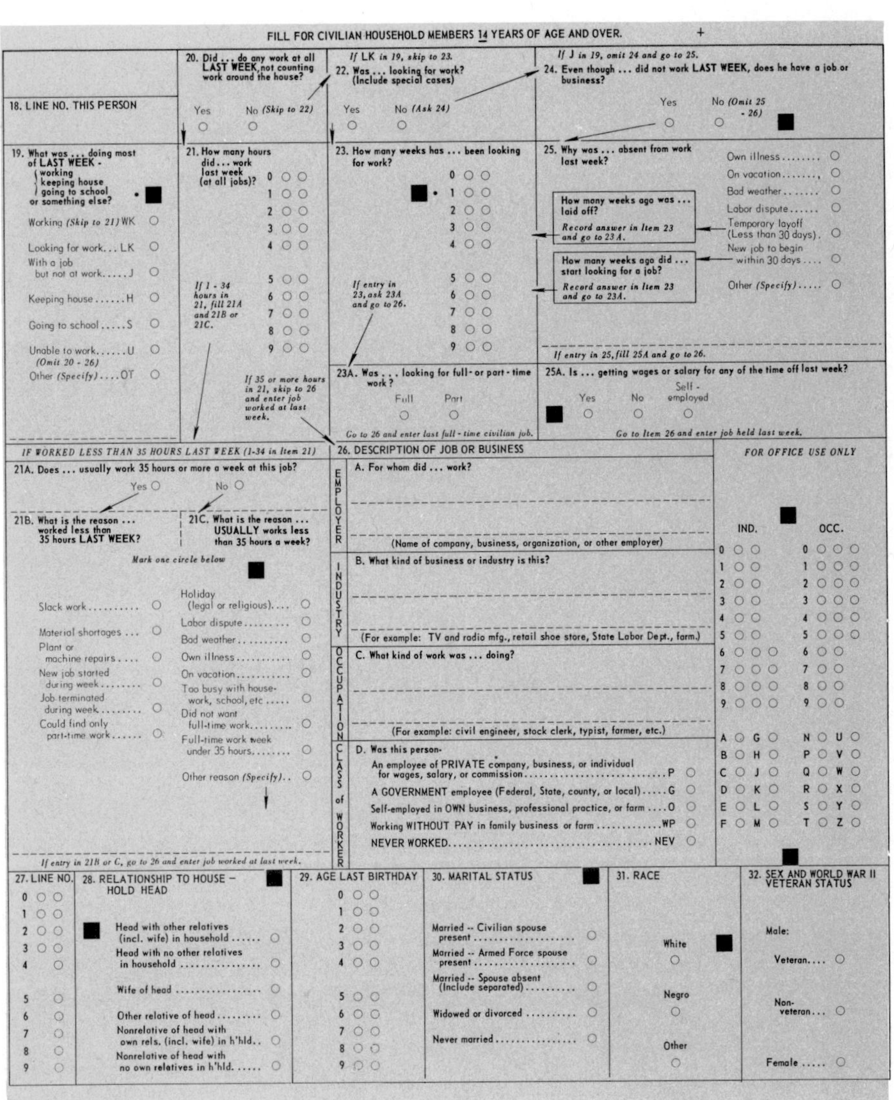

FILL FOR CIVILIAN HOUSEHOLD MEMBERS 14 YEARS OF AGE AND OVER.

18. LINE NO. THIS PERSON

20. Did ... do any work at all LAST WEEK, not counting work around the house?
Yes ○ No *(Skip to 22)* ○

If LK in 19, skip to 23.
22. Was ... looking for work? (Include special cases)
Yes ○ No *(Ask 24)* ○

If J in 19, omit 24 and go to 25.
24. Even though ... did not work LAST WEEK, does he have a job or business?
Yes ○ No *(Omit 25 - 26)* ○

19. What was ... doing most of LAST WEEK - working, keeping house, going to school or something else?
- Working *(Skip to 21)* WK ○
- Looking for work ... LK ○
- With a job but not at work ..... J ○
- Keeping house ...... H ○
- Going to school ..... S ○
- Unable to work ...... U ○ *(Omit 20 - 26)*
- Other *(Specify)* .... OT ○

21. How many hours did ... work last week (at all jobs)?
0 ○ ○
1 ○ ○
2 ○ ○
3 ○ ○
4 ○ ○
5 ○ ○
6 ○ ○
7 ○ ○
8 ○ ○
9 ○ ○

If 1 - 34 hours in 21, fill 21A and 21B or 21C.

If 35 or more hours in 21, skip to 26 and enter job worked at last week.

23. How many weeks has ... been looking for work?
0 ○ ○
1 ○ ○
2 ○ ○
3 ○ ○
4 ○ ○
5 ○ ○
6 ○ ○
7 ○ ○
8 ○ ○
9 ○ ○

If entry in 23, ask 23A and go to 26.

25. Why was ... absent from work last week?
- Own illness .... ○
- On vacation .... ○
- Bad weather .... ○
- Labor dispute ...... ○
- Temporary layoff (Less than 30 days) . ○
- New job to begin within 30 days .... ○
- Other *(Specify)* ..... ○

How many weeks ago was ... laid off? *Record answer in Item 23 and go to 23A.*

How many weeks ago did ... start looking for a job? *Record answer in Item 23 and go to 23A.*

If entry in 25, fill 25A and go to 26.

23A. Was ... looking for full- or part-time work?
Full ○ Part ○
Go to 26 and enter last full-time civilian job.

25A. Is ... getting wages or salary for any of the time off last week?
Yes ○ No ○ Self-employed ○
Go to Item 26 and enter job held last week.

IF WORKED LESS THAN 35 HOURS LAST WEEK (1-34 in Item 21)

21A. Does ... usually work 35 hours or more a week at this job?
Yes ○ No ○

21B. What is the reason ... worked less than 35 hours LAST WEEK?

21C. What is the reason ... USUALLY works less than 35 hours a week?

Mark one circle below

- Slack work .... ○
- Material shortages ... ○
- Plant or machine repairs .... ○
- New job started during week .... ○
- Job terminated during week .... ○
- Could find only part-time work ...... ○
- Holiday (legal or religious) .... ○
- Labor dispute .... ○
- Bad weather .... ○
- Own illness .... ○
- On vacation .... ○
- Too busy with house-work, school, etc ..... ○
- Did not want full-time work .... ○
- Full-time work week under 35 hours .... ○
- Other reason *(Specify)* .. ○

If entry in 21B or C, go to 26 and enter job worked at last week.

26. DESCRIPTION OF JOB OR BUSINESS

EMPLOYER
A. For whom did ... work?
(Name of company, business, organization, or other employer)

INDUSTRY
B. What kind of business or industry is this?
(For example: TV and radio mfg., retail shoe store, State Labor Dept., farm.)

OCCUPATION
C. What kind of work was ... doing?
(For example: civil engineer, stock clerk, typist, farmer, etc.)

CLASS of WORKER
D. Was this person-
- An employee of PRIVATE company, business, or individual for wages, salary, or commission .... P ○
- A GOVERNMENT employee (Federal, State, county, or local) ..... G ○
- Self-employed in OWN business, professional practice, or farm .... O ○
- Working WITHOUT PAY in family business or farm .... WP ○
- NEVER WORKED .... NEV ○

FOR OFFICE USE ONLY

IND.	OCC.
0 ○ ○	0 ○ ○ ○
1 ○ ○	1 ○ ○ ○
2 ○ ○	2 ○ ○ ○
3 ○ ○	3 ○ ○ ○
4 ○ ○	4 ○ ○ ○
5 ○ ○	5 ○ ○ ○
6 ○ ○ ○	6 ○ ○
7 ○ ○ ○	7 ○ ○
8 ○ ○ ○	8 ○ ○
9 ○ ○ ○	9 ○ ○
A ○ G ○	N ○ U ○
B ○ H ○	P ○ V ○
C ○ J ○	Q ○ W ○
D ○ K ○	R ○ X ○
E ○ L ○	S ○ Y ○
F ○ M ○	T ○ Z ○

27. LINE NO.
0 ○ ○
1 ○ ○
2 ○ ○
3 ○ ○
4 ○
5 ○
6 ○
7 ○
8 ○
9 ○

28. RELATIONSHIP TO HOUSEHOLD HEAD
- Head with other relatives (incl. wife) in household ...... ○
- Head with no other relatives in household .... ○
- Wife of head .... ○
- Other relative of head .... ○
- Nonrelative of head with own rels. (incl. wife) in h'hld.. ○
- Nonrelative of head with no own relatives in h'hld. ...... ○

29. AGE LAST BIRTHDAY
0 ○ ○
1 ○ ○
2 ○ ○
3 ○ ○
4 ○ ○
5 ○ ○
6 ○ ○
7 ○ ○
8 ○ ○
9 ○ ○

30. MARITAL STATUS
- Married -- Civilian spouse present .... ○
- Married -- Armed Force spouse present .... ○
- Married -- Spouse absent (Include separated) .... ○
- Widowed or divorced .... ○
- Never married .... ○

31. RACE
- White ○
- Negro ○
- Other ○

32. SEX AND WORLD WAR II VETERAN STATUS
Male:
- Veteran.... ○
- Non-veteran... ○

Female ..... ○

Fig. 3-2

probing enough and was missing a very significant number of workers. A new schedule was therefore designed and introduced in July 1945. It immediately produced 1.6 million additional employed persons over and above the old schedule's estimate—proving again that the kind and sequence of questions can make a difference of millions in the figures. Data obtained before July 1945 were adjusted accordingly, so that we still have a continuous, comparable-as-possible series back to 1940.

The "New" Schedule

The "new" schedule (Fig. 3-2), now in use, tries not to take anything for granted, but keeps asking the respondent a series of questions—in three major sequences—to assure conforming as closely as possible to our concepts.

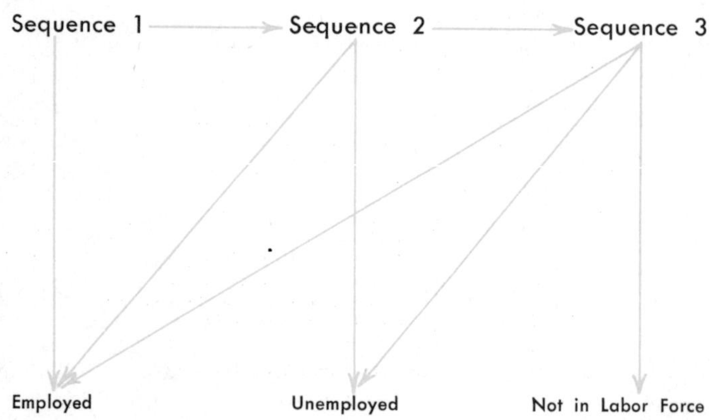

Fig. 3-3

Sequence 1: Questions 19, 21, 26

This sequence takes care of all those whose initial response puts them unequivocally into the group at work, for whom information on hours of work, occupation, industry, and class of work is then obtained.

(Others can *still* be classified as employed on the basis of later questions by the interviewer.)

19. The first question here is: "What was this person doing most of the week—working, keeping house, going to school, or something else?" It gives us the first major sorting out of the people being enumerated. In this first go-around the beginning slot is for those whose initial response classifies them as working.

21. For these the next question refers to hours of work.

21 A-B-C. For those who worked less than thirty-five hours a week, these questions elicit the facts about and the reasons for part-time work.

26. The worker is asked for details concerning his particular job or business. He is classified as to whether he is employed in private enterprise, works for the government, owns his own business, or works without pay.

Sequence 2: Questions 19, 20, 22, 23, 26

This sequence sorts out those who have actively sought work and are therefore classified as unemployed. Information on the length of joblessness and on occupation, industry, and class of work on their last full-time job is then obtained. (Others can still be classified as unemployed on the basis of later questions.)

Note that the starting point and destination are the same as for the unequivocally employed—Question 19 and Question 26—but there is a considerable series of "probing" questions in between.

19. The initial query, as we have shown, concerns the respondent's principal activity during the week.

20. Every person not classified as working as a result of his answer to Question 19 (except for those who take themselves out of the running by saying they are unable to work) gets the first "probe" —did the person do any work *at all* last week? If so, he is classified as employed, and is returned to Question 21 and Sequence 1.

22. If "no," he gets the next "probe"—did he *look for work?* If he did, he is clearly unemployed and we move into Sequence 2.

23. How long has he looked for work? And was he looking for full-time or part-time work?

26. Here again, the responses classify the job seeker as to private or government enterprise, work in family business, proprietor of a business, or new job seeker who has never worked.

Sequence 3: Questions 24, 25

This sequence sorts out the remaining persons to be enumerated. It returns to the employed category all persons with a job but not at work. It returns to the unemployed category those who are on temporary layoff or awaiting a new job. It retains in nonworker (not in labor force) status those who are students and awaiting a new job, as well as all those who were initially classified in that status and remained so through the intervening screening questions.

24. This question probes still further among those who remain and asks, "Even though this person did not work last week, does he have a job or business?" If the answer is "no," the person remains in the nonworker class. If the answer is "yes," we move to Question 25.

25. "Why was this person absent from work last week?" Here is where we get our information on those with a job but not at work—because of illness, vacation, bad weather, labor dispute, and other reasons. All these persons are counted as employed, of course, and go on to Question 26. Those who are on temporary layoff and waiting to start a new job within thirty days go back to Question 23 and Sequence 2 as unemployed. Students who say they are waiting to start a new job stay as nonworkers.

Proposed Changes in the Schedule

It should be noted that one set of probes in the "old" schedule is no longer present. The question on why a person did not seek work is gone. The only categories of the inactive unemployed now overt on the schedule are in Question 25—temporary layoff and awaiting a new job. Enumerators are, indeed, instructed to note such categories as those who were not actively seeking work because of temporary illness or because they believed no work was available. But no specific probes are currently included that would elicit such information.

Many labor force experts think that the present survey procedure understates the size of the unemployed group—particularly the group who no longer look for work after considerable long-term joblessness and may get to be recorded as out of the labor force altogether, especially during recessions. (1)

That additional probing would result in a different count of the unemployed was documented by a test conducted for August 1955. Persons who were enumerated as neither employed nor looking for work (except those unable to work) were asked, after all the questions had been completed for everyone in the household, whether they had actually taken any steps to find work within the past *two months;* persons who still responded in the negative to that question were then asked why they were not looking for work.

Without going into all the facets of this experiment (2), suffice it to say that it resulted in a significantly different level and composition of joblessness. Just a little over 1 million persons, classified as not in the labor force in the original interview, showed up as having actively sought work during the preceding two months—adding almost 50 percent to the published estimate of unemployment for August 1955 of 2.2 million. Most of these additions were, as might be expected, from the more marginal groups: one-third were teen-agers, more than half were women.

Once again we emphasize: Stipulating any agreed-upon set of concepts, we get different quantitative results as we vary the specific questions asked and the sequence in which they are asked.

Special Questions

We have been focusing our attention on that section of the schedule form in which the labor force questions are asked. The remainder of the form covers information on the identity and location of the household and on personal characteristics of those being interviewed, such as age, sex, race, and marital status. There is also room for special questions, which change each month, depending on what is being investigated.

These special questions have become a very important feature of the survey. The demand is so great that there is a long waiting line for the limited additional space, and a new panel of respondents has been set up recently in the form of a separate quarterly sample just for this purpose.

The regular schedule still carries special questions that range from subjects such as the labor market status of high school dropouts to job changing by workers. Some of these special surveys, such as those relating to income, migration, and work experience, are now scheduled for specific months in each year and give us annual information on a wide range of social and economic problems that we would not otherwise have available except for the decennial census years.

These supplementary questions have to be watched carefully for any possible effect on the regular returns. For example, in March 1942 each person who was counted as not in the labor force was asked —as a special question—if he would take a full-time job within thirty days; each was also asked when he last had a full-time job.

The enumerators were very carefully told not to go back and change any entries on account of the answers to these questions. Nevertheless, the employment figure that month was about 1 million higher than was expected for that time of the year, and a corresponding decline took place in the figure for nonworkers. In the following months, when no special questions were asked, the figures moved back to their previous levels.

The Enumerators

That enumerators also play a critical role in the final results is perhaps clear in view of the great importance of the schedule questions and of making sure that they are asked in the indicated form and sequence.

The Bureau of the Census devotes a significant amount of time and resources to familiarizing its enumerators with the precise techniques to be used. Three months intensive training is given each new enumerator. Experienced interviewers are given refresher training each month. Each month, all returns are inspected both at the regional level and in Washington. Daylong group training and review sessions are scheduled at least four times a year; twice a year each enumerator is observed by a supervisor in actual enumeration.

About three times a year a sample of each enumerator's work is reinterviewed. A supervisor or some other specially trained individual repeats the interview and in most cases then proceeds to discuss with the household respondent any differences between the information he got and that which came from the original interview by the enumerator. The results are discussed with the original enumerator and they become a good device for training and for improving the accuracy of subsequent interviews.

During the five-year period 1956–60 a quarter of a million persons were enumerated by reinterview. After differences between the two interviews were reconciled as far as possible, the remaining differences averaged out as follows:

Classification	*Percent Difference*
Labor force	1.1
Employed	.9
Agriculture	1.8
Nonagriculture	.8
Full time	.6
Part time	6.7
With a job but not at work	0
Unemployed	3.8
Not in labor force	1.4

The differences between the two are hardly to be assigned entirely to the enumerator. Misunderstandings on the part of the respondents are no doubt part of the picture. The differences are generally quite small, but the larger figures for such items as unemployment and part-time work are a continued warning that some of the concepts are difficult to get across.

The results also emphasize that one key to the returns lies in the person-to-person relationship at the point of interview, when the training and understanding of the enumerators become critically important.

Reference Notes

1. For other points and issues on the *Monthly Report on the Labor Force* schedule and questions, see *Measuring Employment and Unemployment,* issued by the President's Committee to Appraise Employment and Unemployment Statistics, Washington, D.C., 1962 (Gordon Committee Report).
2. The details will be found in Appendix C, "Results of the Experimental Study on Unemployment, August 1955," in the Gordon Committee Report.

Readings

See Chapter V and Appendix L in

Measuring Employment and Unemployment. (Gordon Committee Report.) Washington, D.C.: President's Committee to Appraise Employment and Unemployment Statistics, 1962.

On earlier development of problems involved in schedule construction and design, see Chapter II in

DUCOFF, LOUIS J., and HAGOOD, MARGARET J. *Labor Force Definition and Measurement.* (Social Science Research Council Bulletin No. 56.) New York: the Council, 1947.

See also

BANCROFT, G., and WELCH, E. H. "Recent Experience with Problems of Labor Force Measurement," *Journal of the American Statistical Association,* Vol. 41 (September 1946).

CHAPTER FOUR

From Sample to Publication

We now come to one of the most important problems in getting a count of the labor force. It can be summed up as follows: Having agreed on our concepts and definitions and on how to translate them through a set of questions on a properly designed form, in what places and for which households and to whom shall we put the questions?

At any given time there exists a theoretically perfect, precisely correct figure on unemployment, or on persons not in the labor force —or on any other statistical item that we would like to know.

That "true" figure is called the *parameter.* It is well-nigh impossible to achieve when we are dealing with millions of people in so extraordinarily complex a society as ours.

This is the case even in taking the decennial census, a "full" count of the population. The U.S. Constitution requires a total count of the population every ten years; yet postenumeration checks in connection with the 1950 census, for example, showed that several million persons were not counted at that time.

The Sample

The *Monthly Report on the Labor Force* is not a full enumeration of the labor force. It is based on a carefully selected sample—at present about 35,000 households per month.

Even if a census or total count were as nearly perfect an operation as possible (Census Bureau procedures are making our decennial counts more nearly perfect all the time), it would be prohibitively expensive to take one each month. Further, a full census could probably not be processed in time to provide the desired *current* data each month. Also, it is possible to get just as good, or better, results from a carefully devised sample count as from a full census, considering the difficulties of training the many persons who would be required for a full count.

The goal, then, is to design a sample that will contain no bias and that will represent the current situation with as much precision as possible. This must be done in the light of such nontechnical considerations as the funds available for the operation.

Primary Sampling Units and Strata

The first decision involves a choice of the basic building blocks to be used in constructing the sample—a decision as to which geographic areas shall be our primary sampling units.

Among the basic governmental units are the 3100-odd U.S. counties (in some instances called parishes and independent cities). To enumerate a sample in all of these would be quite expensive and difficult, requiring interviewers, visits, controls, and supervisory units in each.

The Census Bureau therefore combines the counties into 1891 *primary sampling units* (each abbreviated as a PSU). Some counties are big enough and heterogeneous enough to constitute a PSU by themselves. The bureau combines others in pairs or in sets of three or more.

Each PSU should as far as possible be compact enough to be sampled efficiently without too much travel time and cost. It should also include urban and rural residents, high, medium, and low income groups, and different occupational and industrial groups because of their effect on labor force, employment, and unemployment.

The PSU total of 1891 is still too formidable a number to visit. So the 1891 units are grouped into 357 *strata.* These are the basic sampling areas.

A stratum is a single PSU or set of units, brought together on the basis of being as alike as possible in such characteristics as rate of population growth, proportion living in urban areas, principal industries, proportion of the population that is nonwhite.

Of these 357 strata, 112 are important enough to constitute strata by themselves. They are called "self-representing" and are included in the sample automatically. They include a little over 100 million of the 1960 U.S. population of about 180 million.

In the remaining 245 strata, a single PSU in each is chosen to represent that stratum in the sample. The bigger the population of the PSU, the better its chance of being selected to represent its stratum. These are "non-self-representing strata."

We end up, therefore, with 357 areas in which the sample survey is taken; 112 of them are strata by themselves; 245 of them represent each of the strata to which they belong.

The 357-area sample now in force represents a gradual growth in the size of the MRLF sample from an original 68 areas in 1940 to 230 areas in February 1954 to 330 areas in May 1956 to 333 areas when Alaska and Hawaii joined the Union.

Sampling Ratio

Now that we have the 357 sampling areas, we must decide which households are to be visited in each. These are chosen principally through the use of census enumeration districts, represented generally by clusters of six housing units listed on every third line at some point in the 1960 decennial census books. Special techniques are used for institutions, sparsely settled rural areas, and some other situations.

Each of the 357 areas has a sampling ratio assigned to it which indicates what percentage of its households will be sampled. This will vary by PSU, according to the proportion that the given unit's population bears to the population of the stratum it represents.

It is very important to note that this is a ratio, for example one in every 150 households—and not a fixed number. If, as time goes on, the total number of households in an area goes down, then a ratio (for example, one in every 150) results in a declining number of sample households; if the total goes up, then the sample take of households also goes up. In this way the sample reflects the ebb and flow of population change.

Sample Households

Each household chosen is kept in the sample for four months in a row, dropped out of the sample for the next eight months, and then brought back in for another four final months. This minimizes the burden of enumeration on the same households and also strengthens the over-the-year estimates.

The operation is phased so that in any given month 75 percent of the sample households were also in the sample the previous month, a factor which is used in the preparation of the final estimates.

The result is a list of sample addresses totaling about 42,000. In any given month about 35,000 of these are actually enumerated. Some addresses (about 5500 in recent years) are found to be nonresidential structures, unoccupied places, or buildings that have been torn down. At about 1500 addresses the people are temporarily absent or not found at home after repeated visits. Fewer than 1 percent of the households refuse to be interviewed.

Preparing the Estimates

The schedules (questionnaire forms) are received in Washington by the end of the week after enumeration. The process of quickly converting the raw data on each of the forms (accomplished with the help of electronic computers) is quite complex.

The estimation procedures call first for an adjustment for those occupied dwelling units where no interview was obtained. These, we will recall, run to about 1500 or somewhat less than 5 percent of the occupied dwellings. This first adjustment attempts to reduce any bias that could result if the noninterviewed persons had markedly different labor force characteristics from those who were interviewed. The result is an adjustment of the weights of the sample households, made separately for each color and residence group of households.

Once this adjustment has been made, the computation of our

estimates can be accomplished by taking the number of persons showing up in the sample for each group for which we want a figure—for example, men fourteen years of age and over and unemployed—and multiplying them by the weight each has at the time of the survey. For example, in April 1962 each person in the sample had a weight of about 1600.

This can be improved upon by a second weighting procedure which involves the use of so-called ratio estimates. The basic idea here is that there are certain population characteristics that are very closely associated with labor force, employment, and unemployment, such as age, color, sex, farm-nonfarm residence. The population being sampled at any time may differ somewhat in these characteristics from the total population of the country. Sample estimates can be improved by weighting the original returns in such a way as to bring them into as close agreement as possible.

This is done in two stages. The first involves the 245 non-self-representing strata, where a single PSU is used to represent the stratum to which it belongs. Here weights are adjusted for individual sample groups, cross-classified in twenty-four different ways—by four regions (northeast, north central, south, and west), by three residence classifications (urban, rural nonfarm, and rural farm), and two color groups (white and nonwhite) in accord with the distribution of the population in these various groups at the time of the last census. The aim is to reduce stratum sampling variability, reflecting the fact that in each of the 245 strata only one PSU is used as the sample.

The second stage takes into account differences between the population distribution of the sample and the distribution prevailing in the country. This is done as follows:

Each month the Census Bureau makes an independent estimate (as already noted) of the U.S. population by age, color, and sex. Its basis is the last decennial census population count. For each successive month, births and immigration are added and deaths and exits from the country are subtracted. These independent estimates are made for each of fifty-six different nationwide "cells"—for fourteen age groups, each differentiated into the two color groups, and into the two sex groups.

The sample MRLF returns—all adjusted now—might show for some month that the relevant distribution of white males twenty to twenty-four years of age was as follows: 90 percent were in the labor force and 10 percent not in the labor force; of the 90 percent in the labor force, 85 percent were employed, 5 percent unemployed. Each of these MRLF percentages is then applied to the Census Bureau's independently estimated monthly total population of white males twenty to twenty-four years of age in that month to get the estimated total numbers in this group and in and out of the labor force, employed and unemployed. The overall national totals are the end products of doing these steps for each of the fifty-six cells (fourteen age groups × two color groups × two sex groups) and adding up the results.

Still a third process is involved before the final figures are ready to be published. Known as the "composite estimate," it is based on the fact that 75 percent of the households in each month's sample were also in the sample the month before (one-eighth of any month's sample is brand-new, one-eighth is back again after having been in the sample four months and then dropped for eight months and six-eighths—three-fourths or 75 percent—are continuing on from last month's sample).

Under certain conditions—which happen to be true in the case of labor force items—the best way to estimate change from one point of time to another is to use the same sample at both points. The commonality of 75 percent of the sample in two adjacent months fits this requirement. The Census Bureau therefore makes a first estimate for the current month as already described, then an estimate based only on the common part of the current and the past month's sample. The two are averaged to give the final estimates for a given month's labor force, employment, and unemployment.

Accuracy of Results

In commenting on the census sample, the Gordon Committee Report said: "The complexities of the CPS sample design and estimation procedures were examined in relation to sampling theory, and no theoretical reason was found to suggest that any portion of the design would be a significant source of bias in the final results." Yet inherent in every operation of this sort are circumstances that can lead to "error." The more important sources of possible error are:

The enumerative situation itself. Possibility of error may inhere in the questionnaire or schedule used—in the translation of the concepts of labor force, employment, and unemployment upon which we have agreed.

The respondent. He, too, is not always a perfect answering medium. He does not always have at his fingertips all the nuances of information we seek.

The interviewer. He may list a household that does not belong in the sample or fail to list one that does, or he may miss someone in the household—all possible sources of error.

Telephone interviews. Every household that is a newcomer to the sample is interviewed person-to-person. But with rising costs, there has been an increasing amount of telephone interviewing of households that have already been in the sample; the proportion of these cases has gone up to about 25 percent. Can we really be sure that we get the same results in a telephone and in an at-the-household interview?

Reporting patterns. Another interesting item—and a bit of a mystery—is the fact that in good times and bad, households tend to report a higher unemployment rate the first time they are in the sample than in the following months when they continue in the sample.

Tabulation. There is always the possibility of error in editing and coding the questionnaires and transferring this processed information onto the magnetic tapes for tabulation. Here, excellent quality control by the Census Bureau has minimized errors.

Estimating procedures. Possible biases, of course, are also inherent in the complex estimating procedures used. To name an almost obvious one: We have shown how independently determined monthly Census Bureau estimates on the population are used in preparing the final results from the monthly sample survey. Any errors that involve the decennial census figures plus continuing monthly estimates of births, deaths, immigration, and emigration can have a direct effect on the labor force, employment, and unemployment data that are published.

Sampling process. Even if our measurements were perfect and our estimates bias-free, we would of course still have "errors" generated by the fact that we are taking a sample rather than a full count. Always we have to ask ourselves, With what precision is the statistic, say for unemployment, measuring the "true" figure, or parameter, on unemployment? In other words, how far off are we, by virtue of having taken a sample, from the results of a census—had we been able to complete one—with the use of the same techniques, procedures, and schedules?

Calculations for Error

Present-day theory permits calculations for sampling errors in our estimates, if a probability sample of the kind used in the MRLF is executed as intended.

A range of sampling variability, or *standard error* as it is called, can be computed that measures the variations in the estimates due to the fact that a sample and not a full count is taken. If the sample taken is large enough, successive estimates fashion themselves in the form of a normal distribution. In these circumstances the chances are about 2 out of 3 that any sample estimate will be within one standard error of the true figure.

Table 4-1 shows the standard error of some of the major estimates coming out of the MRLF sample recently.

TABLE 4-1
Average Standard Error of Selected MRLF Labor Force Categories (In Thousands)

	Average Standard Error of Estimate	
Labor Force Status	For a Given Month	For a Change Between Consecutive Months
In labor force	250	180
Total employment	250	180
Agricultural employment	300	120
Nonagricultural employment	300	180
Unemployment	100	100

Let us say that a month's figure on unemployment from the MRLF is 3,500,000. Referring to Table 4-1, we see that one standard error of a given month's unemployment figure is 100,000. This means that the chances are about 2 out of 3 that the true figure is 3,500,000 (our sample estimate) plus or minus 100,000—or somewhere in the interval 3,400,000 to 3,600,000. This interval (known as the "confidence" interval or limit) describes the range within which we can say with some confidence—in this case 2 out of 3—that the true figure lies.

Suppose we want an interval with even a greater degree of confidence. In that case we can use two standard errors, in which case the chances are 95 out of 100 that the true figure on unemployment is 3,500,000 ± 200,000, or between 3,300,000 and 3,700,000.

Or, if we want to be even closer to certainty, we can increase the span of our confidence interval to three standard errors, giving us 3,500,000 ± 300,000; the chances are now more than 99 out of 100 that the true unemployment figure for the given month is between 3,200,000 and 3,800,000. Obviously, the surer we want to be, the broader must be our interval.

One more illustration, by reference to Table 4-1 again: Let us say that the same month's MRLF estimates show nonagricultural employment at 68,500,000. The chances are 2 out of 3, if we use one standard error, that the actual figure is somewhere between 68,200,000 and 68,800,000 (68,500,000 ± 300,000), since Table 4-1 tells us that the standard error of a given month's nonagricultural employment estimate is 300,000.

If we use two standard errors, the chances are 95 out of 100 that the actual figure is between 67,900,000 and 69,100,000 (68,500,000 ± 600,000).

Table 4-1 indicates also that standard errors can be calculated for the amount of change that is shown in a given classification from one month to the next. Similar calculations can be made for other categories as well.

Publication of Results

Each month the MRLF first appears in the form of a brief release with appended tables summarizing some of the major labor force categories. The major effort is to publish as quickly as possible the first returns from the survey.

Currency of First Release

The enumeration takes place during the third week of a given month (the week containing the 19th) and the first results are released by the Department of Labor to the public typically during the first week of the following month. In some cases the data come out in the very same month. Here, for example, are the dates on which each month's returns were released during 1962:

First Returns for the Month of	*Were Released on*
January	January 31
February	March 7
March	April 6
April	May 9
May	May 31
June	July 5
July	August 1
August	September 5
September	October 4
October	October 31
November	December 5
December	January 10

Publication of Complete Data

About a week or so later a more nearly complete release is made, including detailed information by age, sex, color, marital status, industry, and occupation. Included also are the first returns from the establishment reporting system and data from the unemployment insurance system (both described in the succeeding chapters). This permits a more extensive analysis of the month's returns.

About two weeks later a monthly *Employment and Earnings* bulletin is issued that contains all the published details, including further cross-tabulations from the MRLF as well as the other systems. Once a year a supplement to this bulletin brings together a computation of yearly averages of many of the major statistical series. Special reports on various aspects also are published in such organs as the *Monthly Labor Review* issued by the Bureau of Labor Statistics, U.S. Department of Labor.

This three-stage publication process—initial MRLF returns during approximately the first week of the month, a more detailed release the next week, and a final bulletin putting all the detail together two weeks after that—has been the pattern of presentation that has been followed since the beginning of 1961. Before 1961 the

Census Bureau published the MRLF results separately; subsequently the Department of Labor would publish the results of its employer reports separately. This often resulted in different kinds of assessments of the month's labor force, employment, and unemployment picture, based as they were on different systems of information. In 1954 it was decided to issue a joint release by the two departments, so that all figures could be brought together and an analysis published that would be based on all available data. This meant holding up the early MRLF returns until the results of the employer reports were ready for publication, and a great deal of pressure was built up to release initial data as soon as they became available. This resulted in the present three-phase pattern initiated in 1961.

Obviously, simultaneous publication of all the data—household, establishment, and social-insurance statistics—would be most desirable. This is why the Gordon Committee Report recommended consideration of means to accelerate the employer reports. In the meantime there has been some expansion in the MRLF information presented in the initial release.

The Decennial Census Enumeration of Labor Force

Every ten years, during the month of April, when the decennial census, which includes certain labor force information, is taken, we have a very interesting experiment: The regular MRLF is, as usual, also conducted during the same month and we can compare the results from the two.

Substantial differences have been found between the two. In April 1950, the census figure for unemployment was 20 percent below the comparable figure from the MRLF for the same month. The overall labor force figure from the census was 5 percent below that of the sample survey. The figure on persons not in the labor force was 8 percent higher in the census than in the MRLF. For some specific groups in the population the differences were even bigger; for example, there was a difference of 29 percent in the figure on unemployment for nonwhite males.

With improved procedures, the Census Bureau has successfully pared down these differences, as can be seen from Table 4-2.

Differences, of course, still appear and they are still noticeably higher in some of the groups not shown in Table 4-2. For example, the difference between census and sample results in 1960 for non-

TABLE 4-2
Comparison of Labor Force, Employment, and Unemployment Estimates, Decennial Census and Monthly Sample Survey April 1960

Labor Force Status, Sex, and Color	Difference of Census from Sample Survey	
	In Thousands	As a Percent
Both sexes—all persons 14 and over	+ 377	+ 0.3
Labor force	−1,675	− 2.4
Employed	−1,520	− 2.3
Unemployed	− 155	− 4.2
Not in labor force	+2,052	+ 3.9
Both sexes—white	+ 274	+ 0.2
Labor force	−1,273	− 2.0
Employed	−1,263	− 2.1
Unemployed	− 10	− 0.3
Not in labor force	+1,546	+ 3.2
Both sexes—nonwhite	+ 104	+ 0.8
Labor force	− 402	− 5.2
Employed	− 257	− 3.7
Unemployed	− 145	−18.7
Not in labor force	+ 506	+10.2

Source: Gordon Committee Report, *op. cit.*, Table J1, p. 377.

white males unemployed was about 22 percent; and the difference for youths fourteen to seventeen years of age in the labor force was 14 percent. The Census Bureau plans involve further checks, including a cross match of the same persons found in the census and sample enumerations. These should help explain some of the differences and suggest methods for improvement.

Considering that the figures came from two substantially different enumerating systems and that the decennial census enumerators are temporary workers and tend to be less well trained in labor force concepts, the differences are not surprising. It is noteworthy that the biggest differences are in the more marginal labor force groups, such as the very young and the very old, and certain groups in agriculture. The manner in which the Census Bureau apparently was able to improve its appraisal of labor force status in the 1960 decennial operation is instructive. The bureau made certain technical improvements, such as the distribution of persons who did not respond to the labor force questions. It also improved the wording of some questions. The bureau operated through partial self-enumeration on labor force questions, and while the total population was enumerated for decennial purposes, the census actually used only a 25 percent sample for the decennial labor force queries. In most areas the sample counts were made after the complete count stage of the operation and permitted the use of special, highly skilled enumerators.

In the official government statistics on the labor force for April 1950 and April 1960, it is the sample results from the MRLF that are used. The census returns are of course still enormously useful and provide much detail—including details of labor force geography—not available from the MRLF.

Readings

On the sample of the MRLF and its operations, see

Frankel, L. R., and Stock, J. S. "On the Sample Survey of Unemployment," *Journal of the American Statistical Association,* Vol. 37 (March 1942). (The authors pioneered the development of the original sample design.)

Hansen, M. H., and Hurwitz, W. N. *A New Sample of the Population.* Washington, D.C.: Department of Commerce, Bureau of the Census, September 1944. (The authors had the major responsibility for carrying forward on the new sample design and other technical features of the MRLF.)

Some of the basic principles of sampling upon which the MRLF is predicated can be found in

Hansen, M. H.; Hurwitz, W. N.; and Madow, W. G. *Sampling Survey Methods and Theory.* New York: John Wiley & Sons, 1953.

See also

Hansen, M. H.; Hurwitz, W. N.; Nesselson, H.; and Steinberg, J. "The Redesign of the Census Current Population Survey," *Journal of the American Statistical Association,* September 1955.

Less technical presentations are found in

Concepts and Methods Used in the Current Employment and Unemployment Statistics Prepared by the Bureau of the Census. (Series P-23, No. 5.) Washington, D.C.: Department of Commerce, Bureau of the Census, May 9, 1958.

Also see explanatory notes found in each month's

Employment and Earnings (bulletin of the Bureau of Labor Statistics, Washington, D.C.).

See especially Chapter V and IX and Appendixes D, E, J, and K in

Measuring Employment and Unemployment. (Gordon Committee Report.) Washington, D.C.: President's Committee to Appraise Employment and Unemployment Statistics, 1962.

CHAPTER FIVE

Establishment Reporting

As WE HAVE SEEN, THE BASIC REPORTING UNIT IN THE *Monthly Report on the Labor Force* is the household. Under this system, appropriate information is obtained by personal enumeration for all members of the respondent's household who are in civilian, noninstitutional status and are fourteen or over, at a specified time during the month.

We now turn to another type of data, which is obtained through the mail from individual business units, or establishments, that report payroll information to various agencies.

Establishment reporting was the earliest method of obtaining U.S. employment statistics on a current basis. Current monthly employment data in nonagricultural industries were first collected in this country by the Bureau of Labor Statistics (BLS) from establishments in four manufacturing industries in October 1915. A year later —in November 1916—these establishment surveys were increased to include thirteen industries.

In the 1920s this BLS system was expanded substantially and extended gradually to cover nonmanufacturing industries. By 1937 an overall national series on employment in all industries (except agriculture) had become available. Since then the system has expanded to become one of the major sources of information on the labor force.

The Employer Reports

An establishment is formally defined as a single physical location—such as a factory, mine, store, or mill—where business is conducted and for which separate pay records are maintained. Note that this is *not* a company. A company—for example, General Motors or the A & P—may have a number of establishments, and the reporting units refer to those separate establishments rather than the company as a whole. Different establishments may be in different areas and may be producing quite different goods or services. As a result of making individual establishments the focus of attention, this reporting system provides substantial data on the industrial and geographic distribution of employment in the United States.

The reference time is the payroll period ending nearest the 15th of the month (industry and business payroll practices vary a good deal in this country; some are weekly, some are biweekly, some cover a calendar week, some cut across calendar weeks). This reference period and that of the *Monthly Report on the Labor Force* are very close; for all practical purposes, they may be considered to cover the same period of time. (1)

Payrolls

Payrolls are the basic source record from which the employer reports each month the number of his employees and their hours (full or part time) and earnings.

With the advent of the social security system in this country in 1937, requiring employers to file quarterly information on their employment and payrolls, and with the passage of the Fair Labor Standards Act of 1938, calling for overtime pay for work above forty hours a week, payroll practices improved considerably.

The result is some very important economic indicators such as payroll employment and hours of work. These are more reliable than comparable figures available from the MRLF, because they come directly from employer payroll reports, with a geographic and industrial detail almost completely lacking in the MRLF.

At the same time, this system is limited in a number of ways. Since these are payroll reports, they obviously cannot supply information on unemployment. Further, they are limited to wage and salary workers, that is, people who appear on payrolls. Thus the self-employed are excluded as well as domestics and unpaid family workers. Only workers who have received some pay during the reference period are included. Thus a person on paid vacation is included—but not a person on unpaid vacation.

Establishment and Household Reporting Compared

Remembering that the key word in any description of establishment reporting is *payroll,* let us examine how the different labor force groups are treated by household and establishment reporting:

Item	*Household Enumeration*	*Establishment Reporting*
Labor force	Enumerated	Not enumerated
Unemployment	Enumerated	Not enumerated
Employment		
Agricultural	Enumerated	Not enumerated
Nonagricultural		
Self-employed	Enumerated	Not enumerated
Domestics	Enumerated	Not enumerated
Unpaid family workers	Enumerated	Not enumerated
Wage and salary workers		
At work	Enumerated	Enumerated
With a job but not at work		
On vacation	Enumerated	Only if on paid vacation
Temporarily ill	Enumerated	Only if on paid sick leave
On strike	Enumerated	Not enumerated
Idle because of bad weather	Enumerated	Only if paid
Away for personal reasons	Enumerated	Only if paid
Not in labor force	Enumerated	Not enumerated

The touchstone in establishment reporting, as we have said, is the payroll. Only if a wage or salary worker was on the payroll for any time during the payroll period ending nearest the 15th of the month is he counted as employed. For example, during the 116-day steel strike of 1958, most of the 500,000 steelworkers were not included in the count of payroll employment from the establishment reports. They did continue to be included in the employed category of the *Monthly Report on the Labor Force* (they were recorded in the MRLF as unemployed if they registered for unemployment insurance in the states where they were eligible).

There are other differences between the two systems. The MRLF has an age cutoff at fourteen; establishment reports have none. In the MRLF, a person is counted once and only once. If he has two jobs or three during the week of reference, he gets enumerated only once in the MRLF employment total. In establishment reporting, a person appearing on more than one payroll gets into the count as many times as he appears on different payrolls. He may be in this position because he holds down more than one job during the reference payroll period, or he may move from one job to another during that time. For very understandable reasons, this is why payroll employment information is often referred to as a count of jobs filled rather than of persons employed.

Factors that tend to make the establishment report figure higher are the double or multiple counting of persons concurrently or successively holding more than one job during the reference period and the fact that it also includes persons under fourteen years of age (the latter effect is of course quite small).

Tending to make the MRLF nonagricultural wage and salary figure higher is its inclusion of persons not on payrolls (those with a job but not at work and unpaid).

And then, of course, there is the fact that the two systems come from different sources and use different samples and sampling techniques to get their results.

The net effect is that the nonagricultural wage and salary figure is generally higher for the establishment reports than for the MRLF. The two series show very similar long-term trends and they show the same general cyclical ups and downs.

They usually come closer to each other in periods of recession because of a sharper decline in the establishment series—apparently a result of the reduction in multiple job-holding during recessionary periods. (2)

The Shuttle Schedule

Figs. 5-1 and 5-2 are copies of one of the so-called shuttle schedules used in obtaining information from individual establishments. (The number 790 is the one assigned to these Bureau of Labor Statistics forms; 790C, reproduced here, is used for establishments in manufacturing; those with other letters are used for other industries.)

The schedule is tightly constructed. Column 1 presents the dates to which the information applies, and incidentally indicates why these are called shuttle schedules. Each month the establishment being queried is sent a copy of this schedule, which it fills out and sends back. The information is taken off and combined with all the rest to yield the needed data; then the very same schedule, with last month's information still on it, goes back to the establishment, which fills out the new month's information and returns the form; and the cycle goes on from there again. In January each year a new form goes out, with the information for the December just past written in as a point of reference.

The columns under the heading "Period Reported" cover the time reference period, the payroll period (preferably a week) ending nearest the 15th of the month. As indicated before, many firms have payroll periods of more than one week and the form asks for some of this information so that estimates can be prepared on a weekly basis. (1)

Columns 7 and 8 ask information on the number of employees in the establishment. Note the one piece of demographic information regularly collected—employment by sex.

The next bank of columns (9 through 12) relate to "production workers" only and it is for them that data on hours and earnings are collected. This term is defined in detail on the other side of the form (Fig. 5-2). Here it can be briefly described as those directly engaged in the production process itself—from the foreman down. As the schedule indicates, it excludes executive, legal, medical, advertising, sales, and similar personnel, who are nonproduction workers.

The distinction between the so-called production and nonproduction workers has become important because of the very different trends in employment as between the two groups. Table 5-1 summarizes what has happened to the two during the period following World War II; it should be remembered that both of these groups are within manufacturing—the factory sector of nonfarm employment

BLS Codes

State	Report No.	Ind.		

Form BLS 790 C

Before entering data please see explanations on other side

LOCATION OF ESTABLISHMENT(S) COVERED IN THIS REPORT

(Number of establishments)	(City)	(County)	(State)

YEAR AND MONTH	PERIOD REPORTED					ALL EMPLOYEES		PRODUCTION AND RELATED WORKERS					YOUR COMMENTS
	PAY PERIOD One pay period only (*preferably 1 week*) ending nearest 15th of month		NUMBER OF DAYS during the pay period shown in cols. 2 and 3 on which the majority of employees worked *plus* holidays and vacation days paid for. (*Nearest ½ day*)			NUMBER Include all persons who worked during or received pay for any part of period regardless of type of work performed		Enter in these columns the number of production and related workers who worked during or received pay for any part of the period reported, the pay earned, and all hours worked or paid for. Include pay and man-hours for overtime, sick leave, holidays, and vacations					Please enter in column 13 the main factors responsible for significant month-to-month changes in employment, average hours worked (col. 11 ÷ col. 9), average hourly earnings (col. 10 ÷ col. 11), etc., as indicated by this report. Examples are: *Strike*; *Seasonal expansion*; *Partial shut-down for repairs or inventory-taking*; *More higher paid workers*; *Less piecework*; *Weather*; *Premium pay for holiday work*; *Less incentive pay*; *Materials shortage*; *Hiring due to new contracts*. If any general wage-rate changes (not individual changes for length of service, merit, or promotion) have occurred since last month's report, note the amount of increase or decrease (as +2%, −5¢), the effective date of the change, and the approximate number of production workers affected.
	From— (*Both dates inclusive*)	Through	During the entire period	During 7-day period ending nearest 15th of month	DO NOT USE L/P	Both sexes	Women only	NUMBER OF PRODUCTION WORKERS	PRODUCTION-WORKER PAYROLL (*omit cents*)	TOTAL PRODUCTION-WORKER MAN-HOURS INCLUDING OVERTIME MAN-HOURS (*omit fractions*)	DO NOT USE Expl. Code	OVERTIME PRODUCTION-WORKER MAN-HOURS Included in column 11 (*omit fractions*)	
(1)	(2)	(3)	(4)	(5)	(6)	(7)	(8)	(9)	(10)	(11)	(12)	(11X)	(13)
1961 Dec.									$				
1962 Jan.													
Feb.													
Mar.													
Apr.													
May													
June													
July													
Aug.													
Sept.													
Oct.													
Nov.													
Dec.													

(Person to be addressed if questions arise regarding this report)

(Position)

☆ U.S. GOVERNMENT PRINTING OFFICE : 1961—O-603168

FIG. 5-1

BLS 790 C
MANUFACTURING

U. S. DEPARTMENT OF LABOR
BUREAU OF LABOR STATISTICS
WASHINGTON 25, D. C.

CONFIDENTIAL REPORT
ON
EMPLOYMENT, PAYROLL, AND HOURS
COOPERATIVE PROJECT

Budget Bureau No. 44-R745.12
Approval expires January 31, 1964.

(CHANGE MAILING ADDRESS IF INCORRECT—INCLUDE POSTAL ZONE NUMBER)

Please handle carefully and return promptly each month in the enclosed envelope which requires no postage

EXPLANATIONS FOR ENTERING DATA ON REVERSE SIDE

Data on production and related workers should be supplied for the same classes of employees each month. All payroll and man-hour figures reported should relate to employees defined as production and related workers.

Columns 2 and 3. PERIOD REPORTED—PAY PERIOD.—Give the first and last dates of the pay period reported.

Columns 4 and 5. PERIOD REPORTED—NUMBER OF DAYS.—Enter in column 4 for the entire pay period reported, the sum of the number of days on which the majority of production and related workers performed work *plus* the number of holidays and vacation days during the period for which the majority were paid. When the period is longer than a week, enter in column 5 the number of such days worked or paid for during the 7 consecutive day period which ends nearest the 15th of the month and falls entirely within the period reported in columns 2 and 3.

Column 7. ALL EMPLOYEES—BOTH SEXES.—Enter the total number of persons on the payroll(s) covered by this report who worked full- or part-time or received pay for any part of the period reported. Include salaried officers of corporations and executives and their staffs but do not include proprietors, members of unincorporated firms or unpaid family workers. Include persons on vacations and sick leave for which they received pay directly from your firm for the period reported but *exclude* persons on leave without company pay the entire period and pensioners and members of the Armed Forces carried on the rolls but not working during the period reported.

NOTE.—If the total reported on this form is different from the total which will be reported to your State unemployment compensation agency, please explain differences in column 13 on the reverse side.

Column 8. ALL EMPLOYEES—WOMEN ONLY.—Report number of women employees included in column 7.

Column 9. NUMBER OF PRODUCTION AND RELATED WORKERS.—Enter the number of production and related workers, both full- and part-time, on your payroll(s), whether wage or salaried, who worked during or received pay for any part of the pay period reported. Include persons on paid sick leave, paid holidays, and paid vacations.

The term "production and related workers" includes working foremen and all nonsupervisory workers (including leadmen and trainees) engaged in fabricating, processing, assembling, inspection, receiving, storage, handling, packing, warehousing, shipping, trucking, hauling, maintenance, repair, janitorial, watchman services, product development, auxiliary production for plant's own use (e. g., power plant), and recordkeeping, and other services closely associated with the above production operations.

The term "production and related workers" excludes employees engaged in the following activities: Executive, purchasing, finance, accounting, legal, personnel, cafeterias, medical, professional, and technical activities, sales, sales-delivery (e. g., routemen), advertising, credit, collection, and in installation and servicing of own products, routine office function, factory supervision (above the working foreman level), and force account construction employees on your payroll engaged in construction of *major* additions or alterations to the plant who are utilized as a separate work force. (Employees in the above activities should be excluded from column 9 but included in column 7, All Employees.)

Column 10. PAYROLL.—Enter amount of pay earned during the pay period by the production and related workers reported in column 9. Payrolls should be reported before deductions for old-age and unemployment insurance, group insurance, withholding tax, bonds, and union dues but after deductions for damaged work. Include pay for overtime and for holidays, vacations, and sick leave paid directly by your firm to employees for the pay period reported.

Do not include bonuses (unless earned and paid regularly each pay period) or other pay not earned in pay period reported (e. g., retroactive pay). Do not include value of free rent, fuel, meals, or other payment in kind.

Column 11. TOTAL MAN-HOURS.—Enter the sum of man-hours worked (not scheduled hours) during the pay period by the production and related workers reported in column 9 *plus* hours paid for stand-by or reporting time and holiday hours, and man-hours equivalent to pay received by employees directly from your firm for sick leave and for holidays and vacations for the pay period reported. Do not convert overtime or other premium paid hours to straight-time equivalent hours.

Column 11X. OVERTIME MAN-HOURS.—Enter the number of man-hours included in column 11, for which premiums were paid because the hours were in excess of the number of hours of either the straight-time workday or workweek. Include Saturday and Sunday hours (or 6th and 7th day hours) only if overtime premiums were paid, and holiday hours only if pay for the holiday hours plus pay for hours worked is *in excess of double* the straight-time rate. Exclude hours for which only shift differential, hazard, incentive, or other similar types of premiums were paid. If none, enter "0" in column 11X.

FIG. 5-2

in the United States. It will be seen that nonproduction workers have steadily increased in numbers, holding their own and sometimes even going up during recessions. They now account for more than one out of every four factory employees.

The production worker is likely to be the man or woman who gets paid by the hour and for whom hours and earnings are more readily obtainable. The nonproduction worker includes many on a salary for whom actual hours are difficult to ascertain. With nonproduction workers now a formidable proportion of workers in manufacturing as well as other sectors of the economy, there is great need for at least hours-of-work information on them. Steps are being proposed to obtain this kind of information.

TABLE 5-1
Production and Nonproduction Workers in Manufacturing 1950–1962

Year	Number (In Thousands)			
	Total	Production Workers	Nonproduction Workers	Percent Nonproduction Workers
1950	15,241	12,523	2,718	17.8
1951	16,393	13,368	3,025	18.5
1952	16,632	13,359	3,273	19.7
1953	17,549	14,055	3,494	19.9
1954	16,314	12,817	3,497	21.4
1955	16,882	13,288	3,594	21.3
1956	17,243	13,436	3,807	22.1
1957	17,174	13,189	3,985	23.2
1958	15,945	11,997	3,948	24.8
1959	16,667	12,596	4,071	24.4
1960	16,762	12,562	4,200	25.1
1961	16,268	12,046	4,222	26.0
1962	16,750	12,417	4.333	25.9

Source: U.S. Department of Labor, Bureau of Labor Statistics.

The final column (13) is for employer comments on any unusual developments for the month and often is a good clue to why a firm has had some big change in its employment, hours, and earnings at some particular time.

Federal-State Cooperation

A significant aspect of establishment reporting is the cooperative manner in which the data are collected. At the national level, the enterprise is a joint project of the Bureau of Labor Statistics and the Bureau of Employment Security of the Department of Labor, which share the total cost of the operation. The Bureau of Labor Statistics takes the leadership in the technical aspects of the work at the national level, and in cooperation with the Bureau of Employment Security designs the schedule form that we have reproduced. This is the standard form used in all collection of these data.

The actual collection of the data is done on contract by each of the fifty states and the District of Columbia. In forty-five of these jurisdictions, the state employment security agency affiliated with the federal Bureau of Employment Security carries out this operation. These cooperating state agencies mail the shuttle schedules to the reporting establishments, get them back, edit them, and take off the information for their own states and labor market areas. They then send on the assembled data to the Bureau of Labor Statistics, which prepares the national estimates. This system has the great advantage of using one standard form and one response each month from the employers to yield national, state, and area estimates—eliminating duplication of reporting.

Sampling

Like the MRLF, the system of establishment reporting is based on a sample. Unlike the MRLF, however, the BLS sample is not a probability sample. It has evolved over the years, to get as big a sample as possible among the larger organizations in most industries that account for most of the volume and change in employment. Recently, smaller firms have been introduced into the sample. In 1961, size-of-firm stratification was introduced into the national sample for a number of industries, including a little over half of the manufacturing industries.

The sample coverage differs quite extensively by industry sector. It is excellent in a number of them, not so good in others, practically nonexistent in still others. In such volatile fields as construction, where small and ever changing units are typical, the sampling problem is particularly difficult.

Table 5-2 shows the recent sample coverage in the BLS system. About 180,000 separate establishments report on employment, hours, and earnings each month; they employ about 25 million wage and salary employees. This very large sample is necessary in order to get the amount of geographic and industrial detail this system produces.

TABLE 5-2
Sample Coverage in BLS Establishment Reporting System March 1962

	Employees in Sample	
Industry Division	Number (Thousands)	Percent of Total
Mining	301	47
Contract construction	581	23
Manufacturing	10,767	65
Interstate railroads	775	97
Other transportation and public utilities	1,622	53
Trade	2,212	20
Finance, insurance, real estate	983	36
Service	1,362	18
Federal government	2,294	100
State and local government	3,414	50

Source: U.S. Department of Labor, Bureau of Labor Statistics.

The coverage varies substantially—from all employees in the federal government (through the U.S. Civil Service Commission) and practically all employees of railroads (through the Interstate Commerce Commission) to relatively small samples in construction, trade, and services. Work is going forward in the BLS and state agencies to improve the samples in many of these sectors.

Accuracy of Estimates

Since, unlike the MRLF, the BLS sample is not a probability sample, we cannot compute the mathematical measures of sampling error and the confidence limits described in Chapter 4 for household enumeration figures.

There does exist, however, a method for checking the estimates of employment from the payroll reports. As will be noted in Chapter 6, in which we discuss social security statistics, periodic tabulations of employment data are made, industry by industry, by the various state agencies on the basis of quarterly reports filed by *all* employers covered under state unemployment insurance laws. Some firms, however, are not covered by unemployment insurance laws—in some states, for example, concerns with fewer than four employees—and in such instances the information is supplemented by similar reports required by the U.S. Bureau of Old-Age and Survivors Insurance for the regular social security program, where coverage is more complete. These data form the best periodic total or universe count of establishment employment by industry for one given period of time in the United States. It is against this benchmark that the sample estimates are checked just about every year. (3)

TABLE 5-3
Difference Between Sample and Benchmark Estimate in 1962

Industry	In Thousands	As a Percent
Total	−386	−0.7
Mining	5	−0.8
Contract construction	−152	−6.1
Manufacturing	− 93	−0.6
Transportation and public utilities	15	0.4
Trade	10	0.1
Finance, insurance, and real estate	− 3	−0.1
Service	−158	−2.0
Government	0	0

Source: U.S. Department of Labor, Bureau of Labor Statistics.

Table 5-3 shows how the sample estimates checked out against the benchmark in 1962, a fairly representative year. Overall, there was a difference of less than 1 percent (.7 percent) between the sample and the benchmark figure—about 390,000 on a base of over 54 million wage and salary workers in nonagricultural establishments. Five of the eight major industry divisions had differences that were also less than 1 percent. The biggest variation, as always, occurred in construction, a highly seasonal industry abounding in small firms, many existing just for one project. In 1962 the contract construction sample estimate was off by some 6 percent.

The difference between benchmark and sample estimate is small for manufacturing, where the size of sample is substantial. Here too, however, some of the industry groups within manufacturing have large differences. In 1962, for example, the difference was about 3.4 percent for the stone, clay, and glass industry, 2.9 percent for the textile mill industry. (4)

Making Monthly Estimates

After each benchmark check, the sample of employer reports provide the ensuing months' estimates until the next year's benchmark check, when the figures are revised again and the cycle goes on.

Let us say that the benchmark figure for Industry A is 125,000 wage and salary workers. The BLS reporting sample of ninety establishments in that industry for the following month shows that wage and salary workers in those establishments went up from 25,000 to 26,000—a 4 percent increase. We would apply the 4 percent increase to the 125,000 figure, getting an increase of 5000, and the published figure for that month for Industry A would be 125,000 + 5000, or 130,000. Successively, the month-to-month change shown by identical establishments in each industry sample is used to move the benchmark figure up to the time of the next revision.

The estimates would move off considerably from the true situation without these benchmark revisions. One reason why the differences between sample and benchmark have been quite small is the practice of making so-called bias adjustments in the monthly figures. Each month the estimates from the sample employer reports are adjusted in anticipation of benchmark revisions. This is done on the basis of past experience in comparing sample with benchmark and knowing that the present system does not make adequate provision for the inclusion in the sample of new firms, especially among the smaller establishments. The statisticians in the Bureau of Labor Statistics do a capable job in these anticipatory "bias adjustments."

Additional research on improving these operations, as well as the benchmarks themselves, is now going on. Eventually social insurance statistics should be able to provide a well-structured universe with enough information on geography, size of firm, and industrial classification so that a satisfactory probability sample can be chosen. This will enable establishment reporting to achieve the technical level of sampling now realized by the MRLF household surveys.

Industrial Classification

Once a year the Bureau of Labor Statistics sends to its respondent establishments a "product supplement" form on which they record the nature of their business activity and what and how much they produced and sold. This information is the basis for classifying each establishment in its appropriate industry. With these data it becomes possible to estimate and publish payroll employment information by detailed industry classification, one of the most important sets of data in the labor force field.

Principles of Classification

One of the first problems in the complex task of classifying an organization by industry is to choose a basis for classification. Should one aggregate individual establishments into an "industry" on the basis of similar industrial processes or technology? or on the basis of usage of similar raw materials? or on the basis of the utilization of certain kinds of power and fuel and energy? Each would be meaningful and useful in studying the economy. For our purposes, all establishments engaged in making similar end products have been combined. *What the establishment produces is used as the yardstick.*

This, of course, is only the beginning. Hundreds of goods and services are produced by U.S. industry. The problem is how to combine organizations into meaningful groups, not so large as to mask trends, but not so small as to be insignificant in number of organizations and volume of business. In addition, the "industries" we use have to be meaningful in relation to our subject: they must have attributes that make it worthwhile to make separate estimates for them regarding employment problems, earnings, and hours of work.

Suppose that various different products are manufactured by a single establishment, and a substantial part of its work force (especially the nonproduction workers) works on all of them. Suppose, for example, that a company engages workers both for job printing and for publishing a newspaper; to produce both refrigerators and agricultural tractors. On the basis of what end product shall we classify these firms?

Let us take the establishment producing both refrigerators and farm tractors. Let us say that it produced 40,000 refrigerators and 26,000 tractors. One solution would be to put it into the "refrigerator" industry because it made more refrigerators. Another solution would be to use as our criterion the gross income generated by the sales of the different products. In this case the gross sales from the tractors would doubtless exceed those from the refrigerators and lead us to classify the firm in the "tractor" industry. That is what would happen in actual practice. *We classify multiproduct establishments on the basis of sales.*

An establishment is classified once and only once in some particular industry. All of its employment is assigned to the principal product as measured by the dollar value of its sales. In the circumstances there is not an exact allocation of employment and related information by end product or industry.

There are two categories that require special comment: contract construction and government establishments.

Contract Construction

One major industry division for which monthly payroll employment information is published is contract construction. This classification includes wage and salary workers engaged by establishments performing construction work on contract. Thus, if a person hires a builder to have a home constructed, the employees of the builder are in contract construction.

In addition, thousands of construction workers work for companies whose business is not construction. Many nonconstruction companies, for example, have electricians and carpenters on their payrolls to perform repair and other work as needed. They are called "force account" construction workers, and data concerning them are included in the reports of the firms and, therefore, of the particular industries in which those firms are classified. Speculative home builders also employ large numbers of construction workers. These are classified in an entirely different division—"finance, insurance, and real estate."

Government Establishments

There is no problem in classifying an executive department of the federal government. But how about a naval weapons plant or arsenal? It produces ammunition, say, and is literally engaged in manufacturing—in fact, in a separate manufacturing industry for which a separate industrial classification is available, known as "ordnance." Shall it be classified in government or in manufacturing?

Government activity at all levels cuts into many different phases. Army post exchanges are engaged in trade, for instance, and the Military Air Transport Service in transportation. All such cases are in fact classified in government.

Consideration is being given, however, to a twofold classification that will permit a count of all government activities and also industry information based on the agency's principal activity.

Government agencies engaged in the collection of reports from establishments follow these policies as well as the detailed structure embodied in the latest edition of the *Standard Industrial Classification Manual*, prepared by the U.S. Bureau of the Budget.

Major Industry Divisions

The Bureau of Labor Statistics publishes payroll information for the following eight major industry divisions, which constitute the overall total of "wage and salary workers in nonagricultural establishments."

Manufacturing
Mining
Contract construction
Transportation and public utilities
Wholesale and retail trade
Finance, insurance, and real estate
Service and miscellaneous
Government

TABLE 5-4
Employees on Nonagricultural Payrolls, by Industry Division 1919–62 (In Thousands)

Year	Total	Mining	Contract Construction	Manufacturing	Transportation and Public Utilities	Wholesale and Retail Trade	Finance, Insurance, and Real Estate	Service and Miscellaneous	Government
1919	27,088	1,133	1,021	10,659	3,711	4,514	1,111	2,263	2,676
1920	27,350	1,239	848	10,658	3,998	4,467	1,175	2,362	2,603
1921	24,382	962	1,012	8,257	3,459	4,589	1,163	2,412	2,528
1922	25,827	929	1,185	9,120	3,505	4,903	1,144	2,503	2,538
1923	28,394	1,212	1,229	10,300	3,882	5,290	1,190	2,684	2,607
1924	28,040	1,101	1,321	9,671	3,807	5,407	1,231	2,782	2,720
1925	28,778	1,089	1,446	9,939	3,826	5,576	1,233	2,869	2,800
1926	29,819	1,185	1,555	10,156	3,942	5,784	1,305	3,046	2,846
1927	29,976	1,114	1,608	10,001	3,895	5,908	1,367	3,168	2,915
1928	30,000	1,050	1,606	9,947	3,828	5,874	1,435	3,265	2,995
1929	31,339	1,087	1,497	10,702	3,916	6,123	1,509	3,440	3,065
1930	29,424	1,009	1,372	9,562	3,685	5,797	1,475	3,376	3,148
1931	26,649	873	1,214	8,170	3,254	5,284	1,407	3,183	3,264
1932	23,628	731	970	6,931	2,816	4,683	1,341	2,931	3,225
1933	23,711	744	809	7,397	2,672	4,755	1,295	2,873	3,166
1934	25,953	883	862	8,501	2,750	5,281	1,319	3,058	3,299
1935	27,053	897	912	9,069	2,786	5,431	1,335	3,142	3,481
1936	29,082	946	1,145	9,827	2,973	5,809	1,388	3,326	3,668
1937	31,026	1,015	1,112	10,794	3,134	6,265	1,432	3,518	3,756
1938	29,209	891	1,055	9,440	2,863	6,179	1,425	3,473	3,883
1939	30,618	854	1,150	10,278	2,936	6,426	1,462	3,517	3,995
1940	32,376	925	1,294	10,985	3,038	6,750	1,502	3,681	4,202
1941	36,554	957	1,790	13,192	3,274	7,210	1,549	3,921	4,660
1942	40,125	992	2,170	15,280	3,460	7,118	1,538	4,084	5,483
1943	42,452	925	1,567	17,602	3,647	6,982	1,502	4,148	6,080
1944	41,883	892	1,094	17,328	3,829	7,058	1,476	4,163	6,043
1945	40,394	836	1,132	15,524	3,906	7,314	1,497	4,241	5,944
1946	41,674	862	1,661	14,703	4,061	8,376	1,697	4,719	5,595
1947	43,881	955	1,982	15,545	4,166	8,955	1,754	5,050	5,474
1948	44,891	994	2,169	15,582	4,189	9,272	1,829	5,206	5,650
1949	43,778	930	2,165	14,441	4,001	9,264	1,857	5,264	5,856
1950	45,222	901	2,333	15,241	4,034	9,386	1,919	5,382	6,026
1951	47,849	929	2,603	16,393	4,226	9,742	1,991	5,576	6,389
1952	48,825	898	2,634	16,632	4,248	10,004	2,069	5,730	6,609
1953	50,232	866	2,623	17,549	4,290	10,247	2,146	5,867	6,645
1954	49,022	791	2,612	16,314	4,084	10,235	2,234	6,002	6,751
1955	50,675	792	2,802	16,882	4,141	10,535	2,335	6,274	6,914
1956	52,408	822	2,999	17,243	4,244	10,858	2,429	6,536	7,277
1957	52,904	828	2,923	17,174	4,241	10,886	2,477	6,749	7,626
1958	51,423	751	2,778	15,945	3,976	10,750	2,519	6,811	7,893
1959	53,380	731	2,955	16,667	4,010	11,125	2,597	7,105	8,190
1960	54,347	709	2,882	16,762	4,017	11,412	2,684	7,361	8,520
1961	54,077	666	2,760	16,267	3,923	11,368	2,748	7,516	8,828
1962	55,325	647	2,695	16,752	3,925	11,572	2,794	7,757	9,184

Source: U.S. Department of Labor, Bureau of Labor Statistics.

These data (Table 5-4) are available back to 1919 in a continuous and comparable series. Even a cursory examination of Table 5-4 shows how the United States has changed since the end of World War I from a goods-producing to a services-producing economy. This will be discussed later in detail. We shall particularly discuss the prominent role played by women in service occupations.

Industry Groups

For each of the major industry divisions, there is another level of detail—the industry groups. Manufacturing, for instance, is broken down into twenty-one subsidiary industry groups, each with separately estimated and published monthly data:

MANUFACTURING

Durable Goods	*Nondurable Goods*
1. Ordnance and accessories	12. Food and kindred products
2. Lumber and wood products	13. Tobacco manufactures
3. Furniture and fixtures	14. Textile mill products
4. Stone, clay, and glass products	15. Apparel and related products
5. Primary metal industries	16. Paper and allied products
6. Fabricated metal products	17. Printing, publishing, and allied industries
7. Machinery	18. Chemical and allied products
8. Electrical equipment and supplies	19. Petroleum refining and related industries
9. Transportation equipment	20. Rubber and miscellaneous plastic products
10. Instruments and related products	21. Leather and leather products
11. Miscellaneous	

In addition to manufacturing, most of the other eight major industry divisions are also broken down into industry groups; in *mining*, for example, we have separate estimates for coal mining, metal mining, crude petroleum and natural gas production, and quarrying and nonmetallic mining.

There is yet another level of detail: further classifications within each industry group.

Thus, under *manufacturing* we have *transportation equipment,* as indicated in the listing above. Within transportation equipment we also have subclassifications for motor vehicles and equipment, aircraft and parts, ship and boat building and repair, railroad equipment, and all other transportation equipment—each industry with separate estimates of payroll employment.

Under *trade,* to take another example, we have *retail trade,* which in turn is subdivided into general merchandise stores, food stores, apparel and accessories stores, furniture and appliance stores, eating and drinking places, and other retail trade.

In many instances there is still another level of detail. For example, in the transportation equipment group, the motor vehicle and equipment industry, we have separate employment data each month for motor vehicles, passenger car bodies, truck and bus bodies, and motor vehicle parts and accessories. For the retail trade industry group, apparel and accessories stores, we have separate estimates for men's and boys' apparel stores, women's ready-to-wear stores, family clothing stores, and shoe stores.

This illustrates what the reader can see in any issue of the Bureau of Labor Statistics monthly bulletin *Employment and Earnings,* which contains payroll, employment, and related information for about 400 industries. These data show the anatomy of employment and are indispensable for making sound judgments on the course of industrial jobholding in the United States. They are also our principal guide to the changing geography of employment, including information available for every state and for almost 150 labor market areas. A look in *Employment and Earnings* will show, for example, such varied information as the most recent figure for wage and salary employment in Alabama, contract construction employment in New Mexico, employment in trade in Sioux Falls, South Dakota, and manufacturing employment in Fresno, California.

Farm Employment

Establishment reporting is also carried out in the farm sector by the Department of Agriculture in a statistical series going back to 1909. So we also have a series on farm employment from both household and establishment reporting.

"Crop Reporter" System

Each month the Agricultural Marketing Service of the Department of Agriculture receives mailed reports from about 25,000 farms. The respondent farm owners are called "crop reporters," and the data they supply pertain primarily to what they produce. But information is also given that permits an estimate of the average employment per farm. This, in turn, is applied to an independently estimated number of farms in each state, resulting in an estimate of farm employment nationally and for most of the states.

The series has many of the characteristics inherent in data collected from establishments. All persons (with no age cutoff) who worked at least one hour in agricultural activities for pay or profit are counted. Unlike the nonagricultural-establishment data, this series includes information on the self-employed (farm owners), since the farm is typically also a place of residence of the family. It also includes unpaid family workers who worked fifteen or more hours on a family farm. Separate statistics are provided on hired workers who received wages.

As with the nonfarm-establishment series, persons who worked on more than one farm are counted more than once. And the series does not include any unpaid persons other than family workers—for example, it does not include those with a job but not at work.

The farm series is also different in its time reference. The data apply to the final week of a calendar month, unless that week contains the last day of the month, in which case the figures apply to the next preceding week.

In summary, then, we have from the Department of Agriculture a monthly farm employment series based on information supplied from a sample of about 25,000 crop reporters. The data—shown separately for about thirty-five states for which estimates can be made—apply to family workers (owners and unpaid family workers) and hired workers of all ages who put in at least one hour of work on the farm during the latter part of each month. Persons are counted as many times as they appear on different farm payrolls.

Limitations

We will recall that the MRLF has an age cutoff at fourteen, includes unpaid persons with a job but not at work, and counts a person once and only once. The last point is significant, since many persons typically work on and off U.S. farms during the same week. Those whose hours of work were higher off the farm do not appear at all, of course, in the MRLF count of agricultural employment.

As a result of these differences, the establishment series on farm employment from the Department of Agriculture produces higher estimates than those from MRLF. Table 5-5 shows how the figures have been running for the past dozen years.

TABLE 5-5
Estimates of Farm Employment
MRLF and Department of Agriculture
1951–62 (In Thousands)

Year	MRLF	Department of Agriculture
1951	7,048	9,546
1952	6,792	9,149
1953	6,555	8,864
1954	6,495	8,639
1955	6,718	8,364
1956	6,572	7,820
1957	6,222	7,577
1958	5,844	7,525
1959	5,836	7,384
1960	5,723	7,118
1961	5,436	6,900
1962	5,190	6,707

Source: U. S. Departments of Labor and Agriculture.

In general, both series show a long-term decline, although not at the same rate. The differences between the two series are quite substantial in terms of levels. The 1961 Agriculture Department figure was 28 percent higher than the MRLF figure, and the differences shifted around considerably each month. As the Gordon Committee Report indicated, in one month (January) in 1961 the Agriculture Department figure was only 5 percent higher than that from the MRLF, but in another month (September) it was 55 percent higher.

At the present time the Department of Agriculture statistics suffer from severe limitations. The estimates they produce are based on benchmarks generated by the quinquennial censuses of agriculture and special enumerative studies. But substantial bias occurs because the data come from a sample of crop reporters representing only those able and willing to report. The evidence is that these reporters tend to be the larger farm owners.

An accurate and reliable establishment series in this important sector of the American economy is needed, especially one that can produce geographic data and relevant information by type of farm. This the MRLF cannot now do, if only because of its small sample size. Work now in process at both the Department of Agriculture and the Bureau of the Census promises some improvement in this series.

Reference Notes

1. Beginning January 1964, the time reference is the pay period "which includes the 12th of the month."
2. There have been a number of attempts at an exact statistical reconciliation of the two series, but this is a very difficult procedure that has not yet met with any real success.
3. Additional benchmark information for industries exempted from these social-insurance programs is also used—for example, data from the Interstate Commerce Commission for railroads; from the American Hospital Association for private nonprofit hospitals; from the U.S. Office of Education and from the National Catholic Welfare Conference for private schools and colleges.
4. See D. Hinton, "New Benchmark Levels for BLS Establishment Employment Estimates," in *Employment and Earnings* (U.S. Bureau of Labor Statistics, September 1963).

Readings

Data for the entire history of the national Bureau of Labor Statistics series are in

Employment and Earnings Statistics for the United States, 1909–1960. (Bulletin 1312.) Washington, D.C.: Department of Labor, Bureau of Labor Statistics, 1961.

Employment and Earnings Statistics for States and Areas, 1939–62. (Bulletin 1370.) Washington, D.C.: Bureau of Labor Statistics, 1963.

Current data on wage and salary workers in nonagricultural establishments are issued monthly in summary form in the regular Department of Labor releases on the employment situation and in detail in

Employment and Earnings (bulletin). Washington, D.C.: Department of Labor, Bureau of Labor Statistics.

The monthly farm employment series is issued in

Farm Labor. Washington D.C.: Department of Agriculture, Statistical Reporting Service, Crop Reporting Board.

Concepts, techniques, problems, and issues involved in establishment reporting programs are discussed in Chapters III, IV, and V of

Measuring Employment and Unemployment. (Gordon Committee Report.) Washington, D.C.: President's Committee to Appraise Employment and Unemployment Statistics, 1962. Also, the BLS bulletin *Employment and Earnings* contains a brief summary of concepts, definitions, and techniques used in the nonagricultural establishment series. Some of the newer developments in this series, including the revisions to the new (1957) Standard Industrial Classification system and the results of the 1959 benchmark revision will be found in

WYMER, J. P. "The Revised and Expanded Program of Current Payroll Employment Statistics," *Employment and Earnings*, November 1961.

On the subject of industrial classification *per se*, a good discussion on the principles involved is presented in

SIMMONS, W. R. "The Elements of an Industrial Classification Policy," *Journal of the American Statistical Association*, Vol. 43 (September 1953).

CHAPTER SIX

Information from Social Security Programs

In 1962 more than seven million workers received a total of about $2.75 billion in unemployment insurance benefits. They received their benefits under an insurance system predicated on the idea that eligible jobless workers unable to find suitable employment should be insured against hardship by replacing a part of their lost income. At the same time these benefit payments help the economy by keeping up national purchasing power.

The Bureau of Employment Security, Department of Labor, is the responsible agency at the federal level for the unemployment insurance program. It is now being operated by all fifty states, the District of Columbia, and Puerto Rico, which, in administering the program, make available significant information in the labor force field.

Coverage of Unemployment Insurance System

At the current stage of its development the unemployment insurance system covers four major groups of workers:

1. The first and preponderant group is covered by the regular network of state-operated programs. A federal unemployment insurance tax is imposed on firms in covered industries that employ four or more workers for twenty weeks. Most of the tax is forgiven if the state in which the firm operates sets up a system of unemployment insurance—which each state has done. The states, under federally prescribed general administrative rules, operate these programs and determine the amount and duration of benefits and other features of the program.
2. Unemployment compensation is paid to eligible ex-servicemen. The present program (alphabetized as the UCX program) began in 1958.
3. Unemployment compensation was extended to eligible federal employees under the so-called UCFE program, begun in 1955.
4. Railroad employees are covered under a program administered separately by a federal agency—the Railroad Retirement Board.

These four groups account for about four out of every five wage and salary workers in nonfarm industries who have this insurance against the risk of unemployment.

At this point it is already clear that any estimate of unemployed persons covered by this system is going to be smaller than the figure on total unemployment, since not all workers are included under unemployment insurance. There are other reasons why this is so; these are enumerated in the following paragraphs.

Exclusions

First, various groups are excluded, wholly or in part, by law:

1. Agricultural labor, domestic workers in private homes, unpaid family workers, and the self-employed. Unemployed persons in these sectors will be counted in the MRLF sample but will not appear in any count of the insured unemployed.

2. Employees of state and local governments. The federal unemployment insurance tax cannot constitutionally be imposed on state or local governments. Many states, however, have chosen to extend coverage to some government employees; one state (Wisconsin) and the District of Columbia cover all the government workers in their jurisdictions.

3. Employees of nonprofit organizations, which currently totals about 1.5 million persons.

4. Employees of firms with fewer than four employees. Although the law applies to firms with four or more employees, states may extend the coverage to those employing fewer workers. About half the states have done so; in fact, in twenty states the coverage has been extended to all of the firms that employ one or more workers.

Thus, the federal law, supplemented by state actions, has so far created a system of inclusions and exclusions from coverage that, at the beginning of 1962, resulted in the pattern of coverage that is shown below.

Covered by Unemployment Insurance (Millions)		*Not Covered by Unemployment Insurance (Millions)*	
Under state programs	40.4	State and local government	6.2
Federal employees (UCFE)	2.4	Domestics	2.6
Ex-servicemen (UCX)	2.6	Agricultural	1.9
Railroad employees	.8	Small organizations	1.8
		Nonprofit organizations	1.5
		Other	.3
	46.2		14.3

Persons Not on Payrolls

There is another very important category that is not covered by the unemployment insurance programs. The tax that the employer pays is based on his payroll—on the number of persons in his employ and the wages they make. Obviously, persons not on payrolls are not included. Thus, youthful job seekers who have never had any work experience—who have not been on payrolls—will not be included. Similarly, married women returning to the work force and actively seeking work will be counted as unemployed by the MRLF but will of course be excluded from these counts.

Persons Not Entitled to Benefits

Concerning unemployment benefits, a similar situation exists among some workers who have made too little in wages to draw unemployment insurance when they become jobless. All states require that claimants for unemployment benefits must have earned some minimum amount ("wage credits") during a specified "base period." In most states this base period is the fifty-two-week period immediately preceding the claimant's first spell of unemployment. (1) Thus, even if a person is in covered employment and loses his job, he must also meet his state's requirements on this score before he can receive unemployment benefits and be counted under this system.

Extremely important to an understanding of how the system works is the fact that in all states there is a limit to the amount of time during which an eligible person can draw benefits. The duration of the benefit period varies from a maximum of twenty weeks in Virginia to thirty-nine weeks in Oklahoma. Most states have a maximum of twenty-six weeks. Thus, there will always be a number of unemployed workers who have exhausted their benefits because they have reached the maximum in their states. Or they may exhaust their benefits before the maximum period because of the small amount of wages they drew during their employment.

Counts of persons drawing unemployment benefits therefore lose their significance as an accurate measure of joblessness during an extended period of unemployment, since those who exhaust their entitlements fall out of the count. Estimates by the Labor Department's Bureau of Employment Security indicate that, at any given time, about 10 percent of all unemployed workers have exhausted their benefits. Exhaustions have run even higher in recession periods, and in 1958 and 1961, Congress voted temporary extensions of unemployment insurance beyond the prevailing maximum.

Earlier we discussed the evolution of the concepts of ability and willingness to work and the fact that the total unemployment figure from the MRLF is *not* based on such factors.

Ability, willingness and availability to work are, however, very relevant to the ongoing system of unemployment insurance. Otherwise-eligible workers may not receive unemployment benefits if they make themselves unavailable for work. To receive their benefits, workers must report to their local state employment service offices each week, and they must be able, willing, and available to take a suitable job. The job must be in the worker's usual line of work and at a wage level comparable with what he had previously been receiving. He may not be referred by his local state employment office to a plant that is on strike.

There also is a whole series of disqualifications written into the various state laws that can bar an otherwise-eligible worker from drawing benefits. Generally prevailing are those that disqualify workers if they voluntarily quit their jobs, are discharged for misconduct, or are directly engaged in a labor dispute. (2) In all such cases, if the individual is actively seeking work, he will be counted as unemployed by the MRLF but will not appear in the counts under this system.

Some eligible unemployed workers never file for benefits. They may look for a job for a few weeks and then, if unsuccessful, file for their benefits; or they may never file at all.

The counts from this system also include some persons who did some work and would be enumerated as employed by the MRLF household count as well as the BLS. States generally permit claimants to do some work and receive wages as well as correspondingly reduced unemployment benefits. This is done in order not to discourage jobless workers from taking some work for fear of losing all their benefits. The numbers vary greatly from state to state, but anywhere from 6 to 10 percent of all claimants have been in this status in recent years.

Data from Claims

We turn now to a description of the unemployment insurance claims procedures, an important by-product of which is the system of unemployment statistics they generate.

Claims Procedure

Upon becoming unemployed, a worker must personally file a claim for benefits in his local employment office. This first claim is known as an *initial claim.* This is the worker's notice to the employment service office of his unemployment—his eligibility still has to be determined. Not all persons filing initial claims will get benefits. Some may find a job very soon thereafter, and some may not be found eligible.

Nevertheless, these initial claims reveal "new" unemployment in covered industries. The Bureau of Employment Security therefore publishes each week the total number of initial claims under the regular state program as well as under UCFE and UCX. (3) These data are available weekly for each of the fifty states, the District of Columbia, and Puerto Rico. These are not sample counts; they are actual totals of everyone in initial claims status. As the Gordon Committee said, "Initial claims are a sensitive indicator of emerging unemployment, and the availability of the series on a weekly basis makes it a very useful tool for analysis." (4)

After the unemployed worker has filed the initial claim and has been found eligible, he files a *waiting period claim.* This is required in all but five states (Maryland, Nevada, Montana, North Carolina, and Texas). During the required week, the claimant must still be out of work and otherwise eligible. He still does not receive benefits. During the second and succeeding weeks of unemployment, the worker files a *compensable claim* for which he receives benefits.

Waiting period claims plus compensable claims are added together into a series called *continued claims,* representing the number of persons who continue in unemployment status. This series, too, is published weekly under the heading *Insured Unemployment* and includes the regular state programs, UCFE, UCX, and railroads. These data are given by state (except for railroad workers) and for the week containing the 12th, for 147 labor market areas. Again, these are *not* sample counts but actual totals.

Comparison with MRLF Data

As already indicated, the MRLF total unemployment figure is larger than insured unemployment but the trends of the two series are very similar. Table 6-1 gives both sets of figures as published and then adjusts the insured unemployment figure—mainly by adding an estimate of the number who exhausted their benefits but continued to be unemployed. From the MRLF figure it subtracts such groups as agriculture, self-employed, unpaid family workers. The adjustment, while not accounting for all the differences between the two series, significantly cuts down the differences.

The Incidence of Insured Unemployment

Who are the people who draw unemployment insurance? The Bureau of Employment Security publishes a monthly bulletin on *The Insured Unemployed* giving many personal and economic characteristics of this group.

Data are published on the age, sex, occupation, industry, and duration of the current spell of insured unemployment—again by state. The information comes from records and interviews with claimants in some 1800 local employment offices. It is derived from a probability sample of claimants under state programs for the week containing the 12th of the month.

TABLE 6-1
Average Annual Unemployment, Total and Insured, Adjusted and Unadjusted (In Thousands)

Year	Total* Unemployment	Insured* Unemployment	Difference	Total† Unemployment	Insured‡ Unemployment	Difference
1954	3,578	1,878	1,700	2,915	2,247	668
1955	2,904	1,236	1,668	2,234	1,569	665
1956	2,822	1,214	1,608	2,112	1,403	709
1957	2,936	1,465	1,471	2,253	1,694	559
1958	4,681	2,520	2,161	3,667	3,267	400
1959	3,813	1,667	2,146	2,830	2,167	663
1960	3,931	1,945	1,986	2,939	2,272	667
1961	4,806	2,258	2,548	3,588	2,932	666

* Original series as published.

† MRLF series minus unemployed who were self-employed, unpaid workers, persons without work experience, persons in domestic service, education, and public administration, and agricultural workers.

‡ Insured unemployment series minus workers partially employed plus persons who have exhausted their benefits.

Source: Gordon Committee Report, p. 107.

These data provide a valuable insight into the impact of unemployment on various groups—at least that part of unemployment that is insured. In the middle of 1963, for example, these data showed that almost six out of every ten of the claimants were men; two out of five were forty-five years of age and over; over half (55 percent) were unskilled and semiskilled; and half were factory workers.

Area Labor Market Trends

From time to time we have indicated the extent to which geographic data are available from the three major sources of information being reviewed. The most advanced geographic information relates to wage and salary workers in nonagricultural establishments emanating from the cooperative establishment reporting system and the insured unemployment series. These data, however, represent only a part of the total picture.

Information Required by U.S. Government Programs

No on-going system now gives a current, systematic, comparable series on labor force, total employment, and total unemployment by state and area. Yet geographic crosscurrents in employment and unemployment increasingly make this information necessary. Industry, business, unions, and local planning officials need it for planning, market research, plant location, and labor recruitment.

A knowledge of the employment situation by area also is basic to the administration of many government programs. The employment security system itself needs these data for its own operations in local labor markets, which involve knowing where job vacancies are, expected trends in employment, job placement, and employee counseling. The same kinds of knowledge are needed for administering the "Buy American Act," the small-business loan program, and various government procurement programs that give certain preferences to areas of relatively high unemployment. Also for administration of the Area Redevelopment Act of 1961 and the Manpower Development and Training Act, the Trade Expansion Act, and the Accelerated Work Projects Act of 1962, information on the unemployment situation in local areas is required. Administrators of some of these programs also require extensive data on current and anticipated job trends by occupation and industry.

Need for Better Data

Data of this sort are collected across the board only once every ten years, at the time of the decennial census. Ideally, an MRLF type of survey on a current basis among the various areas of the United States would fill the bill in the intervening years. We may continue to lack such a survey for quite some time in view of the substantial costs that would be involved. Lacking this, the Bureau of Employment Security (BES) has developed techniques for building on the data that are available. These are used by the states in constructing the desired information.

One of the basic statistics needed, for example, is the rate of unemployment by local labor market area. An estimate of total unemployment is needed; it will serve as the numerator. Also needed is an estimate of total employment, which when added to the unemployment figure yields the labor force, which serves as the denominator for the estimate.

On the employment side, the methods prescribed by the BES involve use of the current nonagricultural employment figure already described. This is bolstered by the use of covered employment adjusted for sectors not covered—as described in the preceding chapter's discussion of the benchmark operations.

On the unemployment side, one begins with the insured unemployment sector. Then are added estimates of all the groups excluded —such as those who are in noncovered employment, those who delayed or never filed claims, those who have exhausted their benefits, new entrants into the labor force, and all the other excluded groups enumerated in this chapter.

Such procedures are highly complicated. Data for making these kinds of estimates are often unavailable, and practices vary from one place to another. It is difficult to make checks on the validity, comparability, and reliability of those estimates that are made. Steps are being taken to improve this work, and the possibility is being considered, for example, of using surveys of the MRLF type in selected areas from time to time to yield some hard data for the purposes of checking the estimates.

Area Classification

In the meantime the BES uses available information in a number of ways. Every month it publishes a bulletin on *Area Labor Market Trends* that first classifies 150 major labor market areas according to their employment/unemployment situation. What determines an area's classification is basically the extent of unemployment it is experiencing, supplemented by the area's labor supply-demand outlook and by the seasonal forces at work in the area.

Under the classification system that has been used since May 1955, a major labor market area can fall in one of six categories.

Group A includes areas of current overall labor shortage that is expected to continue through the next few months and where the unemployment rate is less than 1.5 percent.

Group B includes areas where the job opportunities for local workers are pretty much in balance with the supply—now and expected for the ensuing few months. The prevailing rate of unemployment falls between 1.5 and 2.9 percent.

Group C covers areas where job seekers, now and again for the next few months, are moderately in excess of job openings and where unemployment ranges from 3.0 to 5.9 percent.

Areas in Groups A, B and C, often labeled as those with "overall labor shortages," "moderately low unemployment," and "moderate unemployment" respectively, thus all fall under the 6 percent unemployment mark.

Groups D, E, and *F* are characterized as areas of "relatively substantial unemployment." In these, job seekers are substantially in excess of job openings and the prognosis is for either declining employment or at best no significant change in status over the next few months; neither is their situation traceable to temporary or seasonal forces. The three are differentiated by their rates of unemployment as follows:

Group D—6.0 to 8.9 percent
Group E—9.0 to 11.9 percent
Group F—12.0 percent and over

Thus, the area classification system is based on a combination of estimates of unemployment rates and judgmental factors regarding the area's outlook. Needless to say, the demarcations should be considered approximate.

Areas classified in Groups D, E, and F are considered as meeting the requirements for official designation as "areas of substantial unemployment" for certain purposes. When they are so designated, they are eligible for special assistance under various federal programs relating to government contract awards, redevelopment area assistance, public works, and small business loans.

Here is how the 150 major areas were classified in a recent year:

Labor Supply Group	*August 1962*	*August 1963*
A	0	0
B	11	16
C	92	97
D	38	28
E	6	7
F	3	2
Total	150	150

Note that between August 1962 and August 1963, the number of "areas of substantial unemployment" (Groups D, E, and F) moved from 47 to 37, in line with overall changes in economic activity.

These 150 major labor market areas account for about 70 percent of all nonagricultural wage and salary workers. In addition, the BES classifies smaller areas (down to a labor force of 15,000), designating them as "smaller areas of substantial unemployment"—although these are not categorized separately in D, E, and F classes. They also can receive preference under appropriate government assistance programs.

Areas of Persistent Unemployment

All "areas of substantial unemployment" are assessed against additional criteria that could designate them as "areas of substantial and persistent unemployment" (for example, 17 of the 37 major labor market areas classified as areas of substantial unemployment in August 1963 were also designated as areas of substantial and persistent unemployment). The same process is applied to the smaller areas and one additional group—the very small areas, with work forces below 15,000. These get first preference under relevant procurement programs. The Area Redevelopment Act of 1961 and the Public Works Acceleration Act of 1962 also make these areas eligible for various government loans, grants, and training and retraining programs, and public works.

To be classified as an area of substantial and persistent unemployment, an area must meet the following criteria:

1. Unemployment must be 6 percent or more, discounting seasonal or temporary factors.

2. The annual average unemployment rate must have been
   a) at least 50 percent above the national average for three of the four preceding calendar years;
   b) at least 75 percent above the national average for two of the three preceding calendar years;
   c) at least 100 percent above the national average for one of the two preceding calendar years.

As an example of the geography of unemployment, we list below all the *major* labor market areas designated in August 1963 as having "substantial unemployment"; those in italics also meet the criteria of "substantial and persistent unemployment."

California:	Fresno, San Diego, San Jose, Stockton
Connecticut:	New Britain, Waterbury
Florida:	Miami
Massachusetts:	Brockton, *Fall River*, Lawrence-Haverhill, *Lowell*, *New Bedford*, Springfield-Chicopee-Holyoke
Minnesota:	*Duluth-Superior*
New Jersey:	*Atlantic City*, Jersey City
New York:	Buffalo, Utica-Rome
North Carolina:	Durham
Ohio:	Hamilton-Middletown
Pennsylvania:	*Altoona*, *Erie*, *Johnstown*, Philadelphia, *Pittsburgh*, *Scranton*, *Wilkes-Barre-Hazelton*
Puerto Rico:	*Mayagüez*, *Ponce*, San Juan
Rhode Island:	*Providence-Pawtucket*
Tennessee:	Chattanooga
Texas:	Beaumont-Port Arthur
West Virginia:	*Charleston*, *Huntington-Ashland*, *Wheeling*

Noncurrent Sources of Employment Data

As we close Part I, it should be noted that we have considered only those sources that yield *current* (monthly and weekly) data.

For instance, we have not gone extensively into data enumerated by the decennial censuses—although we will be using them when we trace the history of labor force growth and occupational trends.

Similarly, in the case of establishment reporting, we have highlighted the current data sources. Noncurrent establishment collections are in fact made by, for example, the Census Bureau in its censuses and surveys of manufacturing, business, government, and agriculture. These also gather important information from establishments on employment and production.

In the case of social-insurance statistics, we have alluded to the importance of the *covered employment* information from the unemployment insurance system. We mentioned its use as the benchmark in checking current data on wage and salary workers in nonagricultural establishments. More than two million employers in private industry are subject to state unemployment insurance laws. They must submit quarterly reports to their respective state agencies giving information on monthly employment and quarterly wages for their establishments. These reports, together with reports from federal government establishments and those state and local units that are covered, supply quarterly published data on covered employment and wages.

The data are classified by industry in substantial detail (also in accord with the standard industrial classification system) and—since 1959—by nine different size-of-firm groupings. They are also, of course, available by state, furnishing a pretty complete record for studying trends in covered employment. The data have a wide range of uses within the employment security system itself, including their use as a frame from which samples may be chosen for research and operational work and use in actuarial studies of state unemployment insurance funds.

Also available in the field of social insurance data is information on covered employment under the federal old-age and survivors insurance system. Quarterly reports are issued on employment and related data for this system by the Bureau of Old-Age and Survivors Insurance (BOASI) in the Department of Health, Education, and Welfare. Close to 90 percent of all persons in paid employment are covered now, with both the employer and the employee paying a tax that is credited to each worker's account and that cumulates toward the time when he retires and receives his pension. This is why (as indicated in the preceding chapter) this system is used to supplement the unemployment insurance covered-employment statistics when used as a benchmark.

The BOASI also publishes quarterly information on age and sex distributions of workers as well as a number of series on wages. Potentially, as it nears almost complete coverage, this system has all the attributes of becoming a primary source of information on employment in this country.

Reference Notes

1. Five states (Idaho, Maine, New Hampshire, Oregon, and Washington) have a uniform benefit year—the same for all persons no matter when they file a claim.
2. New York and Rhode Island do permit payment of benefits to otherwise-eligible workers, but only after serving a disqualification period (in addition to a one-week waiting period) of seven weeks in New York and six weeks in Rhode Island.
3. Although federal programs, the last two are administered by the states; thus, if a federal worker becomes unemployed in California he receives the same amount of benefit and the same duration of benefit as other workers in that state do. Initial claims are not filed under the Railroad Retirement Board system.
4. Gordon Committee Report, p. 87.

Readings

Current data on unemployment insurance claims are released weekly by the Bureau of Employment Security (Department of Labor), Washington, D.C.; relevant data for the midmonth period are also included with the rest of current labor force, employment, and unemployment statistics in the

Monthly Report on the Labor Force. Washington, D.C.: Department of Labor, Bureau of Labor Statistics.

The BES also issues information on the personal and economic characteristics of persons claiming unemployment insurance in the monthly periodical

The Insured Unemployed. Washington, D.C.: Department of Labor, Bureau of Employment Security.

Listings of areas and their labor market classifications according to relative degree of unemployment, a description of the areas, and other factors are contained in the monthly bulletin

Area Labor Market Trends. Washington, D.C.: Department of Labor, Bureau of Employment Security.

Concepts, techniques, problems, and issues involved in social-insurance information programs are discussed in Chapters III, IV, and VII of

Measuring Employment and Unemployment. (Gordon Committee Report.) Washington, D.C.: President's Committee to Appraise Employment and Unemployment Statistics, 1962.

The technical aspects of these programs are comprehensively summarized in

"Insured Unemployment and Wage Statistics; Their Source, Nature, and Limitations," *The Labor Market and Employment Security*. Washington, D.C.: Department of Labor, Bureau of Employment Security, March 1960.

An excellent series of articles on the many facets of these programs will be found in

"The Role of Unemployment Insurance Today and Tomorrow," *Employment Security Review* (U.S. Bureau of Employment Security, August 1962).

Details of provisions of various state laws are found in

Summary Tables for Evaluation of Coverage and Benefit Provisions of State Unemployment Insurance Laws as of Dec. 31, 1961. Washington, D.C.: Department of Labor, Bureau of Employment Security, July 1962.

PART TWO

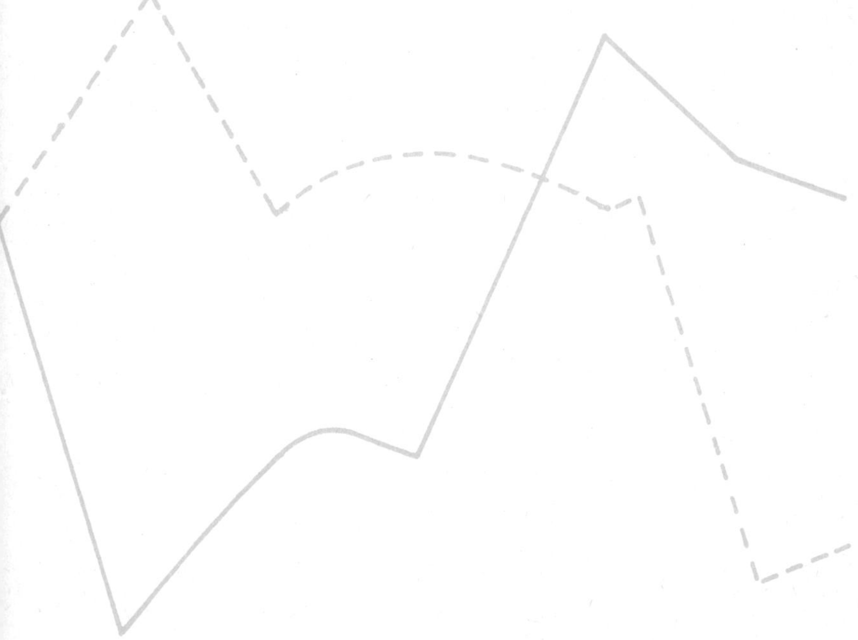

The American Labor Force: Patterns and Trends

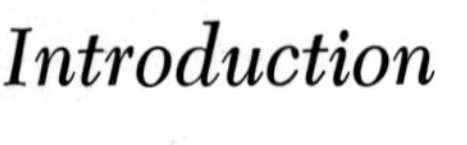

Introduction

In this, Part II of our story, we will begin to describe and analyze the materials that are available from sources of information we reviewed in Part I.

Three overriding themes emerge from these materials. The first is the enormous change that has occurred in the length of our working lives, in the United States and many other countries. This has had significant implications not only for the people involved, but also for the manpower potential and posture of their countries.

As we will see, techniques have been developed that enable us to construct Tables of Working Life, very similar to actuaries' life tables. In such tables one can find figures representing the average lifetime remaining and the average number of years remaining of labor force activity for persons of that age. What has happened to U.S. work-life expectancy and its relation to life expectancy is one of the major stories of this century.

To give one example: While it is commonly expected that most boys will go on to become members of the labor force, it is comparatively little known that the average high school girl today—who typically will go on to get married and have children—will nevertheless spend twenty-five years of her remaining lifetime in the labor force.

The second theme can be stated as follows:

The most important factor affecting a country's labor force is its population's *demographic* characteristics (from the Greek *demos*, meaning "people"). For any given period of time, it is the personal characteristics of the population—their age, sex, color, and marital status, for example—that are the prime determinants of labor force size and composition.

These demographic characteristics change very slowly. Normally—barring any disastrous events—the proportion of the population that is male or female, white or nonwhite, married or unmarried, for example, changes very slowly over the years. Knowing how labor market participation varies with these demographic characteristics, we might be able to make very good estimates of the size and composition of the labor force in the years ahead—*if* these demographic variables were the only ones that counted.

There is a third theme. It turns out that the *nondemographic* factors—the changes in social, economic, and political conditions over a period of time—are overriding influences. These, of course, are extremely difficult to foretell.

To give an obvious example: The rate at which married women participate in the labor force varies with such demographic factors as their age, whether they have children or not and, if they do, the ages of their children. Given the age distribution of married women for the period 1951–61 and the increasing numbers with children, the total number of U.S. married women in the labor force should have stayed the same even though there were about 4.5 million more married women in 1961 than in 1951. As a matter of fact, the number of married women workers went up by more than 4 million during that period. This increase in married women's labor force activity accounted for almost half of all the labor force increase among U.S. females during that decade. Obviously, it was not the demographic factors, but the increasing propensity of these women to work outside the home, that made the difference.

We now turn, in Chapters 7 to 9, to a detailed consideration of these demographic and social and economic trends and their influence on labor force.

We shall conclude with Chapter 10 showing how this information is used to project the labor force into the future.

CHAPTER SEVEN

The Length of Working Life

We shall continue our study of the labor force with a review of two prime forces affecting all of us: how long we live and how long we work, as well as the manner in which these two forces have interacted during the twentieth century.

The lengthening expectation of life in the past sixty years has been extraordinary. On the average, a baby boy today will live about eighteen years longer than a baby boy born at the turn of the century, a baby girl twenty-two years longer.

What this has meant in terms of sheer survivorship is shown in Table 7-1. In 1900, 46,452 out of every 100,000 newborn males could expect to survive to age sixty—well under one out of two. By 1960 the figure was closer to three out of four. Incidentally, almost as many boys born in 1960 can expect to live to age *sixty* as could have expected to live to age *twenty* back in 1900.

For women, the situation is even more striking. Eighty-five out of every one hundred girls born in 1960 can expect to survive to age sixty. Many more can expect to live to age *sixty* than could have expected to live to age *fifteen* back in 1900.

Today sixty has become a relatively young age. At the current rate, one out of every four boys born alive can expect to survive to his eightieth birthday—double the rate that prevailed in 1900. Among women the situation again is more striking, and at present the expectations are that more than two out of every five baby girls will live to their eightieth birthdays—triple the rate of 1900.

More Time for Education, Work, and Retirement

In this chapter we shall discuss the working life expectancy for various age groups, which can be estimated in a manner similar to that of standard life tables. We shall pay particular attention to the effects of the longer life expectancy and longer working life expectancy that prevail today.

TABLE 7-1
*Number Living out of 100,000 Born Alive at Selected Ages, by Sex, 1900–60**

	Male		Female	
Age	1900	1960	1900	1960
15	78,037	96,071	80,680	97,003
20	76,376	95,472	78,978	96,744
40	64,954	91,502	67,935	94,526
60	46,452	73,502	50,752	84,290
80	12,266	24,639	15,349	42,549

*Data for 1900 are based on whites in death-registration states.
Source: U.S. Department of Health, Education, and Welfare, National Vital Statistics Division.

One important development has been that the average member of the working force, male or female, now has more years of his or her life to spend in education, work, and retirement.

With these changes have also come problems: the need for more education and training, and the increased years spent by young people in school, have challenged our overburdened schools and colleges. Yet, with increased automation, more and more young people will need special training if they are to get decent jobs.

At the other end of the age scale, with longer retirement periods, we now have greater concentration on the problems that are faced by the aged: social security, private pension plans, leisure time, housing, and medical expenses.

The United States, we shall see, is not unique in the increase in its people's life expectancy and working life expectancy. These have also increased in other nations for which we have statistics.

Work Life Expectancy

The very extension of the lifespan has afforded many more possibilities of choice to the population. For example, at 1900 levels and rates, when life expectancy for males was about forty-eight years, "retirement" as we know it now was hypothetical for most. Now retirement is the conventional pattern for most.

Next to life expectancy, there is no more important index of social and economic welfare than the expectation of working life.

In dealing with the length of our working lives, we are of course dealing with the age at which persons enter the labor force, as well as the age at which they exit. Such important factors as time spent in education and time spent in retirement are also involved.

The length of time a person spends in economic activity also reflects a variety of other influences. He must of course survive to an age where he can make his first entry into the labor force. In the United States, as in many other countries, a major part of our increased longevity is traceable to a highly significant reduction in childhood diseases and infant mortality. This has enabled a much greater proportion of a given cohort in the population to reach labor force age.

Legislation may also affect the length of a person's working life. School-attendance laws, or laws stipulating minimum working ages, obviously affect the time of labor force entry; social security laws influence the time of exit from the labor force.

Economic events of various sorts will have their impact. For instance, the increased complexity of work during this century, due largely to technological change, has substantially increased the educational and training prerequisites for employment. This has delayed the first entry of young people into the labor force in order to permit them to acquire the necessary knowledge and skills.

On the other hand, the rapid rise of private pension plans after World War II, especially through collective bargaining, has begun to affect the age at which people retire.

Tables of Working Life

Since the eighteenth century, economists, sociologists, and actuaries have been making estimates of the duration of a person's productive life. In 1908, for instance, Georgio Mortara (1) made such a study in Italy, and in 1951 Mortara, still a student of these affairs, analyzed trends in working life in more than thirty countries.

In 1950 this writer constructed a series of Tables of Working Life for the United States which show the changing length and pattern of working life. They are similar to standard life tables made by actuaries to summarize the mortality experience of a population for some particular period of time. A typical life table starts with a group of persons—usually 100,000—born alive, and then follows the group through successive ages as members of it die. A central concept is "life expectancy"—or the average number of years of life remaining at each specified age.

The Tables of Working Life also follow through successive ages the experience of an initial cohort of 100,000 persons from birth. In addition to showing the attrition due to mortality, calculations are made to show the number who may be expected to be in the labor force during their lifespan; rates at which persons enter and exit from the labor force; and a "work life expectancy"—the average number of years of labor force activity remaining at each specified age. Basically, these tables apply the life-table technique to an analysis of labor market activity. These techniques have been used in many countries, making international comparisons of working life (permitted by standard life-table construction) possible on a more extensive basis.

The reader is referred to the Table of Working Life for Men for 1960 (Table 7-2). We will give three examples from the table to make its use and interpretation clear.

Example 1: Age Eighteen

If one looks at Column 1 (Years of Age) he can find eighteen, which we will use as an example. This is the age at which the average male in this country makes his first entry into the labor force as a full-time worker.

In Column 2, the figure 95,666 represents the number still expected to be living at age eighteen out of an original cohort of 100,000 born in 1960. Columns 3 and 4 show the number that are in the labor force at that age (61,992) and their rate of labor market participation (64.8 percent).

Column 5 shows the "accession rate," that is, the proportion that move into the labor force between one age and the next. Thus the accession rate for males eighteen years of age is shown as 116.8 per thousand. The increase in the size of the labor force among men between eighteen and nineteen years of age—taking account of deaths which occur during that time interval—was at that rate in 1960. This column is of interest because it shows the profile or progression of young men into the labor force. The rate ends at age thirty-three, when it is estimated that just about all men have made their entry into the labor market.

Note that accessions move up steeply among the teen-agers, but a substantial amount still takes place among men in their twenties, as many defer their entry until college graduation or completion of postgraduate work. This phenomenon will be presented graphically in the next chapter, when we discuss how demographic factors such as age affect the pattern of labor force participation.

The next three columns (6, 7, and 8) show the pattern of exits from the labor force among males. For the man of eighteen whom we are following through, the death rate is quite small and there are of course no departures because of retirement. This changes as the ages of our men advance and gets quite steep in the older ages, as we would expect. Note that at age sixty-one retirement from the labor force (whether formal retirement on a pension, or withdrawal for any other reason such as disability) took over, as of 1960, as the main reason for exits from the labor force.

By going through the steps enumerated so far, we arrive at the figures given in Columns 9 and 10, the expectation of life and working life respectively. The former is exactly what one observes in a conventional life table.

At age eighteen the average number of remaining years of life is

TABLE 7-2
Table of Working Life: Males, 1960

	Number Living of 100,000 Born Alive				Separations from the Labor Force (per 1000 in Labor Force)			Average Number of Remaining Years of:	
		In Labor Force							
Years of Age (1)	In Population (2)	Number (3)	Percent of Population (4)	Accessions to the Labor Force (per 1000 in Population) (5)	Due to all Causes (6)	Due to Death (7)	Due to Retirement (8)	Life (9)	Labor Force Participation (10)
x	L_x	Lw_x	w_x	$1000\ A_x$	$1000\ Q^s_x$	$1000\ Q^d_x$	$1000\ Q^r_x$	$\overset{o}{e}_x$	$\overset{o}{ew}_x$
	(In Year of Age)				(Between Years of Age)			(At Beginning of Year of Age)	
14	96,102	14,800	15.4	52.0	.9	.9	—	55.2	48.3
15	96,020	19,780	20.6	119.9	1.1	1.1	—	54.2	47.3
16	95,918	31,269	32.6	143.8	1.2	1.2	—	53.3	46.3
17	95,800	45,026	47.0	177.8	1.4	1.4	—	52.3	45.4
18	95,666	61,992	64.8	116.8	1.5	1.5	—	51.4	44.4
19	95,523	73,075	76.5	63.9	1.5	1.6	—	50.5	43.5
20	95,374	79,065	82.9	33.9	1.7	1.7	—	49.6	42.6
21	95,211	82,167	86.3	26.0	1.8	1.8	—	48.6	41.6
22	95,039	84,490	88.9	18.9	1.8	1.8	—	47.7	40.7
23	94,865	86,137	90.8	14.0	1.8	1.8	—	46.8	39.8
24	94,692	87,306	92.2	11.0	1.8	1.8	—	45.9	38.9
25	94,526	88,193	93.3	9.0	1.8	1.8	—	45.0	37.9
26	94,360	88,887	94.2	8.0	1.7	1.7	—	44.1	37.0
27	94,197	89,487	95.0	7.0	1.7	1.7	—	43.1	36.1
28	94,033	89,990	95.7	5.9	1.7	1.7	—	42.2	35.1
29	93,869	90,396	96.3	5.0	1.8	1.8	—	41.3	34.2
30	93,697	90,699	96.8	2.0	1.9	1.9	—	40.4	33.2
31	93,522	90,716	97.0	1.0	1.9	1.9	—	39.4	32.3
32	93,341	90,634	97.1	1.0	2.0	2.0	—	38.5	31.4
33	93,151	90,543	97.2	1.0	2.2	2.2	—	37.6	30.4
34	92,948	90,438	97.3	—	3.4	2.4	1.0	36.7	29.5
35	92,728	90,132	97.2	—	3.6	2.5	1.1	35.7	28.6
36	92,493	89,811	97.1	—	3.8	2.8	1.0	34.8	27.7
37	92,238	89,471	97.0	—	4.0	3.0	1.0	33.9	26.8
38	91,960	89,109	96.9	—	4.3	3.3	1.0	33.0	25.9
39	91,659	88,726	96.8	—	4.7	3.6	1.1	32.1	25.0
40	91,326	88,312	96.7	—	5.0	4.0	1.0	31.2	24.1
41	90,964	87,871	96.6	—	5.4	4.4	1.0	30.3	23.2
42	90,568	87,398	96.5	—	5.9	4.8	1.1	29.5	22.3
43	90,131	86,886	96.4	—	6.3	5.3	1.0	28.6	21.4
44	89,654	86,337	96.3	—	7.1	6.1	1.0	27.7	20.6
45	89,106	85,720	96.2	—	7.5	6.4	1.1	26.9	19.7
46	88,534	85,081	96.1	—	9.2	7.1	2.1	26.0	18.8
47	87,904	84,300	95.9	—	10.0	7.9	2.1	25.2	18.0
48	87,206	83,456	95.7	—	12.0	8.9	3.1	24.4	17.2
49	86,428	82,452	95.4	—	13.8	9.6	4.2	23.6	16.4
50	85,596	81,316	95.0	—	16.4	11.2	5.2	22.8	15.6

Years of Age (1)	Number Living of 100,000 Born Alive: In Population (2)	In Labor Force: Number (3)	In Labor Force: Percent of Population (4)	Accessions to the Labor Force (per 1000 in Population) (5)	Separations from the Labor Force (per 1000 in Labor Force): Due to all Causes (6)	Due to Death (7)	Due to Retirement (8)	Average Number of Remaining Years of: Life (9)	Labor Force Participation (10)
x	L_x	Lw_x	w_x	$1000\ A_x$	$1000\ Q^s_x$	$1000\ Q^d_x$	$1000\ Q^r_x$	$\overset{o}{e}_x$	$\overset{o}{ew}_x$
	(In Year of Age)				(Between Years of Age)			(At Beginning of Year of Age)	
51	84,637	79,982	94.5	—	18.6	12.4	6.2	22.1	14.8
52	83,591	78,492	93.9	—	20.8	13.4	7.4	21.3	14.0
53	82,468	76,860	93.2	—	22.8	14.3	8.5	20.6	13.3
54	81,283	75,105	92.4	—	25.1	15.4	9.7	19.9	12.6
55	80,020	73,218	91.5	—	27.0	16.2	10.8	19.2	11.9
56	78,717	71,239	90.5	—	28.3	17.3	11.0	18.5	11.2
57	77,344	69,223	89.5	—	32.1	18.8	13.3	17.8	10.5
58	75,881	67,003	88.3	—	35.2	20.6	14.6	17.1	9.8
59	74,306	64,646	87.0	—	41.1	22.9	18.2	16.4	9.1
60	72,588	61,990	85.4	—	47.8	24.7	23.1	15.8	8.5
61	70,774	59,026	83.4	—	54.0	26.8	27.2	15.2	7.8
62	68,849	55,837	81.1	—	61.8	29.0	32.8	14.6	7.2
63	66,820	52,387	78.4	—	87.3	30.8	56.5	14.0	6.7
64	64,699	47,813	73.9	—	263.7	29.6	234.1	13.4	6.1
65	62,533	35,206	56.3	—	170.1	34.1	136.0	12.8	6.3
66	60,246	29,219	48.5	—	122.5	37.6	84.9	12.3	7.0
67	57,879	25,640	44.3	—	98.4	41.0	57.4	11.8	7.1
68	55,438	23,118	41.7	—	102.6	44.1	58.5	11.2	7.0
69	52,923	20,746	39.2	—	106.4	46.8	59.6	10.7	6.7
70	50,374	18,538	36.8	—	111.7	50.8	60.9	10.2	6.4
71	47,733	16,468	34.5	—	116.5	54.6	61.9	9.8	6.1
72	45,046	14,550	32.3	—	121.5	58.5	63.0	9.3	5.9
73	42,325	12,782	30.2	—	129.7	62.5	67.2	8.8	5.6
74	39,586	11,124	28.1	—	133.6	68.5	65.1	8.4	5.3
75	36,785	9,638	26.2	—	145.2	71.7	73.5	8.0	5.1
76	34,047	8,239	24.2	—	152.3	77.1	75.2	7.5	4.8
77	31,320	6,984	22.3	—	164.1	82.8	81.3	7.1	4.6
78	28,617	5,838	20.4	—	173.3	89.4	83.9	6.7	4.3
79	25,946	4,826	18.6	—	190.8	99.6	91.2	6.3	4.1
80	23,245	3,905	16.8	—	200.8	105.5	95.3	6.0	3.9
81	20,669	3,121	15.1	—	220.4	115.0	105.4	5.6	3.7
82	18,159	2,433	13.4	—	243.3	125.6	117.7	5.3	3.6
83	15,734	1,841	11.7	—	256.9	139.1	117.8	5.0	3.6
84	13,408	1,368	10.2	—	265.4	140.4	125.0	4.7	3.6
85 and over	55,525	4,386	7.9	—	—	—	—	4.5	3.6

Source: *The Length of Working Life for Males, 1900–60* (Manpower Report No. 8, U.S. Department of Labor, Office of Manpower, Automation, and Training, July 1963).

51.4, and of working life 44.4. In other words, at 1960 mortality and labor force rates, a man of eighteen could look forward to about fifty-one and a half more years of life, about forty-four and a half years as a worker and about seven years in retirement. These, of course, are averages; some eighteen-year-olds will die before their nineteenth birthday; others will survive to an advanced age and spend considerably more years in retirement.

Example 2: Age Forty

Now let us look at the figures for a man of forty. By that age a little more than 91,000 of the 100,000 live-born baby boys remain alive. That just about every adult male in this country works is shown by the labor force participation rate of 96.7 percent (Column 3) for this age cohort. Exits from the labor force are quite small and whatever "retirement" takes place is almost entirely forced by such circumstances as disability. At age forty life expectancy is 31.2 years, work life expectancy is 24.1 years.

Note that this gives the man of forty a life expectancy of 71.2 years. The eighteen-year-old we just discussed had an average of 51.4 years of life remaining, adding up to a life expectancy of 69.4 years. Having survived the intervening years between eighteen and forty, the survival chances of our man of forty have gone up, by approximately two years.

At age forty, under 1960 conditions, he still has almost a quarter of a century (24.1 years) of working life remaining, with a retirement expectancy of 7.1 years (life expectancy of 31.2 years minus 24.1 years).

Example 3: Age Sixty-five

Finally, let us look at men aged sixty-five. By now death has taken more than a third of the original cohort of 100,000 baby boys born alive—about 62,500 survive. The worker rate has moved down to about 56 percent, and separations from the labor force are quite heavy —partly because of deaths, but much more because of retirements. At this age the sixty-five-year-old man—under 1960 mortality conditions—still has almost thirteen years of life expectancy and about six and a half years of work life expectancy.

Female Work Life Tables

Stuart Garfinkle of the U.S. Department of Labor has prepared similar working life tables for women. Table 7-3 shows the figures for selected age groups for women, for 1940 and 1950.

The story here is more complex, since labor force participation varies substantially by marital status. Later we will discuss this factor and present 1960 data on labor market participation among women. The 1960 data will corroborate Table 7-3 in revealing the increased labor force activity and length of working life for women.

In the meantime, Table 7-3 indicates that married women have the lowest work life expectancy. This is because they are not predominantly the prime financial support of families and because bearing and rearing children restricts female labor market activity. Married women, however, did show the biggest increase in work force activity between 1940 and 1950 and this increase has continued since then.

The columns for single women are of some interest. In 1950, for example, at age fifteen a single girl had a work life expectancy of sixteen years. Most girls of that age are single, and most of them will

TABLE 7-3
Work Life Expectancy for Women, by Age and Marital Status 1940 and 1950 (In Years)

Years of Age	All Women		Single Women		Married Women		All Others	
	1940	1950	1940	1950	1940	1950	1940	1950
15	12.9	15.8	13.0	16.0	8.8	13.2	23.1	25.6
20	11.9	14.5	14.0	15.1	8.5	12.2	22.0	24.1
25	9.7	12.4	15.2	18.3	7.5	10.9	19.4	21.7
30	8.1	10.9	15.9	21.6	6.5	9.7	16.4	18.9
35	6.6	9.4	15.3	20.6	5.4	8.4	13.3	15.9
40	5.3	7.8	13.5	17.6	4.4	7.0	10.3	12.8
45	4.2	6.1	11.2	14.1	3.5	5.4	7.5	9.7
50	3.1	4.5	8.6	10.8	2.6	4.0	5.2	7.0
55	2.2	3.2	6.3	7.8	1.9	2.8	3.3	4.6
60	1.4	2.0	4.0	5.1	1.2	1.8	1.8	2.6

Source: *Tables of Working Life for Women, 1950* (Bureau of Labor Statistics, Bulletin No. 1204, 1957).

marry and have children. Note that the work life expectancy figure for the group goes *up* in succeeding years, and by age thirty, for example, work life expectancy has risen to 21.6 years. This indicates, first, that by age thirty most of the single girls have married and are in the "married" column. Secondly, from age thirty on, relatively few single women get married; most fall within the characteristic labor force pattern of single females for the rest of their lives.

Use of Tables

These Tables of Working Life, for both men and women, have had some uses that we did not anticipate. For example, they have been widely used in civil damage suits when injury or death in an accident terminates a person's working activity and an estimate is needed of the loss that this entails. Such a loss, actuarially at least, can be calculated from an estimate of the person's expected annual income and his remaining years in the labor force. More relevant to our subject, however, is their use in estimating the labor force needs in various occupations due to death and retirement.

Labor force practitioners are often called upon to estimate the total number of workers needed in a given occupational group over a period of time. Here, for example, is the story on skilled workers for the decade 1960–70:

BALANCE SHEET FOR SKILLED WORKERS IN THE UNITED STATES 1960–70

Estimated Requirements	*Millions*
Estimated number of skilled workers needed in 1970	10.9
Number of skilled workers in 1960	8.6
Estimated net increase	2.3
Transfers out of skilled occupations 1960–70	1.0
Deaths and retirements of skilled workers 1960–70	1.7
Total losses from occupations	2.7
Total number of skilled workers needed to be trained 1960–70	5.0

It is estimated that in addition to the anticipated 2.3 million increase in skilled workers, 1.0 million will transfer out and 1.7 million will die or retire, thus there will be a total of 5.0 million skilled workers we shall need to train. The number needed due to deaths and retirements (1.7 million) accounts for one out of every three of all the skilled workers who will need to be trained during the 1960s. To omit this dimension of the problem would of course be to seriously underestimate the task involved.

The technique for making this kind of estimate involves getting an age distribution of persons in the occupational group we are interested in and applying our labor force life-table functions to that distribution. In this way we get the resulting total of deaths and retirements for the group.

Ideally, labor force life tables should be developed for different occupational categories, but so far mortality information by occupation has been inadequate to permit this kind of construction. The overall table functions are therefore applied, which assumes that there are no differences in mortality by occupation. This, in turn, is becoming truer because of increasing social and economic improvements for most population groups.

Long-Term Trends

Now let us briefly describe what has happened to the average American's working life expectancy over the past half century or so. Table 7-4 tells that story in a few figures. Perhaps the most important part of the story is what the population has done with the substantial extension of its lifespan.

Years In and Out of the Labor Force

For men, the additional eighteen and a half years of life expectancy between 1900 and 1960 have been divided between an increase in working life and an increase in years spent outside the labor force. The latter increase has come partly from delayed entry into the work force for more education and training, partly from exits out of the labor force for retirement.

To put it another way, despite a marked delay in entry into

working status and an earlier exit from the labor force, men today put in many more years of work. And despite more years of labor force activity, men today spend more of their lives in retirement—the answer to this apparent paradox being the added years of life we have today.

As Table 7-4 shows, the same general pattern has developed among the women—although the increases have been higher across the board. Their twenty-two and a half additional years of life since 1900 have been divided as follows: fourteen more years have gone to their working lives, while eight and a half more years have gone to their education, training, marriage, motherhood, and, eventually, retirement.

TABLE 7-4
Life and Working Life Expectancy in the United States 1900–60 (In Years)

	Men			Women		
Year	Life Expectancy	Work Life Expectancy	Years Outside Labor Force	Life Expectancy	Work Life Expectancy	Years Outside Labor Force
1900*	48.2	32.1	16.1	50.7	6.3	44.4
1940	61.2	38.3	22.9	65.9	12.1	53.8
1950	65.5	41.9	23.6	71.0	15.2	55.8
1960	66.6	41.4	25.2	73.1	20.1	53.0

*Data for 1900 are based on whites in death-registration states.
Source: Seymour L. Wolfbein, *Changing Patterns of Working Life* (U.S. Department of Labor, Office of Manpower, Automation, and Training, August 1963).

We therefore come to this major point: *life, work life, and years spent outside the labor force have all three increased for the population in recent years.*

Increased Manpower Input

All these factors have increased the productive manpower potential of our society, allowing us to take full advantage of technological change as it occurs. We can derive the following picture:

A Group of 100,000 Persons Born Alive in the United States Would Produce the Following Man-Years of Work During their Lifetimes (In Thousands)

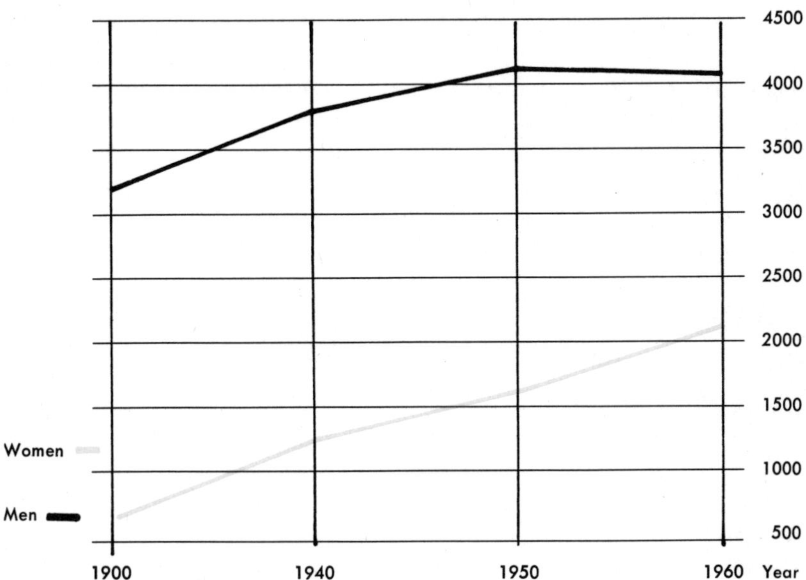

A group of 100,000 boys born alive and experiencing the mortality and labor force conditions existing today will put in about a million more man-years of work during their lifetimes than did their counterparts under 1900 conditions—an increase of almost one-third. A comparable group of girls today will almost triple the performance of their 1900 counterparts.

Here, in a few specific figures, is perhaps the best indication of the huge increase in the manpower potential of our population since the turn of the century. All of this has been accompanied by an equally impressive increase in the years spent outside the labor force.

When one adds to this factor the forces of technological change and the resulting increase in output per man-hour, it is understandable that we have been able to triple the gross national product per capita in this country during the past fifty years.

This increase in productivity has also been important to the individual, in terms of the increased education, training, and retirement time available to him. The increased length of his working life has brought increased lifetime earnings, as well as more time for career development in today's complex occupational world.

Resultant Social Problems

These trends form the basic frame within which the rest of our picture is drawn. It is impossible to note any dimensions of the labor force and related developments that are not involved in life–working-life chain.

As an illustration, let us start with today's "older-worker problem," a natural consequence of the trends in life expectancy. It is difficult to envisage much of an older-worker problem when a man's life expectancy at birth is forty-eight. If only because of the sheer numbers of the elderly we now have, we deal with a problem of enormous social, economic, and political significance. Increasing life expectancy and the concentration of exits from the labor force around age sixty-five have given us the new and important galaxy of problems involved in retirement.

For example, here is the situation for a man twenty years old:

Under 1900 conditions:	
A man of twenty had a life expectancy of	42.2 (years)
And a work life expectancy of	39.4
Thus his outlook was for a period of retirement of	2.8
Under 1960 conditions:	
A man of twenty had a life expectancy of	49.6
And a work life expectancy of	42.6
Thus his outlook was for a period of retirement of	7.0

The average number of years spent by men in retirement is two and a half times today what it was in 1900, and all the evidence shows that it is on the increase.

In 1900 a man of twenty could expect to spend less than one out of fifteen of his remaining years of life in retirement; at today's rates a man of twenty can look forward to spending a little more than one out of seven of his remaining years of life in retirement.

With life and work life changing as they have, we are challenged by such problems as social security, private pension plans negotiated in collective bargaining, income adequacy, and housing and medical care for the elderly. With increasing retirement have come substantial demands for many leisure-time services.

As we have seen, these developments have been matched by the delay in entering the labor force due to increased requirements of education and training, and the resultant challenge to our educational system.

Recent Developments

The problems we have just reviewed have been brought into sharp focus by what has happened to working life during the past decade. The length of working life among men actually declined between 1950 and 1960, for the first time in this century. Despite an increase in life expectancy of a little over a year, work life expectancy fell by half a year because of a substantial dip in labor force activity among older men.

As a matter of fact, the sixty-fifth year of life has now become the conventional age of retirement in this country. From 1950 to 1960 the rate of retirement between ages sixty-four and sixty-five actually tripled. In 1960, 234 out of every 1000 men in the labor force retired at that age; the comparable rate was 83 per 1000 in 1950, and 70 per 1000 in 1940 (Fig. 7-1).

Contrary to the experience among men, work life expectancy continued to go up among women during the 1950s; in fact, for the first time this century the increase in work life expectancy for women exceeded their increase in life expectancy. Work life expectancy among women is now running at about half the corresponding figure for men; in 1950 it was only a little over one-third that of men; in 1900, less than one-fifth.

As a result, the expected years of life spent outside the labor force by women went down for the first time this century during the past decade. Labor force participation has continued to increase among women up to the present, and their work life expectancy in 1960 was more than three and a half times the figure for 1900, a third higher than just ten years ago.

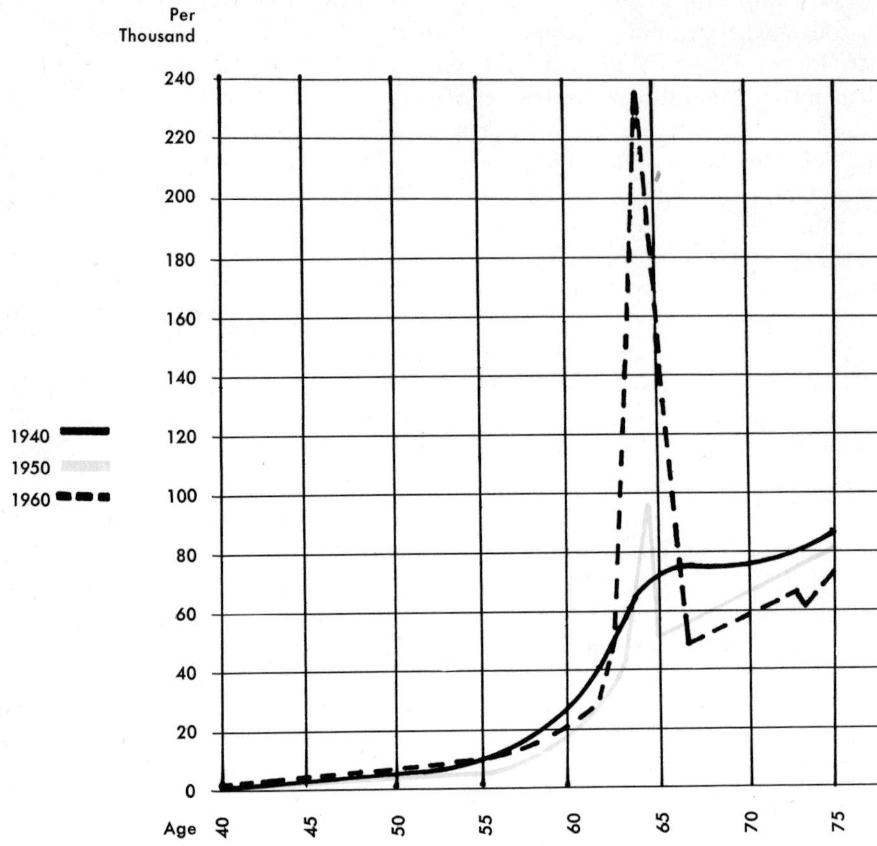

Source: *The Length of Working Life for Males, 1900–60* (U.S. Department of Labor, Manpower Report No. 8, July 1963).

FIG. 7-1 *Retirement rates for men, by age: 1940, 1950, 1960.*

World Work Trends

We complete this chapter with a review of similar surveys and studies done abroad. Each country's labor force development varies, of course, with its own history, its customs, its occupational and industrial trends. But whatever the variations have been, the recent evolution of life, work life, and nonlabor force activity in industrialized nations has been remarkably the same.

TABLE 7-5
Life and Working Life in Selected Countries (In Years)

Country	Time Period	Life Expectancy	Work Life Expectancy	Non-Work-Life Expectancy
Sweden	1816–40	41.47	25.59	15.88
	1931–35	64.24	38.09	26.15
France	1864	39.85	23.93	15.92
	1933–38	58.71	35.66	23.05
Germany	1871–80	36.97	22.74	14.18
	1932–34	61.29	37.04	24.25
Switzerland	1876–80	41.86	25.91	15.95
	1933–37	62.59	38.06	24.53
Italy	1881–90	35.40	26.40	14.00
	1930–32	54.85	32.92	21.93
Australia	1881–90	48.97	29.80	19.17
	1932–34	65.26	39.00	26.26

Source: G. Mortara, "Durée de la vie économiquement active suivant la mortalité" *Bulletin of the International Statistical Institute,* Part IV: "Demography and Labor Statistics," 33 (1951), pp. 147–74.

Georgio Mortara published estimates on these factors for a number of countries in 1951. Some of these figures are presented in Table 7-5. They show how the three functions we have discussed have gone up. More recently, tables of working life have been constructed for various countries and they reveal the same tendencies.

P. Depoid performed this exercise for France, with results as shown in Table 7-6. The trends are very close to ours, despite the difference of national history and development. In France, too, a substantial increase in age of entry into the labor force has occurred, as has a decline in age of exit. Yet, Depoid points out, "Despite the reduction in age of entry and earlier retirement, work life expectancy has continued to increase under the important influence of declining mortality." (2) This was exactly our comment on U.S. trends.

The picture on the other side of the world in New Zealand (Table 7-7) is the same. Again, considering the many differences between the United States and New Zealand, the similarities are quite striking.

TABLE 7-6
Expectancy of Life and Working Life at Birth for Men in France (In Years)

Year	Life Expectancy	Work Life Expectancy	Years Outside Labor Force
1906	46.9	32.3	14.6
1936	55.9	37.0	18.9
1946	61.6	41.0	20.6

Source: P. Depoid, "Tables françaises concernant la population masculine (1906–1946)," *Bulletin of the International Statistical Institute*, Part IV: "Demography and Labor Statistics," 33 (1951), pp. 131–46.

TABLE 7-7
Life and Work Life Expectancy in United States and New Zealand (In Years)

	Male Life Expectancy		Male Work Life Expectancy	
Age	U.S.	New Zealand	U.S.	New Zealand
15	53.6	55.3	47.8	46.7
20	48.9	50.7	43.1	42.0
25	44.4	46.2	38.5	37.5
30	39.8	41.6	33.9	32.8
35	35.2	37.0	29.3	28.1
40	30.8	32.4	24.9	23.5
45	26.6	27.9	20.6	18.9
50	22.6	23.7	16.6	14.6
55	19.0	19.7	13.0	11.0
60	15.7	16.1	9.8	7.6
65	12.7	12.8	7.4	6.7

Source: See Readings at end of chapter.

Reference Notes

1. "La durato media della vita," *Revista italiana di sociologia,* Anno XII, Fasce IV–V, Luglio–Ottobre 1908.
2. *Op. cit.*, p. 140.

Readings

The development of concepts and techniques of labor force life tables in this country can be seen from

GARFINKLE, S. H. "Changes in Working Life of Men: 1900 to 2000," *Monthly Labor Review,* Vol. 78 (March 1955).

____. *The Length of Working Life for Males, 1900–60.* (Manpower Report No. 8.) Washington, D.C.: Department of Labor, Office of Manpower, Automation, and Training, July 1963.

____. *Tables of Working Life for Women in 1950.* Bulletin 1204, Bureau of Labor Statistics, 1957.

SLAVICK, F., and WOLFBEIN, S. L. "The Evolving Work-Life Pattern," *Aging and Society: A Handbook of Social Gerontology,* ed. C. TIBBITTS. Chicago: Univ. of Chicago Press, 1961.

Tables of Working Life. Bulletin 1001, Bureau of Labor Statistics, August 1950.

WOLFBEIN S. L. "The Changing Length of Working Life," *Proceedings of the Seventh Annual Meeting, Industrial Relations Research Association,* December 1954.

____. *Changing Patterns of Working Life.* Washington, D.C.: Department of Labor, August 1963.

____. "The Length of Working Life," *Population Studies,* Vol. III (December 1959).

____. "The Length of Working Life," *Proceedings of the Fourth Congress of the International Association of Gerontology* (Merano, Italy, 1957), Vol. III. Fidenza, Italy: Tipografia Tito Mattioli, 1959.

Comparisons of working life trends here and abroad are reviewed in Chapter III of

WOLFBEIN, S. L., and BURGESS, E. W. "Employment and Retirement," *Aging in Western Societies,* ed. E. W. BURGESS. Chicago: Univ. of Chicago Press, 1960.

Specific references for individual countries include

DARIC, J. *Vieillissement de la population et prolongation de la vie active.* (Institut National d'Etudes Demographiques, Travaux et

Documents No. 7.) Paris: Presses Universitaires de France, 1948.

Depoid, P. "Tables françaises concernant la population masculine (1906–46)," *Bulletin of the International Statistical Institute*, Part IV, 1951.

Mortara, G. "Durée de la vie économiquement active suivant la mortalité," *Bulletin of the International Statistical Institute*, Part IV, 1951.

Naville, P. "Measurement of Working Life and Employment of Older Workers in France," *Aging and Social Health in the United States and Europe*, ed. C. Tibbitts. Ann Arbor: Univ. of Michigan, 1959.

Table of Working Life, 1951: Male Population (Including Maoris). Wellington, New Zealand: Census and Statistics Department, 1955.

CHAPTER EIGHT

The Labor Force in Its Demographic Setting

DURING 1960, 58 PERCENT OF THE NONINSTITUTIONAL CIVILIAN POPULATION fourteen years of age and over were in the labor force. In other words, a little short of six out of every ten of the noninstitutional civilian population aged fourteen and over were economically active, either employed or unemployed.

This overall figure masks a multitude of differences in the labor market participation rates of different groups. Thus, during 1960 the participation rate was 22.3 percent for boys fourteen and fifteen years of age, and 98.2 percent for men thirty to thirty-four; it was 10.6 percent for white females sixty-five years of age and over, and 60.5 percent for nonwhite females forty-five to fifty-four; it was 44.1 percent for single women, and 10.2 percent for married women whose children were under three years of age.

Importance of Demographic Factors

Age, sex, color, marital status, the presence of dependent children in the family, and urban or rural residence all bear directly upon labor market participation in a fundamental way.

Various patterns emerge. For instance, more men work, on the whole, than women. Nearly all men work in their middle years. Women as a group work less during the years of bearing and rearing children than before and after. Many married women today enter the labor force in their middle forties. Nonwhite males over forty-five have a lower labor force participation rate than whites over forty-five; but nonwhite females over forty-five have a greater participation rate than white females over forty-five. Participation rates for both single men and single women are similar. Presence of young dependent children in the household directly affects the economic activity of married women. Rural men start working earlier in life and stop working later in life than city men, but rural women have less work opportunities than city women.

We can establish these patterns for any period of time for which statistics exist. But if we examine statistics covering long periods, we discover that other than demographic factors play the central role in labor force change. For instance, the fact that a woman is married does not have the same influence on work activity today as it did fifty or even twenty-five years ago.

Clearly, these nondemographic influences are at work—such as changing concepts of women's economic role, automation, and the shift toward a "white collar" and "service" economy. Let us keep this fact in mind as we discuss the six major demographic factors in turn.

Sex

The most familiar demographic factor affecting labor market participation is sex. Although the sex differential in worker rates has been narrowing, women as a group still have a lower rate of labor market participation than men. The factors of marriage and childbearing are, of course, responsible for maintaining the difference.

As can be seen from Table 8-1, the worker rate for men in the middle years is more than twice the corresponding rate for women; the same table shows that the differential exists age for age, and for both whites and nonwhites. In almost any way we break down the overall labor market participation rate, the sex differential remains.

Age

The influence of the age factor on worker rates is apparent from Table 8-1 and perhaps a little more so from Fig. 8-1, which portrays the age pattern of work participation for men and women.

For men, labor force rates move up steeply through the teens; for those eighteen to nineteen years of age, 70 percent are in the labor force (age eighteen is the average age of high school graduation in the United States). The rate continues up among men in their early twenties. From age twenty-five to fifty-four just about all men are workers, with the labor market participation rate running 95

TABLE 8-1
Labor Force Status of Noninstitutional Civilian Population Fourteen Years and Over, by Age, Sex, and Color 1960

Age and Sex	Total	White	Nonwhite
Total	57.5%	57.0%	61.9%
Male	80.4%	80.5%	79.4%
14–19	43.8	43.6	45.0
20–24	88.1	87.8	90.4
25–34	97.2	97.7	96.2
35–44	97.7	97.9	95.5
45–54	95.7	96.1	92.3
55–64	86.8	87.2	82.5
65 and over	33.1	33.3	31.2
Female	36.7%	35.5%	46.3%
14–19	30.0	30.7	25.8
20–24	46.1	45.7	48.8
25–34	35.9	34.1	49.7
35–44	43.4	41.5	59.8
45–54	49.8	48.6	60.5
55–64	37.1	36.2	47.3
65 and over	10.6	10.6	12.8

Source: R. L. Stein and H. Travis, *Labor Force and Employment in 1960* (Bureau of Labor Statistics, Special Labor Force Report No. 14, April 1961).

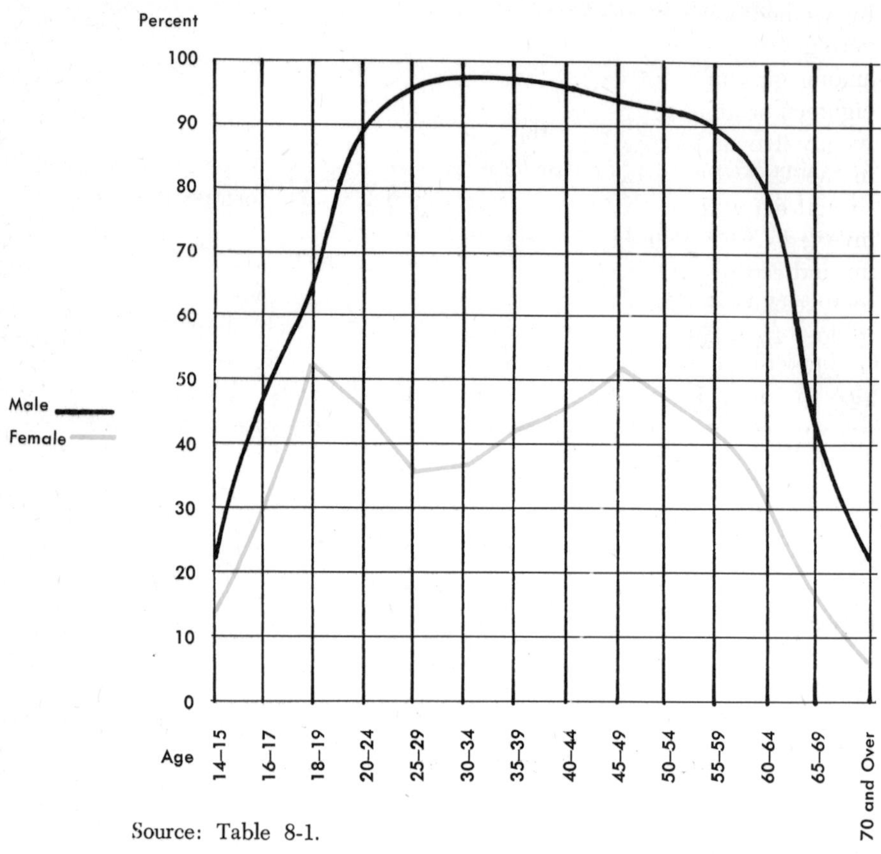

Source: Table 8-1.

FIG. 8-1 *Labor market participation rates, by sex, by age, 1960.*

percent or higher. The rate begins to shade off for men in their fifties and then falls steeply for those in their sixties, when retirement begins to take over. For men seventy and over, the rate is close to that of boys fourteen and fifteen years old.

As Fig. 8-1 shows, the age progression for men takes the form of a large inverted letter *U*. At both ends the movement is quite steep—upward on the younger side, downward on the older side; in between are the adult males, practically all of whom are in the labor force.

The picture given by the age pattern of labor force participation by women is quite different—roughly it is in the shape of two inverted *U*'s. The rate of worker participation also goes up steeply among girls in their teens and reaches the 50 percent mark by age eighteen or nineteen. Then marriage takes over and for those between twenty-five and thirty-four—the prime childbearing ages of women in the United States—the rate falls to about one-third.

At age thirty-five the curve reverses and gradually starts another inverted *U*; as the children get older, labor market participation goes up and returns to the 50 percent mark for women forty-five to fifty-four years of age, after which the rate moves steeply down again as it does for men.

Note that our first factor—the sex differential—still holds age for age; the worker rate remains higher for men than women.

Color

Note that the age progression we have just described also holds by color (Table 8-1), but other significant labor force differentials exist between the white and nonwhite sectors of our population. These, too, vary according to sex.

For the whole of the noninstitutional civilian population fourteen years of age and over, whites have a *lower* labor market participation rate than their nonwhite colleagues. The difference of about 5 percentage points in 1960 is much less than it used to be, but it is still significant.

Among the men, however, a significant color difference appears at about age forty-five: labor market participation is *lower* among nonwhite males forty-five to sixty-four years of age than for whites of that age group. Why this is so for nonwhite males in such prime working ages is difficult to prove. It may be that the continued lack of job opportunities for many in this age group leads to the phenomenon known as "labor force disappearance," where individuals exit from the work force altogether, knowing that the outlook for their employment is poor. This phenomenon has emerged only in the past twenty years and may be related to the movement of job opportunities away from the farm to the city.

Among women the opposite is true. As can be seen from Table 8-1, labor market participation rates are much *higher* for the adult nonwhite female than for her white counterpart. In the age group thirty-five to forty-four, the rate for nonwhite women is about 50 percent higher than for white women; in the age group forty-five to fifty-four the differential is about 25 percent. Reasons for these differences are also difficult to prove. Perhaps the greater pressure for family income in the nonwhite family groups, where joblessness is much greater, is a primary factor.

Marital Status

The picture of how labor market participation varies with marital status is shown in the following data from the MRLF for March 1960:

LABOR FORCE PARTICIPATION BY MARITAL STATUS

	Men	Women
Single	55.5%	44.1%
Married	88.9%	30.5%
Other*	59.3%	40.0%

* Includes widowed, separated, divorced.

As might be expected, married men have the highest labor market participation rates and married women the lowest.

Fig. 8-2 explores this matter in a little more detail, showing how marital status and labor force status are related age by age. It also makes several other interesting points:

Married men have a higher rate of labor market activity than single men at every age level. This, no doubt, is due to the fact that family responsibilities require this activity. It may also be due, in some part, to the fact that marriage is a selective process. The lower labor market activity of single men in the adult age groups may be due to factors of disability affecting both employability and marriageability.

The rates for married women, which are at the lowest end of the scale, show the familiar age progression already discussed. Our next section on dependency status will go a long way toward explaining this phenomenon.

Single men and women have very similar patterns of labor market participation by age. Between the ages of twenty-five and fifty-

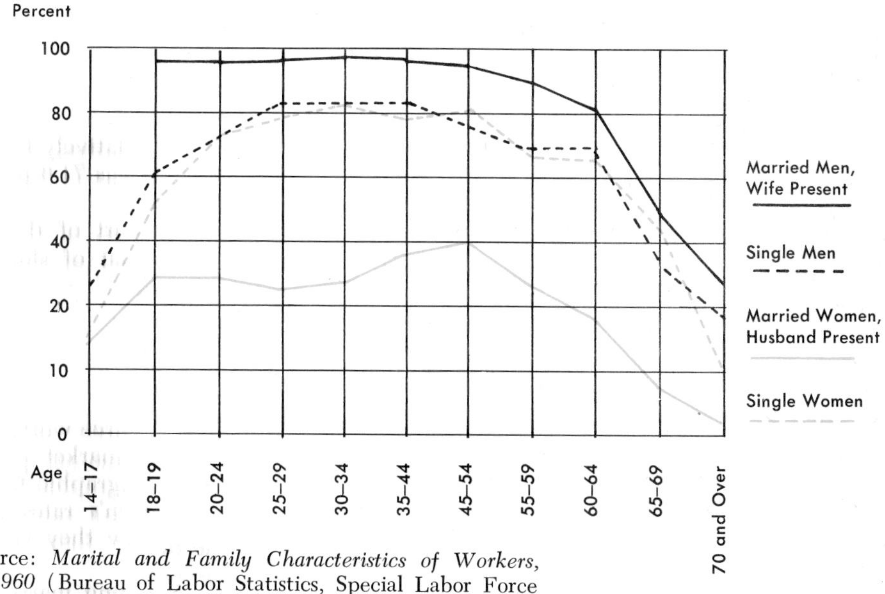

Source: *Marital and Family Characteristics of Workers, March 1960* (Bureau of Labor Statistics, Special Labor Force Report No. 13, April 1961).

FIG. 8-2 *Labor market participation rates, by marital status, by age, March 1960.*

five, about four out of every five single women work, and their higher rate of labor market participation in relation to married women prevails throughout their lives.

Finally, a word about those who are widowed, divorced, and separated. Although not depicted on the chart, the data show that women in that status participate much more extensively in the labor force than their counterparts who are married and whose husbands are present. Age by age, their rates lie roughly between those of single and married women.

In this last category of women, the highest labor market rate prevails among divorced women, the lowest among widows. The former category tends to include many younger women with family and financial responsibilities, while the latter tends to be in the older age ranges where labor market participation is already relatively low. Thus in March 1960 the labor market participation rate was 71.6 percent for divorced women, 29.8 percent for widows.

On the male side, labor market activity on the part of those divorced, widowed, and separated is very similar to that of single men.

Dependency Status

With women now accounting for about one out of every three workers in the United States, the factors affecting their labor market participation are of some importance. Staying with the demographic factors, we have noted so far in this chapter how women's rates of labor force activity compare with those of men, and how they vary with age and marital status.

One other set of factors is of prime importance among married

TABLE 8-2
Labor Market Status of Married Women–Husbands Present, by Age and by Presence and Age of Their Children
March 1960

Age of Women and Presence and Age of Children	Labor Market Participation Rate
Total	30.5%
No children under 18 years of age	34.7%
14–34 years	61.1
35–44 years	55.1
45–54 years	43.0
55 and over	17.1
Children 6 to 17 years of age only	39.0%
14–34	41.4
35 and over	38.5
Children 3 to 5 years of age—none under 3	25.1%
14–34	26.7
35 and over	22.8
Children under 3 years of age	15.3%
14–34	15.1
35 and over	16.6

Source: *Marital and Family Characteristics of Workers, March 1960* (Bureau of Labor Statistics, Special Labor Force Report No. 13, Table G, April 1961).

women: whether or not they have children and, if they do, the ages of the children in the household.

Table 8-2 tells the story. The overall labor market participation rate for married women was 30.5 percent in March 1960, but the variations in that rate, depending on the presence and ages of children, were very great.

As might be expected, the highest labor force rates prevailed among married women who had no children eighteen or younger. This is somewhat masked by the overall rate for this group because of the inclusion of elderly women who tend to have no children under eighteen and whose labor market participation is generally low. This is why we have included an age breakdown in some detail for this group. It will be noted that for married women who are fourteen to thirty-four years of age and have no children under eighteen, the labor market participation rate is 61.1 percent—significantly and substantially higher than for members of their age group who do have children under eighteen. In fact, their 61.1 percent rate is quadruple that of one particular group (those who have children under three years of age), whose rate is 15.1 percent.

The progression by age of children is quite clear after that. Married women with children of school age (six to seventeen) have a labor market participation rate (39.0 percent) about 50 percent higher than that of married women whose children are of preschool age (three to five years). The latter rate (25.1 percent) is, in turn, almost double that (15.3 percent) of married women whose children are under three years of age.

One other point: The presence in the family of an additional person—even another child of school age—is associated with a *higher* labor market participation rate for married women with children under six. For example, if one takes all married women with children under six, the labor market rate was 18.6 percent in March 1960; if they also had a child of high school age, their rate went up to 23.8 percent; and if there was another adult in the household who could presumably take care of the children, the rate went up to about 30 percent.

Urban-Rural Residence

The five factors discussed so far—age, sex, color, marital status, and dependency status—are quite clearly demographic or personal characteristics of the people involved. The matter is not so clear for the sixth factor—urban and rural residence. There are those, such as this author, who consider this an economic factor related to an individual's occupational deployment. Urban-rural residence, however, has been traditionally considered part of the demographic constellation, so we will discuss it at this point as well as later.

Briefly, the available data point up the longer length of working life for men on the farm, who begin their working lives earlier and end them later. Overall, the labor market participation rates are higher for both whites and nonwhites in the rural areas. The difference in labor market participation rates is particularly marked in the early ages for the farm youth.

At the other end of the age scale, for both whites and nonwhites, labor market participation rates are significantly higher for the older farm men. The farm, of course, is typically a place where an older person can continue in some kind of employment (most often self-employment) to a much greater extent than he can in the urban, industrialized parts of the country.

The opposite is true for farm women's labor force activity: labor market participation is higher for both white and nonwhite urban women than for those in rural areas. On an overall basis, women in urban areas have a rate almost double that of women in rural areas. The great growth in job opportunities for women has taken place in the urban industrial and occupational complex; employment opportunities for women remain relatively limited on the farm.

Summary

These then are the six major demographic factors that exert a dominant force on the structure of the American labor market at any given time. The following important points emerge as the demographic setting for the labor force:

Men have a higher labor market participation rate than women.

Highest rates prevail among adult males, almost all of whom are in the labor force.

The age progression among men is the classic inverted *U*, rising steeply at the younger age side, falling steeply at the older age side, the high middle plateau representing the adult males.

For women, the age progression in labor force activity is more in the shape of a double inverted *U*, as marriage and children constrain labor force activity for a substantial proportion of adult women.

Overall, nonwhites have a somewhat higher labor market participation rate than whites.

Adult nonwhite males' labor market activity is below that of adult white males.

The opposite is true for women: nonwhites have markedly higher rates of labor market activity than whites.

Age for age, married men have the highest labor force rates; married women have the lowest.

Single men and single women have similarly high rates of labor market participation.

Widowed, separated, or divorced men have a labor market participation rate much like that of single men, whereas women in that status participate at a rate between the rate of single and that of married women.

For married women, labor market activity in general depends on whether they have children.

Particularly important in determining the activity of married women in the labor force is the age of their children.

For men, labor market participation is higher on the farm than off the farm.

For women, employment opportunities and labor market activity are higher in urban than in rural areas.

Socioeconomic Factors

These demographic characteristics are fundamental to the structure of the labor force of a country *at any given time.* These characteristics tend to change very slowly. *If all other things remained equal,* the composition of the labor force would change only slightly over a period of time and its size would change with changes in population size.

But these demographic factors have not been all-determining

in real life. Overriding forces, other than demographic, have effected major changes in labor market participation over the years. This was first documented in a quantitative manner in 1946 by this author and A. J. Jaffe, now at Columbia University.

Suppose we were living in 1890 and we had the results of the decennial census of that year showing the gainful worker rates for various groups in the population. Suppose further that we were able to foretell exactly what would happen to the various demographic characteristics between then and 1930, forty years later, and made our projections accordingly. How close would we have come to the actual gainful worker rates of 1930? The results of such a computation are shown in Table 8-3.

On the basis of demographic changes alone, we would have projected a decline in gainful worker rates for all workers, male and female, both married and unmarried (line 3 of Table 8-3). We would have done this because virtually every demographic change in those forty years pointed in that direction. The number of males per one hundred females went down between 1890 and 1930. The proportion of married women, who have a lower rate of labor market participation, went up during that period. The proportion of the foreign-born population (which has a higher participation rate) went down during these forty years, and the proportion of nonwhites (who as a whole have a higher rate) also went down.

Actually, between 1890 and 1930 the gainful worker rate went down *for males only* (line 2), and here we would have underestimated the downward movement by quite a mark. As Table 8-3 shows, we would have projected a decline of .4 of a percentage point in the male gainful worker rate; we actually got a 2.5 percentage point drop. Most of the actual change was due not to the changing demographic structure, but to socioeconomic (nondemographic) causes.

Among the women the actual results are even more startling. For married women, for example, we would have projected a small decline, from 4.6 to 4.0 percent, in the gainful worker rate, although it actually went up to 11.7 percent, or two and a half times the 1890 figure. Obviously, nondemographic forces exerted dramatic changes. To put the figures for married women shown in Table 8-3 in percentage terms: between 1890 and 1930 there was a 154 percent *increase* in their gainful worker rate. This was the net result of a 13 percent *decline* ascribable to changing demographic factors and a 167 percent *increase* due to socioeconomic forces.

Similar studies of long-term demographic and nondemographic

forces in labor force change have been made for this and other time periods and for this and other countries, and they show basically the same results.

TABLE 8-3
Effect of Demographic and Other Socioeconomic Changes on Gainful Worker Rates for Population Fifteen Years Old and Over, 1890–1930

Effect of Demographic and Other Socioeconomic Changes	Total	Male	Female		
			Total	Not Married	Married
1890 gainful-worker rates as enumerated	54.8%	88.7%	18.9%	37.7%	4.6%
1930 gainful-worker rates as enumerated	55.9	86.2	24.8	45.4	11.7
1930 gainful-worker rates expected on basis of changing demographic factors	52.6	88.3	16.0	34.9	4.0
Influence of demographic factors (line 3 minus line 1)	−2.2	−0.4	−2.9	−2.8	−0.6
Influence of other socioeconomic factors (line 2 minus line 3)	3.3	−2.1	8.8	10.5	7.7

Source: S. L. Wolfbein and A. J. Jaffe, "Demographic Factors in Labor Force Growth," *American Sociological Review,* August 1946.

Readings

Information on the labor force, classified by the various demographic factors, is available each month from the U.S. Department of Labor, especially the Bureau of Labor Statistics' *Employment and Earnings.* The Special Labor Force Reports series of the Bureau of Labor Statistics also contains excellent materials on this subject. For example, the annual series, based on supplementary questions to the MRLF, gives information on labor force activity by age, sex, marital status, presence and age of children, and so forth. The latest in this series is

SHIFFMAN, J. *Marital and Family Characteristics of Workers in March 1962* (Special Labor Force Report No. 26, January 1963).

The relation between demographic factors and socioeconomic forces affecting labor force participation is examined in

WOLFBEIN, S. L., and JAFFE, A. J. "Demographic Factors in Labor Force Growth," *American Sociological Review,* Vol. 2 (August 1946).

See also

BANCROFT, G. *The American Labor Force.* New York: John Wiley & Sons, 1958.

DURAND, JOHN D. *The Labor Force in the United States, 1890–1960.* New York: Social Science Research Council, 1948.

JAFFE, A. J., and STEWART, C. D. *Manpower Resources and Utilization.* New York: John Wiley & Sons, 1951. Pp. 299–302.

CHAPTER NINE

Labor Force Trends

CONSIDERING THE ENORMOUS CHANGES THAT HAVE OCCURRED IN THIS COUNTRY since 1900, it may come as a surprise that the proportion of the non-institutional civilian population fourteen years and older in the labor force has hardly changed in that period of time.

Some years ago John D. Durand performed a notable service by revising the decennial census statistics on labor market participation by age, sex, and color (from 1890 and 1930) in order to make them as comparable as possible to the 1940 decennial census. (1) By adding the decennial census results of 1950 and 1960, we can present the best available historical series on what has happened to labor force participation over the years. This information will be found in Table 9-1.

We want to emphasize that these are adjusted decennial census data, used only for making these valuable comparisons over long period of time. Labor force data are available from the *Monthly Report*

TABLE 9-1
Labor Force Participation Rates, by Age, Color, and Sex 1890–1960 (Adjusted Data—Decennial Census Levels)

Age, Color, and Sex	1890	1900	1920	1930	1940	1950	1960
Total	52.2%*	53.7%	54.4%	53.2%	52.7%	54.0%	55.3%
White	51.0	52.3	53.3	52.1	52.1	53.7	55.2
Male	84.0	85.4	84.3	81.7	79.7	79.7	78.0
14–19	48.2	60.1	50.0	38.2	34.1	39.5	39.0
20–24	90.6	90.5	89.7	88.5	88.4	82.7	86.8
25–34	96.0	95.0	96.4	96.1	96.2	93.5	95.7
35–44	95.9	94.5	95.4	95.7	95.8	95.7	96.3
45–54	93.7	92.6	93.3	93.8	93.0	92.9	94.8
55–64	88.6	85.6	86.0	86.2	84.5	84.1	83.9
65 and over	67.0	61.7	54.1	53.0	41.6	41.3	30.6
Female	15.8	17.2	20.7	21.8	24.5	28.4	33.6
14–19	22.3	23.8	27.5	21.9	18.7	23.6	24.8
20–24	27.9	29.4	36.7	41.4	45.8	44.1	44.7
25–34	14.5	16.8	21.5	24.9	31.8	30.5	33.5
35–44	9.9	12.2	16.5	19.1	25.2	33.7	41.1
45–54	9.8	11.3	15.4	17.3	20.8	32.0	45.8
55–64	9.3	10.2	12.6	13.8	15.7	23.1	34.5
65 and over	6.0	6.7	6.1	6.5	5.5	7.7	10.1
Nonwhite	62.4	65.0	64.2	63.0	58.1	56.3	56.3
Male	86.7	88.5	87.5	85.8	80.0	76.8	72.1
14–19	61.7	74.8	62.7	55.4	46.2	43.6	31.5
20–24	92.9	91.3	91.6	91.9	88.6	81.1	82.0
25–34	95.8	93.6	95.1	95.1	92.1	86.7	88.5
35–44	96.1	94.2	95.4	95.0	91.8	91.1	89.8
45–54	95.3	93.9	94.7	94.2	89.4	88.9	87.6
55–64	93.4	91.0	90.8	90.0	85.5	80.3	75.9
65 and over	81.8	77.3	73.5	68.0	49.1	43.3	29.3
Female	37.7	41.2	40.6	40.4	37.3	37.1	41.8
14–19	38.3	45.4	34.8	29.9	21.6	18.4	17.3
20–24	46.5	45.4	43.1	44.7	44.2	39.7	45.5
25–34	36.2	39.9	42.7	44.6	45.8	44.4	48.6
35–44	35.4	39.2	43.5	45.0	45.0	48.6	55.8
45–54	36.4	39.7	44.9	44.0	39.6	43.6	54.7
55–64	34.9	38.2	39.5	37.9	30.4	31.4	40.3
65 and over	23.4	25.0	24.1	20.3	12.3	10.8	12.9

Source: See Readings at end of chapter.

on the Labor Force sample since 1940, and they are usually preferred to those in Table 9-1 for that period. MRLF data are used in this volume throughout—except when, as in this instance, we want to present the story on a comparable basis over long periods of time.

Overall Work Participation Steady over the Years

As we have already mentioned, the overall labor force participation rate has remained practically unchanged since 1890. Let us take these global rates from Table 9-1 and summarize them as follows:

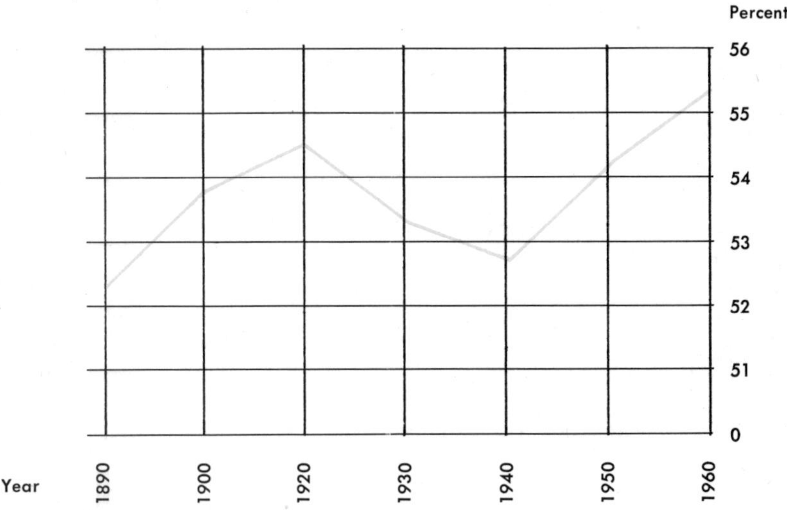

Though the rate has edged up and down within an exceedingly narrow range during the past seventy years, the changes cannot be considered statistically significant. In almost three-quarters of a century of dramatic change in the United States, the economically active proportion of the population has remained about the same, somewhat over 50 percent.

These overall rates again mask enormously significant changes. In general, the stability of the overall rate reflects the counterbalancing effects of significant declines in labor force activity among the young and old, on the one hand, and an equally significant upturn in activity among adult women on the other. Even this generalization hides other notable changes.

Major Long-Run Changes

We now set forth twenty propositions concerning labor force change in this country during the past seventy years. The figures we will be referring to will be found in Table 9-1 and Figs. 9-1 through 9-3. Brief supplementary tables will be shown where needed.

The sex differential in labor force participation has narrowed considerably over the years. (Fig. 9-1)

Males still have a higher rate of labor market activity than females, but the differences have been cut down significantly. The narrowing of these differences stems from the concurrent *declines* in labor force rates for men and *increases* for women.

There was a time around the turn of the century when the labor market participation rate for white males was five and a half times that of white females, and the rate for nonwhite males about two and a half times that of nonwhite females. Today the rate for males is only a little over twice that for females among whites, and much less than that among nonwhites.

The color differential in labor force participation has narrowed considerably over the years. (Fig. 9-1)

The overall labor market participation rates for whites and nonwhites are quite close now. For many years about two-thirds of the nonwhites were in the labor force, and only about one-half of the whites.

The differences have narrowed because of the concurrent small increase in the rate for whites and a significant decline for nonwhites.

Labor market participation has declined significantly among men, both white and nonwhite. (Fig. 9-1)

Among white males, the decline since the turn of the century has been a little less than 10 percent; among nonwhite males the decline has been closer to 20 percent.

Labor market participation has increased significantly among women. (Fig. 9-1)

Virtually all the increase for women has taken place among white women, whose labor market participation rate has doubled so far in the twentieth century.

There has been a substantial decline in labor market participation among teen-agers. (Fig. 9-1)

The decline in worker rates among teen-agers has been especially marked among nonwhites. Reasons are (1) increasing school attendance associated with (2) minimum school-leaving laws and (3) rising educational prerequisites for employment, as well as (4) the shift from farm to city. These have all operated to cut in half the labor market participation rate for nonwhite teen-agers, both boys and girls, since the turn of the century.

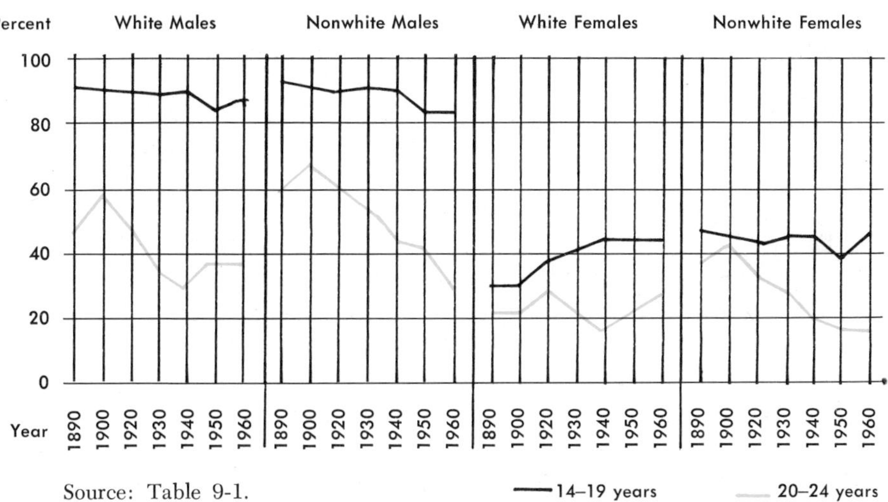

Source: Table 9-1.

FIG. 9-1 *Labor market participation rates, by age, color, and sex, 1890–1960.*

White males fourteen to nineteen years of age also have experienced a marked and persistent decline in labor force activity, with a cut of about 50 percent in the worker rate.

The only exception is represented by white female teen-agers, whose rate has held up over the years. Aside from a rise in 1920 (after World War I) and a drop in 1940 (the rate for all teen-agers was down in 1940 after ten years of depression), the rate for this group has edged up slightly. This has reflected the very great increase in employment opportunities for young white girls in the past several decades, especially in the clerical and sales fields.

White and nonwhite teen-agers have reversed positions on the labor force scale. (Fig. 9-1)

With the greater decline among nonwhite teen-agers, associated with more schooling but also with relatively fewer job opportunities off the farm, the historic position between the races has been reversed in this regard.

For many years the labor force participation rate for nonwhite males fourteen to nineteen years was about 15 percentage points above that of their white counterparts; then the difference began to narrow considerably. This has developed especially since 1940. In 1960 the decennial census showed that for the first time white males fourteen to nineteen years old had the higher labor force rate—by almost 10 percentage points.

Similarly, nonwhite teen-age girls once had a labor market participation rate 15 percentage points and more above that of their white counterparts. Here, too, about 1940 the difference began to narrow. The reversal came in the 1950 returns (before that of the boys) and it persisted through 1960.

Labor market participation has declined among men in their early twenties. (Fig. 9-1)

There have been a number of significant developments in labor force activity among men twenty to twenty-four years of age. For white males in this age group, the rate has been edging down over the years; for nonwhite males in this group, the rate has declined significantly. (2)

More recently, there is evidence of a tapering-off of this decline, but the trend toward more education after high school (technical institutes, junior colleges, universities) continues strong and should hold the rate at least to recent levels.

Among females in their early twenties, the trend has been up. (Fig. 9-1)

Among nonwhite women twenty to twenty-four years old (aside from 1950) the labor force rate has held fairly steady over the years; but the rate is markedly up during this century for white women aged twenty to twenty-four. This statement exemplifies the constant refrain we will be returning to concerning white women: their labor force rates have gone up across the board—sometimes against declines shown by other groups.

White and nonwhite persons twenty to twenty-four years of age have reversed positions on the labor force scale. (Fig. 9-1)

As a result of the developments just discussed, the profile of labor market participation among young adults by color has been redrawn. What was once a slight edge in labor market participation for nonwhite males twenty to twenty-four has given way to a slight edge for white males. What was once a large difference in labor market participation of nonwhite females twenty to twenty-four, over white females twenty to twenty-four, has become almost no difference at all.

Labor market participation has held steady and high among adult white men. (Fig. 9-2)

For white men twenty-five to fifty-four years old, the labor force story can be brief and to the point. Just about all of them used to work and still do.

Labor market participation has tended down among adult nonwhite men. (Fig. 9-2)

For the first several decades of this century, the rates for nonwhite males twenty-five to fifty-four were a shade higher than for whites; but since 1940 the rates for nonwhites have been going down and have reached the point where the positions of the two color groups have been reversed in significant fashion.

It might be noted in this connection that for the first several decades, every nonwhite male age group had a labor market participation rate of 90 percent or better except the teen-agers and those who were sixty-five years of age and over; the 1950 census, however, showed only one group (thirty-five to forty-four) with that high a rate; by 1960 there was none.

Among adult women, white and nonwhite, labor market participation has significantly and persistently moved up. (Fig. 9-2)

Many, if not most, of our points so far have indicated the declines among various sectors in the population—and some of the most striking declines are still to be recounted. But they all have been counterbalanced by the rise in labor force activity among adult women twenty-five to fifty-four years of age.

The upturn in labor force participation among these women may warrant exciting adjectives, but we will stay with the figures for a little while longer. Among white women, the rate has doubled since

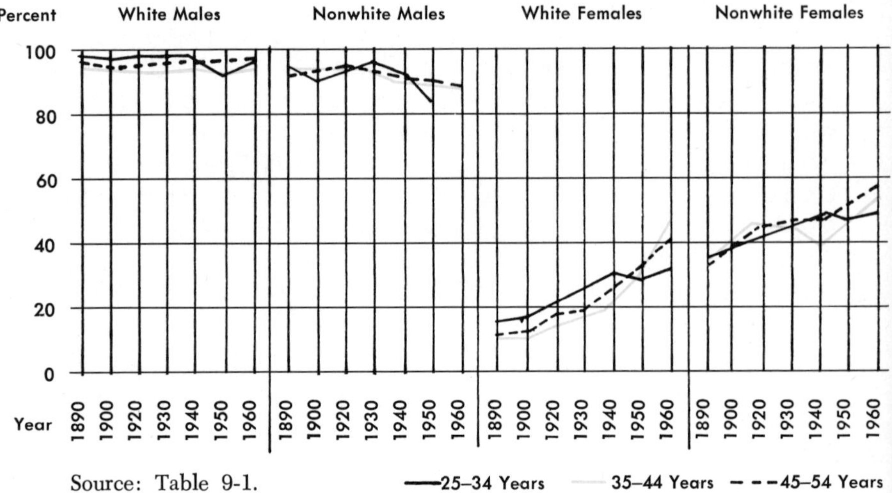

FIG. 9-2 *Labor market participation rates, by age, color, and sex, 1890–1960.*

1900 for the age group twenty-five to thirty-four, gone up three and a half times for those thirty-five to forty-four, and quadrupled for women forty-five to fifty-four. Nonwhite women already had very high rates at the turn of the century, triple and quadruple those for white women of these ages at that time; but they, too, went up significantly.

Men fifty-five to sixty-four years of age have experienced declining labor market participation. (Fig. 9-3)

This age group deserves special mention because it already includes men whose exits from the labor force are affected by the forces of formal retirement, whether they be under federal old age or disability insurance or private plans. White males fifty-five to sixty-four have been experiencing a small decline in labor market participation rates over the years. Among nonwhite males in this age group, the decline has been quite marked, carrying them well below the rate for whites, another reversal in position of the two color groups.

Women fifty-five to sixty-four years of age have increased their rate of labor market participation over the years. (Fig. 9-3)

The upward thrust in worker rates among women has occurred even at the older age levels. Among white women fifty-five to sixty-four the increase has been enormous. At the turn of the century, about one out of every ten of these women was a worker; on an adjusted decennial census level the comparable figure now is one in three; their worker rate has doubled in the last twenty years. The rate for nonwhite women of ages fifty-five to sixty-four has held steady or perhaps shown a slight tendency to move up. The trend is difficult to assess because of the distinct possibility that these women had been underenumerated for some time prior to the 1960 census.

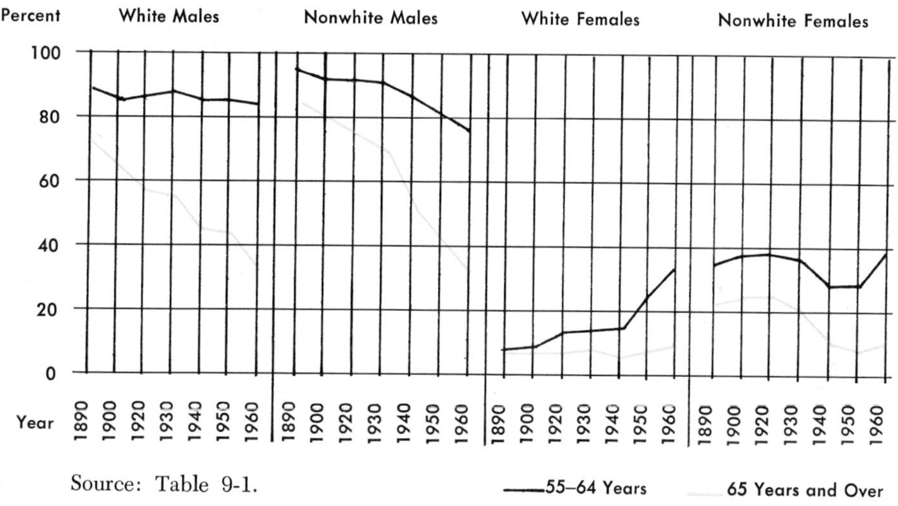

Source: Table 9-1.

FIG. 9-3 *Labor market participation rates, by age, color, and sex, 1890–1960.*

By far the biggest declines in labor force participation have occurred among men sixty-five years of age and over. (Fig. 9-3)

Here, labor market participation has been cut in half for white men, even more than for nonwhite men sixty-five and over. Perhaps the most pointed comment we can make is to note that by now the labor market participation rate for older men is below that of teen-age boys.

Labor market participation has gone up for women sixty-five years of age and over. (Fig. 9-3)

Among white women in this same age group, labor force rates held steady until 1940, but had doubled by 1960, when one out of ten in this age group was a worker.

Among nonwhite women, the trend was distinctly down until 1940, when the labor force rate for this group fell to half of what it was in 1900; but since then it has been holding steady.

Married women have had by far the most significant increase in labor market participation over the years.

Using decennial census data, labor market participation rates for women by marital status look like this:

	1960	1890
Single women	42.9%	36.9%
Married women	30.7%	4.5%
Other	38.7%	28.6%

Each group increased its labor force activity, but the change among married women is almost hard to believe. In 1900 about one out of every twenty married women was in the labor force; now the rate is about one in three.

Single and married women have reversed positions in the composition of the female labor force.

Using decennial census adjusted data again, here is what has happened to the different categories of women workers:

	1960	1890
Single	23.6%	69.3%
Married	55.2%	13.5%
Other	21.2%	17.2%

In 1890 the bulk of women workers (close to 70 percent) were single. Now single women account for less than 25 percent of the entire group and the majority position is held by the married women.

The nonwhite male has declined considerably in his proportion of the labor force.

As a result of the trends enumerated so far, the nonwhite male now makes up a smaller proportion of the American labor force. In 1890 he accounted for about one out of every ten workers; that proportion has now been cut almost in half.

The labor force has gone up considerably in age over the years.

The median age of workers in the United States has moved up significantly since 1890. At that time the average age of men in the labor force was about thirty-two years; now it is closer to forty. Among women the average in 1890 was a little under twenty-five; but with the sharp drop in labor market participation among nonwhite female teen-agers and the big upward shift among adult women, the median age of female workers is now about thirty-eight.

Socioeconomic Factors

It is impossible to measure the precise effects of all the forces that have brought such dramatic changes in the composition of our work force. But it is possible to list the social and economic events these changes clearly reflect. We do this now by reviewing what seem to be the ten leading forces involved. They are not given in rank order of importance—in fact, they are all highly interrelated.

Women and the Family

Let us start with women and point to the change in attitude toward women's participation in activities outside the home. We emphasize the phrase "outside the home" because women usually put in a substantial amount of work at home. Such work does not place them in the labor force, but it is still hard and productive. (In 1900, married women had a much lower labor market participation rate, but the work most women put in round the clock at home was doubtless physically more difficult than the work their granddaughters are doing now outside the home.)

During the twentieth century, two world wars and their aftermaths brought about a change in the concept of the economic role of women. In times of emergency women were called upon for service in government and industry and as members of the armed forces. They performed in virtually every occupation and industry. Women's suffrage has given them political equality, and beginning with the 1920s especially, U.S. mores have changed to the point where women are accepted on a par with men for many jobs. There is still sex discrimination in many places and for many jobs, but no one can gainsay the enormous changes that have taken place in just the past quarter of a century.

Side by side with this factor has been the changing size and composition of the family. Today an increased proportion of adult women are married, but the size of the individual family has become considerably smaller since the turn of the century. Many girls get married earlier now and are younger when their children grow up than several decades ago. And they live longer than they did fifty years ago, which allows many more women to marry, have children, raise them, and still have years of life and good health to work outside the home.

Although attitudes have changed, there is still considerable concern about the role of the working woman, especially the working mother. (3) Half a century ago it was not considered "respectable" in many quarters for a young lady to work—and considering what working conditions were in many places, this attitude may have been brought about by more than snobbery. Times have changed, and working conditions for women have improved.

Today what we hear is concern for the competition women may be giving men for jobs. The author uses as one of the lead economic indicators the letters he gets on this subject. They rise in periods of recession and fall off in periods of high employment. The burden of these letters is that increasing labor market participation by women is taking jobs away from men. One answer to this complaint is that women predominantly fill jobs as typists, nurses, elementary school teachers, and the like. Most unemployed men, as things now stand, would have a difficult time indeed filling these jobs if they were vacated by the women.

Technological Change

Important in the galaxy of social and economic forces we are discussing is technological change. On the farm, in the factory, and at home, technological advance has radically altered the nature and content of work. In the home, automatic ovens, washing machines, diaper service, and fresh-frozen foods are a few of the recent labor-saving developments. In business and industry, work has moved farther and farther away from difficult physical and manual labor. The processes involved and the end products themselves have minimized the sex differential in the efforts required for production. On the farm, technological advances have generated the biggest increase in productivity (or reduction in man-hour requirements).

All of which leads us to make special note again of the great change in our occupational and industrial structure, emphasizing white collar, service-producing activities, with their tremendous opportunities for women workers.

Other Social and Economic Changes

By the same token, we point to the great decline in farm employment and the streams of migration from rural to urban areas. These two are highly correlated with some of the major changes in labor force participation. The decline in labor force activity in a number of groups in the nonwhite population is involved. Also involved is the decline in labor force participation among older men; this, in turn, is in part a consequence of the reduction in agricultural employment, where it is possible to stay at work much longer than in today's urbanized, industrialized society. In 1900 one out of every three persons lived and worked on a farm; today the proportion is well below one in ten.

With these changes has come an increasing emphasis on education and training. Compulsory school attendance, minimum-age school-leaving laws, the growing importance of a high school diploma in getting a job, today's more complex, technologically based working world—all these have raised educational prerequisites for employment. The reduction in labor force participation rates for the young is an inevitable consequence. In this movement toward greater educational attainment, incidentally, the women have joined full-force. A higher proportion of girls graduate from high school than boys, and two out of every five first degrees at the college level go to women. We mention this factor because many women use their educational backgrounds in obtaining jobs as their children grow up and they return to the labor force.

While the length of our working lives has been increasing, the amount of working time on the job as measured by the workweek—or in total hours worked annually—has gone down in practically all sectors of the economy. Technological change, labor-management action in reducing hours and increasing paid vacations and holidays, and changing occupational needs and work patterns have had a twofold impact. There has been a reduction of work hours on full-time jobs and an increase in part-time job opportunities. The biggest increase in jobs for women in the years after World War II, for instance, has come in part-time work. This again has helped increase female labor force participation.

Referring to the reduction of labor force activity by older men, we can briefly note again the emergence of a broadly based social security program and the rapid growth in private pension plans. These are still evolving, as witness the 1961 statute permitting men in the federal social security program to retire at sixty-two.

Finally—and part and parcel of all other factors we have mentioned—is the rising income and standard of living of the general population over the years. Although we still have a long way to go in bringing all sectors of the population up to these high standards, the substantial progress we have seen so far has permitted, for example, a larger and larger proportion of families to support their children in school for longer and longer periods of time.

We point out once more that these are the socioeconomic factors—the nondemographic factors—we talked about in Chapter 8 as being the keys to changes in labor market participation over a period of time. These are the ones that have made the difference as we looked at the labor force changes during this century—and these, of course, are the ones most difficult to foretell.

All of this makes looking ahead in the labor force field a difficult business, especially over long periods of time. But the job of looking ahead is important, and in our next chapter we will discuss what has been done in this field.

Reference Notes

1. *The Labor Force in the United States, 1890–1960* (New York: Research Council, 1948), Appendix A.
2. Labor market participation rates for persons twenty to twenty-four years of age in 1950 should be read in Table 9-1 with the understanding that they were down considerably because of the substantial numbers then going to school under government grants.
3. An excellent discussion of this and related matters can be found in the volume of *Womanpower* by the National Manpower Council (New York: Columbia Univ. Press, 1957).

Readings

The basic data for making comparisons of labor market participation since 1890—done on the basis of decennial census data, adjusted to make them as comparable as possible over the decades since that date—come from the unadjusted decennial 1960 census figures and from

BANCROFT, G. *The American Labor Force.* New York: John Wiley & Sons, 1958.

DURAND, JOHN D. *The Labor Force in the United States, 1890–1960.* New York: Social Science Research Council, 1948.

The long-term trends shown by the data have been reviewed extensively by both Bancroft and Durand for the periods under consideration. Each of the trends we have examined has been the subject of full-scale investigations and reports. Among the more significant are the following:

SMUTS, R. W. *Women and Work in America.* (National Manpower Council.) New York: Columbia Univ. Press, 1959.

Womanpower. (National Manpower Council.) New York: Columbia Univ. Press, 1957.

Work in the Lives of Married Women. (National Manpower Council.) New York: Columbia Univ. Press, 1958.

For the story of the older worker, an excellent source is

TIBBITTS, C. (ed.). *Handbook of Social Gerontology.* Chicago: Univ. of Chicago Press, 1960.

Major developments affecting the young are examined in reports prepared in connection with the 1960 White House Conference on Children and Youth, such as

GINZBERG, E. (ed.). *The Nation's Children.* New York: Columbia Univ. Press, 1960.

CHAPTER TEN

Labor Force Projections

TRYING TO PROJECT WHAT WILL HAPPEN TO THE LABOR FORCE OF A COUNTRY is a valuable, but risky, exercise. Such an exercise requires, first, an estimate of what will happen to the population—its size and its composition in terms of the different age, sex, and other groups; second, an estimate of what will happen to the labor market participation rates for these various groups; and third, the multiplication of one by the other to get absolute figures on the expected labor force.

Underlying these steps are two important sets of assumptions. First we have to project demographic changes—that is, make certain assumptions about what will happen to the size of the population in the future. This involves estimates of the future birthrate and the age or sex or color or marital status or any other demographic variable affecting the composition of the population, depending on how detailed we wish to be.

The second set of assumptions, much more difficult to make, underlies the second step, that of projecting labor market participation rates. It involves estimating the effect of expected social and economic changes on those rates and thus on our overall future labor force figures.

If we are trying, for instance, to project the labor force from 1960 to 1970, we must make assumptions concerning, among other factors, the economic situation in 1970, our international posture in that year, the impact of automation and technological change, the proportion of the college-age population attending institutions of higher learning, and any changes in retirement laws and practices.

Value of Projections

Such an exercise has at least two valuable consequences. First, when finished, one has a picture of the potentialities, the problems, and the promises inherent in the future labor force. This kind of looking ahead is much like what a business organization or a college or a family does from time to time. Each of these groups has to take stock periodically of where it is, its future expectations, and what steps it might take now to prepare for the future.

In going through the projection process for the period 1960–70, it was found that about 26 million new young workers would be coming into the labor market in this country during the decade—about 40 percent more than during the 1950s. This warning of an unprecedented upturn in new young workers can help shape policies for maximizing employment opportunities for these young people. Our discussion of the 1960–70 decade will afford many more illustrations of this kind.

The second opportunity to be found in this exercise lies in the fact that when the period we are projecting is over, we can compare our estimates with what actually happened. We can then discover where we were close and where we were far off. We can better gauge the forces that made for differences between the actual and the projected course of events. A useful result might be the improvement of concepts and techniques for future exercises in this field.

Past Efforts at Looking Ahead

The technique of projection has been improved considerably in the past twenty-five years. The first attempts involved simply making projections of future population and its possible effect on the working population. (1) Changes in the growth and composition of the population, of course, will have a substantial impact on the size and distribution of the labor force. But since labor force patterns themselves can change enormously with time, it is necessary to project labor market participation rates as well.

TABLE 10-1
Live Births in Thousands and Birthrates per Thousand in the United States, 1940–62

Year	Births	Birthrate	Year	Births	Birthrate
1940	2,559	19.4	1952	3,847	24.7
1941	2,703	20.3	1953	3,902	24.6
1942	2,989	22.2	1954	4,017	24.9
1943	3,104	22.7	1955	4,047	24.6
1944	2,939	21.2	1956	4,163	24.9
1945	2,735	19.5	1957	4,285	25.0
1946	3,289	23.3	1958	4,204	24.3
1947	3,700	25.8	1959	4,245	24.0
1948	3,535	24.2	1960	4,258	23.7
1949	3,560	23.9	1961	4,268	23.3
1950	3,554	23.6	1962	4,167	22.4
1951	3,751	24.5			

Source: *Indicators* (U.S. Department of Health, Education, and Welfare, National Vital Statistics Division, March 1963).

In the past quarter of a century it has been seen that social and economic forces can influence population change. For example, during the severe depression of the 1930s, birthrates declined substantially. Most population projections of that time called for continued low birthrates and a leveling off of the U.S. population. The World War II and postwar upsurge in births proved depression-era demographers wrong. (2) This is seen in Table 10-1.

If one makes a projection of the labor force for a ten-year period, however, such as the one we will describe for 1960–70, he avoids trying to gauge what the future birthrates will be. Since labor force age begins at fourteen, everyone who will be a worker in 1970, for example, has already been born by 1960. Thus, our 1960–70 labor force projection does not involve the birthrate-projection problem.

Projections of Wood and Durand for the 1940s

Systematic projections of the working population date back only to the late 1930s. One of the first was done by Loring Wood, for the period 1940 to 1950, on the basis of trends shown from 1900 to 1930. (3) Much more such work was done during World War II, when estimates of the future labor force became important for postwar economic planning. This was particularly difficult, since there was substantial disagreement on how much of the greatly increased World War II labor force would continue to work after the war.

There was another difficulty. The gainful worker concept used in the 1930 census was quite different from the labor force concept used in the 1940 census and thereafter. Yet it was necessary to examine developments between 1930 and 1940. The Census Bureau developed a way to make these two sets of census data comparable and issued a series of labor force projections prepared by John D. Durand and Loring Wood. (4) Basically, what these authors tried was to answer the question: If the social, economic, and demographic forces reflected in changing labor market participation rates from 1920 to 1940 continued, what would labor market participation be in the 1940s?

To answer this question, Durand and Wood made a detailed examination of the changing labor market participation rates by five-year age cohorts and by sex, from 1920 through 1940. They then projected the 1920–40 trends into the ten-year period 1940–50. Applying the resulting rates to an estimate of the population for that period, they came up with what they called a "normal" labor force for the 1940s.

"Normal" was not the best term to apply to these figures, since it implies that any differences from it are "abnormal" or out of the ordinary. The fact that the projections were made during a war period, however, made the use of the word understandable. As we

TABLE 10-2
Differences Between "Normal" and Actual Labor Force by Age and Sex, April 1945 and April 1947 (In Thousands)

	April 1945			April 1947		
Age and Sex	Actual Labor Force	"Normal" Labor Force	Deviation from "Normal"	Actual Labor Force	"Normal" Labor Force	Deviation from "Normal"
Total	66,246	58,163	8,083	60,653	59,555	1,098
Male	46,246	42,406	3,911	44,312	43,049	1,263
14–19	4,737	2,615	2,122	3,363	2,489	874
20–24	5,829	5,401	428	4,980	5,376	− 396
25–34	10,575	10,462	113	10,496	10,732	− 236
35–44	9,453	9,334	119	9,555	9,484	71
45–54	8,017	7,749	268	7,854	7,698	156
55–64	5,385	4,998	387	5,674	5,294	380
65 and over	2,411	1,937	474	2,390	1,976	414
Female	19,839	15,667	4,172	16,341	16,506	− 165
14–19	2,720	1,268	1,452	1,820	1,186	634
20–24	3,405	3,034	371	2,698	3,063	− 365
25–34	4,551	4,365	186	3,649	4,722	−1,073
35–44	4,089	3,404	685	3,583	3,656	− 73
45–54	2,964	2,149	815	2,691	2,343	348
55–64	1,620	1,118	502	1,460	1,195	265
65 and over	490	329	161	440	341	99

Source: Bureau of the Census. Labor force figures include armed forces.

have seen, expectations in this field on the basis of long-term trends are practically always off the mark. The terms now used are more often "projected" or "estimated" or "trend," and imply an extrapolation of past trends into the future.

These projections for 1940 to 1950 were used for the two major purposes we have described: trying to learn what is in store in the immediate years ahead, and trying to learn the reasons for the differences that eventually show up between the projected and the actual labor force.

Labor Force Developments of the 1940s

A concrete demonstration of what we are discussing can be seen from Table 10-2, which contrasts the actual with the "normal" labor force that had been predicted by Durand and Wood. The two sets of figures show labor force participation, first during the peak war period, and then after two years of transition and reconversion to peacetime patterns. The following points stand out:

For April 1945 the labor force (including the armed forces) was about 8.1 million above the projection based on previous long-term trends—showing, of course, the enormous expansion in working population during World War II.

A substantial part of the increase in the male labor force by April 1945 was accounted for by teen-agers who were inducted into the armed forces or who left school to take jobs in war industries. Induction into the armed forces also played a large role in the upturn among males twenty to twenty-four years of age.

For much of the rest of the male labor force, the difference between actual and "normal" was quite small, since most were in the labor force already. However, the differences were substantial for the older men, especially those sixty-five and over, as the previous (and as it turned out, the future) declines in labor market participation were reversed under wartime conditions.

More than half of all the excess of labor force growth over what was anticipated on the basis of long-term trends was accounted for by women. Only a small proportion of this change was due to entries by women into the armed forces. Women provided by far the preponderant supply of "manpower" to meet wartime civilian needs.

Among women, too, it was the teen-agers who accounted for a big part of the difference between "normal" and actual labor force for April 1945. Many, of course, responded to the great increase in employment opportunities. For those girls eighteen or nineteen who were married, labor market participation was still very high because of the absence of many of their husbands in the armed forces.

Some of the much larger than projected increases were accounted for by adult women. There were especially large increases among women thirty-five to fifty-four, whose children were well along in school.

By 1947 the excess of actual over "normal" fell dramatically to a little over one million, about one-eighth of the April 1945 figure. The reduction in the size of the armed forces, the return to the home of many wartime working wives, the beginning of the big upsurge in births, the return to school of many young men, were all important factors in the decline.

It will be noted that the excess of actual over "normal" labor force persisted among the teen-agers, both boys and girls, although it was considerably lower than during the war period. The continued ready availability of jobs in the postwar period and the continued presence of more than a half million teen-age boys in the armed forces were the major reasons for these developments.

Both older women and older men continued their relatively high labor market participation in the period immediately following World War II. For the older women, it was a harbinger of the upturn in labor market participation that was to characterize the next fifteen years. For older men, it represented a revival after the severely depressed depression-era labor force rates. These men, however, would experience a substantial decline in activity in the following decade and a half.

Younger men and women both reversed tracks and were actually the only ones to show a *deficit* rather than an excess in the comparison between actual and "normal" labor force in the years immediately following the war. There were fewer men in the age groups twenty to twenty-four and twenty-five to thirty-four in the labor force in 1947 than were expected on the basis of long-term trends. This deficit was due primarily to former servicemen who took advantage of federal legislation helping them to resume and complete their education. The big upturn in marriages and births accounts for the similar situation among women in those age groups. By April 1947 there were approximately one million fewer women in the labor force of ages twenty-five to thirty-four, the prime childbearing ages, than were to be expected on the basis of long-term trends.

Durand's Projections for the 1950s

Durand, in his volume on the labor force (5), made a series of projections for 1960, working with data available for only a year or two past the end of World War II. He made a detailed analysis of the long-term trends from 1920 to 1940 and of the impact—permanent or temporary—of such factors as the wartime changes in marital status of women. Table 10-3 shows his projections, published in 1948, compared with actual 1960 returns.

TABLE 10-3
Actual and Projected Labor Force Rates for 1960

	Labor Market Participation Rates	
Age and Sex	Projected*	Actual†
Male	76.5%	79.5%
14–19	24.1	42.9
20–24	88.1	87.8
25–34	96.6	96.0
35–44	96.6	96.6
45–54	93.3	94.6
55–64	84.2	85.4
65 and over	30.1	32.7
Female	31.5%	36.0%
14–19	11.7	26.1
20–24	56.5	45.3
25–34	43.5	35.7
35–44	37.6	44.0
45–54	35.8	49.1
55–64	26.8	37.0
65 and over	6.3	10.5

*"Projections adjusted for effects of World War II," Durand, *op. cit.*, p. 257.

†April 1960 MRLF rates.

For many of the age-sex groups, Durand was quite close—for example, for adult men, where the rates have continued at their expected high levels. He was fabulously close for men sixty-five and over, where the 1920–40 trends persisted despite the intervening World War II years.

The wide gap between projected and actual for 1960 for teen-age boys and girls demonstrates how events may reverse long-term trends. From Table 9-1, which shows the long-term labor market participation trends, it can be seen that through 1940 the movement was unmistakably and persistently down for those fourteen to nineteen years old. This phenomenon was noted among the twenty long-term developments in labor force patterns reviewed in Chapter 9.

Since 1940, however, there have been some changes. Among whites fourteen to nineteen years old, labor market participation rates have moved up, among both boys and girls. The rates have continued down among nonwhite teen-agers, but since whites make up about 90 percent of the labor force, they move the overall rate for that age group. It is this recent upturn in white teen-age employment and job seeking that any projection on the basis of previous long-term trends comes up against.

The projections were also lower by a wide margin for the adult female group, thirty-five years of age and over, for reasons that we have already mentioned. No projections known to this author moved the labor participation rate for this group of women close to the actual figure for 1960.

Census Bureau Projections

In the early 1950s the Census Bureau prepared estimates of projected growth in the labor force to 1975. By then, more up-to-date information on labor force trends was available. Certain specific assumptions were made, including some relating to future economic conditions.

In its projections, published in 1952 (6), the Census Bureau used

TABLE 10-4
Actual and Projected Labor Force Rates for 1960

	Labor Market Participation Rates	
Age and Sex	Projected*	Actual†
Male	81.1%	79.5%
14–19	46.7	42.9
20–24	88.0	87.8
25–34	96.5	96.0
35–44	96.9	96.6
45–54	94.2	94.6
55–64	86.8	85.4
65 and over	41.2	32.7
Female	33.8%	36.0%
14–19	27.0	26.1
20–24	48.2	45.3
25–34	37.2	35.7
35–44	43.0	44.0
45–54	40.3	49.1
55–64	29.2	37.0
65 and over	9.2	10.5

*Bureau of the Census, Series P-50, No. 42, December 10, 1952.

†April 1960, MRLF rates.

the trends between 1920 and the period 1947–51. Both 1920 and 1947–51 had high employment rates, and the Census Bureau used them because they wished to prepare projections under high employment conditions in a peacetime economy. The 1952 Census Bureau projections involved a computation of the annual rate of change in labor force participation rates for each age-sex group between 1920 and the middle of the period 1947–51. It was assumed that this rate of change would continue into the future. Table 10-4 shows how the bureau's 1952 projections and the actual 1960 rates compare.

With the information available through the first part of the 1950s, these projections did very well for 1960, with two familiar exceptions. The labor force participation rate of men sixty-five years of age and over was far below the projected level for 1960, and the rates for adult women after World War II were much higher than expected.

The Census Bureau revised its projections in 1956. This time it made not one, but *four* different estimates for the period 1960 to 1975. (7) The first estimate was based on labor force changes from 1920 to an average of 1954, 1955, and 1956; the second projected average annual rates of change in labor force participation rates for the years 1950–55; the third was a combination of the first two; and the fourth extrapolated 1955 labor force participation rates into the future. The reader may want to take a further look at these estimates in the reference cited. The second set—projections based on trends from 1950 to 1955—came the closest to depicting the decline for older men and the increases for the adult women.

Projections for the 1960s

The statisticians have now turned their attention to the 1960s, and by far the most extensively used projections for the current decade are those prepared late in the 1950s by the Bureau of Labor Statistics. (8) The detailed materials from this work formed the basis and the context for a summary document called *Manpower: Challenge of the 1960s* (9), which highlights the expected changes for this decade.

In preparing these projections, the Bureau of Labor Statistics made specific assumptions: that past trends in labor force participation rates would continue; that the economy would continue to expand and provide adequate job opportunities for new workers, ending up the decade with a 4 percent unemployment rate; that there would be no major war; that technological advance would continue at the postwar rate; and that additional school facilities would be available to take care of the anticipated increase in the college population. Thus many of the socioeconomic factors that influence labor force trends were specifically considered.

Projections by Age and Sex Groups

The labor force itself was projected by individual age-sex groups. With past trends as guideposts, each of the age and sex categories was analyzed separately and judgments were made on future trends. Here is a brief description of what was done for the different groups:

Young workers: Because of the importance of increasing educational attainment, data on school enrollment trends since 1920 were examined for boys and girls of ages fourteen to seventeen, eighteen, and nineteen and for men twenty to twenty-four separately. Projected increases in school enrollment for each of the groups were made on the basis of a continuation of these trends. Labor force participation rates were then projected for each of these age groups, for persons both in and out of school. For the girls, additional consideration was given to nonstudents by marital status and presence of young children.

Adult men: Because rates have been relatively stable for the group twenty-five to sixty-four years of age, the decision was made to carry forward the 1955 levels of labor market participation rates.

Men aged sixty-five and over: Analysis of this group was made on the basis of farm and nonfarm residence and for those sixty-five to sixty-nine and those seventy and over. Taking into account the tendency for earlier retirement, the projections call for a much sharper drop in the rate for men sixty-five to sixty-nine than for those seventy and over, where the rate is already quite low.

Adult women: For the group twenty to forty-four years of age, separate consideration was given to the single, to the married with children under five years, and to the married with no children under five years. Labor force rates were developed for each separately, on the basis of surveys done on the subject in 1940, 1948, 1951, 1952, and 1955.

For the group *forty-five years and over,* presence of children is no longer a significant factor. Estimates were prepared on the basis of marital status—single, married with husband present, and other (that is, widowed, divorced, and separated). Past trends were extrapolated, calling for continuing increases in labor market participation by this group.

This brief listing does not do justice to the detailed assessment given to each group. But it indicates that with increasing knowledge of labor force trends the vantage point from which projections are made becomes broader and more sophisticated. Table 10-5 shows the results of this major exercise in population and labor force projections.

Some Highlights

The interested reader will also want to examine Bulletin 1242 of the Bureau of Labor Statistics and *Manpower: Challenge of the 1960s.* Here are some of the highlights:

If we take Table 10-5 and apply our labor force life table functions to the figures, we get the following manpower balance sheet for the 1960s:

Number of workers in 1960	73.6 (millions)
Minus:	
Exits from the labor force because of deaths, retirements, marriage, etc.	−15.5
1960 workers still in the labor force by 1970	58.1
Plus:	
Young workers coming into the labor force in the 1960s	+26.0
Women returning to the labor force during the 1960s	+ 3.0
Number of workers in 1970	87.1

Notice that in moving up from 73.6 to 87.1 million in the number of workers from 1960 to 1970, we project a *net* increase of about 13½ million. This, however, is actually the result of a *gross* change involving exits of 15½ million and entries of 29 million.

An unprecedented 26 million new young workers will be com-

TABLE 10 5
Projected Population and Labor Force Changes, by Age and Sex, 1960–70 (In Thousands)

	Population		Change, 1960–70		Labor Force		Change, 1960–70		Labor Force Participation Rate	
									Percent	
Age and Sex	1960	1970	Number	Percent	1960	1970	Number	Percent	1960	1970
Total	126,528	150,691	24,163	19.1	73,550	87,092	13,542	18.4	58.1	57.8
Male	61,765	73,247	11,482	18.6	49,971	57,443	7,472	15.0	80.9	78.4
14–24	13,921	20,669	6,748	48.5	8,963	13,121	4,158	46.4	64.4	63.5
25–34	11,309	12,614	1,305	11.5	10,913	12,173	1,260	11.5	96.5	96.5
35–44	11,731	11,351	−380	−3.2	11,367	10,999	−368	−3.2	96.9	96.9
45–54	10,180	11,278	1,098	10.8	9,681	10,725	1,044	10.8	95.1	95.1
55–64	7,505	8,936	1,431	19.1	6,484	7,721	1,237	19.1	86.4	86.4
65 and over	7,119	8,399	1,280	18.0	2,563	2,704	141	5.5	36.0	32.2
Female	64,763	77,444	12,681	19.6	23,579	29,649	6,070	25.7	36.4	38.3
14–24	13,565	19,989	6,424	47.4	4,822	7,046	2,224	46.1	35.5	35.2
25–34	11,515	12,608	1,093	9.5	4,364	4,905	541	12.4	37.9	38.9
35–44	12,252	11,639	−613	−5.0	5,268	5,470	202	3.8	43.0	47.0
45–54	10,666	12,028	1,362	12.8	5,141	6,555	1,414	27.5	48.2	54.5
55–64	8,105	10,030	1,925	23.8	3,031	4,313	1,282	42.3	37.4	43.0
65 and over	8,660	11,150	2,490	28.8	953	1,360	407	42.7	11.0	12.2

Source: Bureau of Labor Statistics, Bulletin 1242.

ing upon the job market in this country during the 1960s—about 40 percent more than during the 1950s. This represents a great challenge —how to develop employment opportunities for such an enormous group of newcomers.

This surge in new workers stems, of course, from the upturn and high level of births and birthrates in the period following World War II. (See Table 10-1.)

As a result of all this, Table 10-5 shows that we can expect to have about 13 million more persons in the age group fourteen to twenty-four in 1970 than we had in 1960. Since current labor force projections for this group show no change for the females and just a small dip for the males, we can expect a substantial increase in workers in that age cohort during this decade. If these events do transpire as projected, a little over 23 percent—or almost one out of every four U.S. workers—will be concentrated in this age group (fourteen to twenty-four) in 1970.

Substantial increases are also expected at the other end of the age scale. An increase of about 5½ million in men and women workers forty-five years of age and over is expected between 1960 and 1970.

Note the expected developments in the age group thirty-five to forty-four. In the midst of all of the other increases, an actual decline is expected in the population of these ages during the 1960s. There will actually be about one million fewer men and women thirty-five to forty-four years of age in 1970 than in 1960—because of the low birthrates during the 1930s, when many of these people were born. In other words, just as we have seen the effect of the postwar period in the big crop of young people, so we are now seeing the effect of the depression of the 1930s in one of the prime working ages.

All in all, our manpower posture for this decade is unique, determined by a combination of past events and anticipated future developments, including a continued decline in labor market participation rates among men aged sixty-five and older and a continued advance in activity among adult women. Our manpower profile for the 1960s looks like an hourglass, with big bulges at the ends and a narrow waist in the middle. This profile has enormous implications for manpower policy, ranging from the question of jobs for the coming tidal wave of new young workers, to meeting the coming shortage of personnel in the key working ages of thirty-five to forty-four.

There are many other points we could mention on the basis of Table 10-5, for example the fact that women are scheduled to account for fully 45 percent of the net increase in the labor force during the 1960s, or the anticipated continued advance in worker rates for just about every age group among the women. But those we have enumerated provide some of the desired insight into coming problems in the manpower field.

Revised Estimates for the 1960s

The other benefit described at the start of this chapter will come when the year arrives for which we make our estimates. The first few years of this decade already indicate some questions about the projections just described. In fact, on the basis of the evidence of the recent years, the Bureau of Labor Statistics has issued some changes in its projections for 1970. (10)

The original study was based on data available through part of 1957; the interim revisions are based on data available through part of 1962. These five additional years show evidence of some changes in the pattern of labor force participation which, in addition to revised census projections of population and school enrollment, moved the BLS to make some provisional adjustments to the original study.

We will not go into the details of the revision except to mention one of the most dramatic: the great reduction in labor force participation among men sixty-five years of age and over. As one can see from Table 10-5, the original projection for these men called for a worker rate of 32.2 percent in 1970. The new projection for 1970 is 26.4 for the older men. It turned out that the 32.2 percent participation rate projected for 1970 was exactly the actual rate for 1960. Let us make this clear: *the rate of labor market activity projected for 1970 was actually reached ten years earlier for men sixty-five and over.* As a matter of fact, their actual labor force rate for 1961 was the one originally projected for 1975.

This and other revised estimates cut the size of the projected labor force for 1970 about 1⅓ million. A little over a million of this reduction was due to revised labor force participation rates, the rest to revised population estimates. Whether this will turn out to be a better projection for 1970 we do not know, of course. These five additional years of labor force evidence (1957–62) also coincide with a period of relatively high unemployment rates. Whether this is pertinent to what will prevail in 1970 remains to be seen.

All of which led to the following comment by the BLS in its report on the interim revisions: (11)

> "It should be emphasized that these projections are based on judgments as to future changes in both the population and the labor market participation rates in each age and sex group. . . . Many important factors cannot be accurately anticipated. Among these are institutional changes, such as the recent legislation permitting earlier retirement under the social security system and legislation affecting the ability of young people to continue their education. It is also difficult to predict the kind of decisions people will make between work and other activities at various times of their life. For example, the proportion of adult women who work has been increasing for a long time but may soon reach the point where the proportions who prefer to use their time in some other fashion will not be susceptible to further reduction. Past trends, although very useful, are far from being an

infallible guide to future developments. For these reasons, the projections are subject to review from time to time, and when reviewed may well be modified."

To this, we can only say amen.

Reference Notes

1. Pioneering in a systematic, organized system of population projections was P. K. Whelpton. See his "Population in the United States, 1925 to 1975," *American Journal of Sociology*, Vol. 34 (September 1928).
2. See Joseph S. Davis, *The Population Upsurge in the United States* (Stanford Univ., 1949).
3. "Estimated Growth in the Labor Force: 1940 to 1950," *Monthly Labor Review*, Vol. 53 (November 1941).
4. *Normal Growth of the Labor Force in the United States: 1940 to 1950* (Bureau of the Census, Series P-44, No. 12, June 12, 1944).
5. Durand, *op. cit.*, Appendix C.
6. *A Projected Growth of the Labor Force in the United States Under Conditions of High Employment: 1950 to 1975* (Bureau of the Census, Series P-50, No. 42, December 10, 1952).
7. *Projections of the Labor Force in the United States: 1955 to 1975* (Bureau of the Census, Series P-50, No. 69, October 1956).
8. *Population and Labor Force Projections for the United States: 1960 to 1975* (Bureau of Labor Statistics, Bulletin No. 1242).
9. U.S. Department of Labor, 1960.
10. *Interim Revised Projections of U.S. Labor Force: 1965–75* (Special Labor Force Report No. 24, 1962).
11. *Op. cit.*, p. 1.

Readings

Excellent materials on labor force projections and a good bibliography on the subject can be found in

Durand, John D. *The Labor Force in the United States, 1890–1960.* New York: Social Science Research Council, 1948.

Historically, special reference should be made to

Whelpton, P. K. "Population in the United States, 1925 to 1975," *American Journal of Sociology*, September 1928.

Wood, Loring. "Estimated Growth in the Labor Force: 1940 to 1950," *Monthly Labor Review*, November 1941.

Wood, Loring, and Durand, John D. *Estimated Growth of the Labor Force in the United States: 1940 to 1950.* (Series P-44, No. 12.) Washington, D.C.: Department of Commerce, Bureau of the Census, June 12, 1944.

The juxtaposition of actual and expected labor force during the 1940–50 decade was made and discussed in Chapter 6 of John Durand, *op. cit.*, and in the Bureau of Labor Statistics series of technical memoranda, some of which were published, such as

ESKIN, L. "Sources of Wartime Labor Supply," *Monthly Labor Review*, Vol. 59 (August 1944).

____. and PEARLMAN, L. "Extra Workers in the Postwar Labor Force," *Monthly Labor Review*, Vol. 61 (November 1945).

____. "Teenage Youth in the Wartime Labor Force," *Monthly Labor Review*, Vol. 60 (January 1945).

Bureau of the Census projections of labor force through 1975 were published in

A Projected Growth of the Labor Force in the United States Under Conditions of High Employment: 1950 to 1975. (Series P-50, No. 42.) Washington, D.C.: Department of Commerce, Bureau of the Census, December 1952.

Projections of the Labor Force in the United States, 1955 to 1975. (Series P-50, No. 69.) Washington, D.C.: Department of Commerce, Bureau of the Census, October 1956.

These, with additional data, are discussed in Chapter 6 and Technical Appendix B of

BANCROFT, G. *The American Labor Force.* New York: John Wiley & Sons, 1958.

Labor force projections by the Bureau of Labor Statistics are found in

COOPER, S. *Interim Revised Projections of U.S. Labor Force, 1965–75.* (Special Labor Force Report No. 24.) Washington, D.C.: Department of Labor, Bureau of Labor Statistics, 1962.

Population and Labor Force Projections for the United States, 1960 to 1975. (Bulletin 1242.) Washington, D.C.: Department of Labor, Bureau of Labor Statistics, 1959.

Bureau of Labor Statistics Bulletin 1242 is summarized and its implications discussed in

Manpower: Challenge of the 1960s. Washington, D.C.: Department of Labor, 1960.

PART THREE

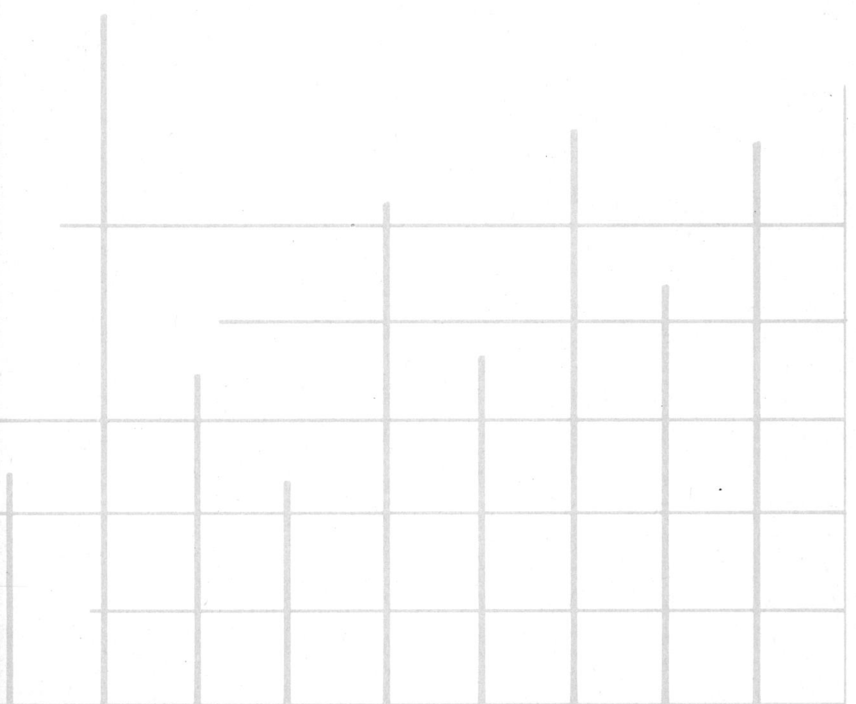

Occupations and Industries

Introduction

In the early days of man just about everyone was in the labor force, to use our modern term. Men, women, even the young, worked nearly full time to provide the necessities—food, clothing, and shelter.

As time went on and as some technological progress took place, a little more leeway developed. There was less need for the constant battle by all for sheer necessities. The young had some time for education and development; the women could attend to more of the home chores; the old got a chance to remove themselves from the battle and even take on roles as elder statesmen. Not everyone who worked had to produce physical goods. Some could spend full time in religious, health, and teaching activities.

In our early society the development of tools and techniques had a significant impact on economic activity and the distribution of end products. On a more sophisticated scale, this has been the story in the United States during the twentieth century. The young now enter the labor market later. The old have more time for retirement.

In the evolution of the modern labor force, we may surmise, the time comes when the decline in activity by women reverses and the curve turns upward again. This seems to happen when the number of gainful jobs begin to shift from the goods-producing industries, always the basic ones, to the service industries, where women's work predominates.

Here again, events in the United States during this century are quite apropos. Our industrial and occupational structure has experienced a radical transformation. We are the only nation in the world that has a majority of its workers in the service-producing, white-collar activities. This development is relatively recent, although for many prior decades there was a very consistent trend in that direction. It goes a long way, we think, in explaining the trends in labor force participation reviewed in earlier chapters and in describing some very important dimensions of our subject that we shall take up later.

CHAPTER ELEVEN

Changing Industrial and Occupational Patterns

HAVING EXAMINED SOME RECENT LABOR FORCE PROJECTIONS, LET US NOW TURN to some of the changing occupational and industrial factors affecting the labor force.

Occupations go a long way in establishing a man's—or woman's—social and economic status. How a country's labor force is deployed also tells much about a nation's social and economic status.

Since 1900 there has been a notable increase in white-collar employment in the United States and a marked decrease in farm employment. The blue-collar factory sector showed a small upturn for the first several decades, but has been relatively stable during the past twenty years. Service occupations, after a slight upward tendency after 1900, have recently begun to show signs of accelerated growth.

• The entry of large numbers of women white-collar and service workers into the labor force since 1900 is one key to recent occupational trends. Women are frequently preferred for the white-collar and service jobs. The ability of women to obtain jobs in these fields reflects a growing public demand for these types of work.

The increasing tempo of industrialization and automation in the U.S. economy, with the consequent emphasis on technology, has brought a rise in jobs in technically oriented, skilled, and semiskilled occupations. Simultaneously there has been a decline in unskilled laboring jobs. These developments have meant greater emphasis on educational prerequisites for employment.

Rise of U.S. Service Industries and Public Services

There are four major goods-producing industries. By far the largest is *manufacturing*, where most of these goods are literally "made": steel, rubber, autos and machinery; processed foods; tobacco; chemicals and paper; furniture; stone, clay, and glass products; textiles, apparel; petroleum; and leather goods. Also included in the goods-producing sector of the economy is *agriculture*, which provides us with food, feed, and fiber; and *mining*, from which come gold, lead, silver, coal, and iron ore. Finally, we have the *construction* industry, which builds highways, homes, bridges, schools, factories, and office buildings.

Since 1950 these goods-producing industries have employed *fewer* workers than the *service-producing* industries. In the service industries we include transportation groups, trade, finance, insurance and real estate, service, and government. Workers in these industries buy and sell; carry goods; provide banking, audit, and insurance services; give a wide range of personal services; and operate the government—federal, state, and local.

In Table 5-4 we presented the 1919-62 figures on the employment trends for nonagricultural establishments by major industry division. By adding agricultural employment we have the nine major sectors—goods and service producing. Their respective movements are shown in Fig. 11-1, revealing the consistent and persistent movement of the service-producing industries to a majority position.

In 1919 the picture looked like this:

(In Thousands)

Employed in Goods-Producing Industries		*Employed in Service-Producing Industries*	
Agriculture	13,243	Transportation and public utilities	3,711
Mining	1,133	Trade	4,514
Construction	1,021	Finance, insurance, real estate	1,111
Manufacturing	10,659	Service	2,263
		Government	2,676
	26,056		14,275

Source: U.S. Departments of Labor and Agriculture.

Right after World War I about 65 percent of the workers were engaged in the goods-producing industries and about 35 percent in the service-producing industries.

In 1962 the picture looked like this:

(In Thousands)

Employed in Goods-Producing Industries		*Employed in Service-Producing Industries*	
Agriculture	5,190	Transportation and public utilities	3,925
Mining	647	Trade	11,572
Construction	2,695	Finance, insurance, real estate	2,794
Manufacturing	16,752	Service	7,757
		Government	9,184
	25,284		35,232

Source: U.S. Departments of Labor and Agriculture.

By 1962, the goods-producing sector was down to about 42 percent of all workers, the service-producing sector up to 58 percent.

Actually, this presentation tends to understate the proportion in the service-producing sector. For the eight major industry divisions outside of agriculture we have used the familiar Bureau of Labor Statistics series on wage and salary workers—the only series available back to 1919 with this kind of industry detail. In other words, we omit groups such as the nonagricultural self-employed, most of whom today are in trade and service and similar divisions.

As Fig. 11-1 and the two summary tables show, a somewhat smaller number of workers were engaged in the production of goods in 1962 than in 1919. In large part, the lack of increase is traceable to the substantial decline in agriculture and persistent downturn in mining. Both construction and manufacturing are up over the long run, but these two divisions have not been areas of major employment growth in recent years.

Service-Producing Industries

The service-producing sector gives quite a different picture. Numbers of workers in *transportation and public utilities* have declined in the last several years because of the railroad industry's laying off thousands of workers. *Finance, insurance,* and *real estate* workers, on the other hand, have more than doubled; but these activities constitute a relatively small division.

It is in the remaining three major industry divisions that the big increase in the service-producing sector really lies. Trade has almost tripled its employment since 1919; service has more than tripled its employment, as has government—the latter under the impact of rising state and local payrolls.

The rise in trade, with the development of widespread distribution systems among cities and areas, and the large demands for personal services on the part of the population are familiar stories that do not have to be retold here. A further word is needed, however, about government employment, which continues to be on the rise right through the current period.

Government Services

Since the end of World War II the total number of wage and salary workers of all categories has increased by about one-fourth; corresponding increases in the government employment were double that figure. About one out of every six nonfarm wage and salary workers is employed in the public sector.

The greatest proportion of these workers are employed at the state and local level. Since World War II the numerical increase in state and local government employment has been two and a half times the upturn in federal government jobs. Nearly three out of every four government workers are in state or local employ.

The largest growth in the states and localities has been in education, where employment has risen well over 100 percent since 1947. In fact, if we take all government employment at all levels, we find that one out of every three workers is in education.

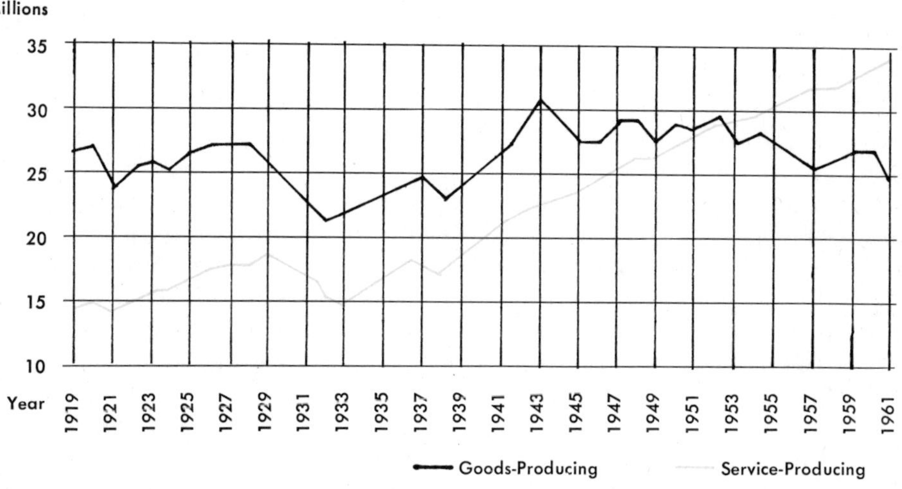

FIG. *11-1 Employment trends in goods- and service-producing industries since 1919.*

Government employment, particularly in the states and localities, has continued in its persistent growth right through the turns in the business cycle. In each of the four recessions of the postwar period, total payroll employment fell by somewhere between slightly more than one million and more than two million workers; in each case government employment went on increasing.

Why this continuing growth in government jobs? One important reason is the burgeoning postwar population. State and local government employment depends especially on the number of people who have to be served. The demand for teachers for the record baby crop and for firemen, policemen, and workers on highways and in hospitals is affected by sheer numbers in the population. In this connection, we must not forget the very substantial movement of people to the suburbs, which, in many cases, had to start from scratch in providing public services.

A second reason is the demand for better services. The postwar period has seen steadily rising incomes and living levels. These have brought about a demand not only for more but for *better* services—better schools, better housing, and, with two and a half times as many autos, better streets and roads. All this, too, has generated increasing demands on the public sector.

Future Trends

Nothing, meanwhile, points to any decline in the demand for state and local services. There is little sign of any abatement in the population rise and in the mass movements of nonurban people into the cities and of former city people out into the suburbs. In fact, our last chapter, on labor force projections for the decade 1960–70, showed large-scale population expansion at both ends of the age scale—among the young and the old. These two groups make the biggest demands for state and local government services. No doubt the increasing demands for better services will continue.

The financing of these government services is of course a major problem and may very well determine—together with the overall level of economic activity—how this sector fares in the immediate years ahead.

Increases are also in store for most of the other service-producing industries, although there are bound to be exceptions—for example, railroads. In contrast, the outlook in the goods-producing industries seems to be for a continuation of past trends, including additional declines in agriculture and mining.

Manufacturing, the biggest sector, has been subject to the most volatile ups and downs with the business cycle. But there has been no real upward thrust in manufacturing employment since the end of World War II.

The outlook for the construction industry, on the basis of recent trends, is for expansion, in view especially of the continued demands for street and highway construction as well as for homes and apartments. In the latter case, the increase in marriageable boys and girls in the late 1960s should generate a substantial surge in family formation and a demand for housing if economic activity remains high.

Occupational Changes

Writing more than twenty years ago, Dr. Alba Edwards, a noted Census Bureau expert on occupations, said (1):

> "The most nearly dominant single influence in a man's life is probably his occupation. More than anything else, perhaps, a man's occupation determines his course and his contribution in life. And when life's span is ended, quite likely there is no other single set of facts that will tell so well the kind of man he was and the part he played in life as will a detailed and chronological statement of the occupation, or occupations, he pursued. Indeed, there is no other single characteristic that tells so much about a man and his status—social, intellectual, and economic—as does his occupation.
>
> "A man's occupation not only tells, for each workday, what he does during one-half of his waking hours, but it indicates, with some degree of accuracy, his manner of life during the other half—the kind of associates he will have, the kind of clothes he will wear, the kind of house he will live in, and even, to some extent, the kind of food he will eat. And actually, it indicates, in some degree, the cultural level of his family."

One's job is of tremendous personal significance. How a country's labor force is deployed occupationally is also an important sign of its social and economic development. It is particularly noteworthy that we are the only country in the world where white-collar workers outnumber any other occupational sector.

The United States did not reach this point until 1957, but the trend in this direction has persisted through much of the twentieth century.

Historical Development of U.S. Occupational Information

For most of our history, data on occupations have come from the decennial censuses. The first to contain some occupational information was the 1820 census; no such information was collected in 1830. In 1840 the information was what we would now term industrial —the data were classified into groups such as manufacturing, mining, agriculture, commerce, navigation of oceans, navigation of rivers and lakes, the learned professions, and engineers.

The 1850 census, for the first time, directed an inquiry limited to free males sixteen years of age and over in specific occupations. The information was grouped alphabetically in an extensive list of 323 occupations, summarized into ten classes. The ten classes may be of some interest to the modern reader, if only the government worker of today, who can see how he was carefully put in a group other than those requiring education:

1. Commerce, trade, manufacturing, mechanic arts, mining
2. Agriculture
3. Labor not in agriculture
4. Army
5. Sea and river navigation
6. Law, medicine, and the divinity
7. Other pursuits requiring education
8. Government
9. Servants
10. Other

In 1860 materials were again collected only for free males sixteen and over, with detail extending to a list of 585 occupations. Beginning with the 1870 census, the occupational inquiry was applied to all persons in the population, and it is from that time that modern occupational statistics date. The decennial censuses since 1870 have of course used different classifications and tabulations in collecting and presenting occupational information; the job content of many occupations has changed over the years. In 1870 we had the "cordwainer," a skilled handicraft shoemaker; today we have the shoe industry, with scores of operations. In 1870 we had the tailor, in a skilled custom-work occupation; today the men's clothing industry, for example, employs a wide variety of persons with different skills and different work to do. Furthermore, new occupations keep coming in while older ones disappear.

In a painstaking, pioneering effort in 1943, Edwards prepared a table giving comparable-as-possible figures on occupational trends from 1870 to 1940.(2) Later, the Census Bureau did the same with the 1950 figures(3) and more recently with the major categories of the 1960 returns. All of this gives us a set of comparable data that we will use later to trace long-term occupational trends.

The *Monthly Report on the Labor Force,* meanwhile, presents current data on occupations, but its relatively small sample does not permit much detail. Though we have substantial industrial data available between the census years, we have few data on occupations. Also, data on occupations from household enumeration—census or current sample—have to be used with care, since the respondent cannot be expected to know the nuances of occupational classification. The ideal method would be to gather this kind of information from employer reports (establishments). In accordance with the Gordon Committee Report, such a system of collection is currently being considered.

Occupational Trends from 1870 to 1930

In Edwards' book the decennial census data from 1870 to 1930 were used to present an analysis of occupational trends during that sixty-year period. He grouped the individual occupations into "general divisions of occupations"—ten in all—which were really a cross between industry and occupational categories. Table 11-1 shows how the data looked.

These data reflected the tremendous transformation in the American economy during the last third of the nineteenth century and the first third of the twentieth, and gave some indication of future trends.

Thus the movement from farm to factory is highlighted by the drop in agriculture and the upward shift in manufacturing. In 1870 about three-fourths of all the gainful workers were reported as engaged in the production of physical goods; by 1930, about one-half.

TABLE 11-1
Percent Distribution of Gainful Workers Ten Years of Age and Over, by General Divisions of Occupations, 1870–1930

General Divisions of Occupations	1930	1870
Total	100.0	100.0
Agriculture	21.4	53.0
Forestry and fishing	.5	.5
Extraction of minerals	2.0	1.4
Manufacturing and mechanical industries	28.9	20.5
Total, physical goods	52.8	75.4
Transportation and communication	7.9	4.2
Trade	12.5	6.8
Public service	1.8	.7
Professional service	6.7	2.6
Domestic and personal service	10.1	9.7
Clerical occupations	8.2	.6
Total, services	47.2	24.6

Source: Edwards, *op. cit.*, p. 100.

Note, too, the doubling of the percent engaged in trade and the significant increases in such white-collar fields as the clerical and professional occupations.

Development of Socioeconomic Groupings

Edwards was a pioneer in developing statistics on occupations that brought together workers belonging to the same socioeconomic group, without regard for the particular industries in which they were employed. He developed this grouping around six major classes and presented statistics on them for the period 1910 to 1940. His six groups were professional persons; proprietors, managers, officials; clerks; skilled workers and foremen; semiskilled workers; unskilled workers.

Edwards felt strongly that each of the six groups really represented a quite distinct class. "Professional persons," he said, "more than most other workers, are engaged in purely intellectual pursuits, as contrasted with other service pursuits directly related to the production, exchange, or distribution of material goods. Professional workers, perhaps more than the workers in any other social-economic group, are pursuing their occupations primarily because of true professional interest in their chosen fields of work, rather than because of monetary or other considerations."

Of the proprietors, managers, and officials he said, "They do most of the hiring and 'firing,' they pay a relatively large proportion of the taxes, they largely control capital, they largely determine (in normal times) what the lines and the extent of production shall be, and, with their assistants, they direct the work of a large proportion of the other workers."

TABLE 11-2
Socioeconomic Classification of Working Population 1910–40

Socioeconomic Group	1910*	1940†
Total	100.0%	100.0%
Professional persons	4.4	6.5
Proprietors, managers, officials	23.0	17.8
Clerks and kindred workers	10.2	17.2
Skilled workers and foremen	11.7	11.7
Semiskilled workers	14.7	21.0
Unskilled workers	36.0	25.9

*Gainful workers fourteen years and over.
†Labor force (except new workers) fourteen years and over.
Source: Edwards, *op. cit.*, p. 187.

Skipping most of the other groups, we cite his description of the unskilled: "The workers in this group are less well educated and more poorly paid than are the workers in any other group; and being lower in economic status than the workers in any other group, they more frequently suffer from unemployment and become the subjects of relief. Inevitably, their views on social and economic questions are influenced by their form of life and labor."

Socioeconomic Changes, 1910–40

Table 11-2 is a summary of what the data showed for the period 1910 to 1940. These groupings, too, are generally in line with what has ensued. Note the pickup in professional and clerical fields, the stability among craftsmen, the sharp drop in the unskilled, the rise in semiskilled operatives.

In fact, Dr. Edwards was not afraid to prognosticate on the basis of these trends, and it is fascinating to see how right he was in most of his projections. He made eight general statements about the future:

> "The labor force will continue to increase." He reasoned That if birthrates continued to decline, the population might become stationary. He refused to believe, however, that the movement of women into the labor force was a temporary phenomenon. "Women," he said, "—particularly married women—will become a larger and larger factor in the nation's labor force and the increase in their numbers will tend to increase the size of the labor force, and, possibly, to change somewhat its social-economic construction." How right he was!
>
> "The professional class will grow in relative importance."
>
> "Farmers will decrease and other proprietors will increase in relative importance."
>
> "Clerks and kindred workers may continue to increase in relative importance."
>
> "Skilled workers probably will decrease in relative importance after the war."
>
> "Semiskilled workers will become the largest group."
>
> "Unskilled workers will continue to decrease in relative importance."
>
> "The upward trend in the social-economic status of the labor force will continue."

We will now spell out what had actually happened by 1960, and we can say that Edwards was much more right than wrong.

The Census Bureau has moved beyond Edwards' eight groups to a listing of eleven major occupational categories. We will use these eleven categories now—available from 1910 to 1960—to review the long-term occupational trends. We owe their availability to the pioneering work of Edwards and to more recent work in the Census Bureau and the Labor Department.

Long-Term Trends

The three-part Table 11-3 (A–C) presents an overview of the changes in the occupational composition of the working population in the United States since the turn of the century. We are using decennial census data for the past sixty years in order to be able to discern the long-term trends.

For more current periods, the occupational data from the MRLF are used.

General Trends

Each of the four broad sectors of the occupational world has moved in a significantly different fashion since 1900.

The *white-collar* occupations are now in first place in the occupational standings, providing a clear-cut plurality of the jobs for American workers, with more than two out of every five workers. The white-collar group is today a two-and-a-half-times larger proportion of the economically active civilian population than in 1900.

At the opposite end of the scale, the *farm* group has moved in 60 years from first to last place in the overall standings. Today the proportion of all workers engaged in farm occupations is only about one-half of what it was in 1950, only one-third of what it was in 1940, and only one-sixth of what it was in 1900.

Most of the loss for the farm group is balanced by a gain for the white-collar sector—which means that the overall changes for the other two categories were relatively small. In the *blue-collar* group the record shows a small upturn since 1900 but a leveling-off during more recent decades: the proportion of the working population in this group is shown as 39.6 percent, on the basis of the census data in Table 11-3A, for both 1930 and 1960. The *service* occupations have tended slightly upward since 1900, with signs of an increase rather than a leveling-off.

White-Collar Occupations

The long-term picture becomes much clearer when we move from these overall sectors to the individual major occupational groups.

Two groups, the professional and the clerical workers, played the major role in putting the white-collar category into first place.

The *professional* occupations have tripled their share of jobs over the past sixty years: more than one out of every ten workers is now a professional or technical person; only about one in twenty-five was performing in these fields in 1900.

The increases among professional and technical personnel reflect a really major change of this century. The persistent technological advances, our continuing industrialization and urbanization, our more recent efforts in research and development have caused groups like engineers to grow more than twentyfold in numbers since 1900; the increasing push for more and more education and training have

TABLE 11-3A

Distribution by Major Occupation Group of the Economically Active Civilian Population, Both Sexes, 1900–60

Major Occupation Group	1900	1910	1920	1930	1940	1950	1960
Total	100.0%	100.0%	100.0%	100.0%	100.0%	100.0%	100.0%
White-Collar	17.6	21.3	24.9	29.4	31.1	36.6	42.3
Professional, technical	4.3	4.7	5.4	6.8	7.5	8.6	11.4
Managers, officials, proprietors	5.8	6.6	6.6	7.4	7.3	8.7	8.4
Clerical	3.0	5.3	8.0	8.9	9.6	12.3	15.0
Sales	4.5	4.7	4.9	6.3	6.7	7.0	7.5
Blue-Collar	35.8	38.2	40.2	39.6	39.8	41.1	39.6
Craftsmen, foremen	10.5	11.6	13.0	12.8	12.0	14.1	14.3
Operatives	12.8	14.6	15.6	15.8	18.4	20.4	19.9
Laborers (except farm and mine)	12.5	12.0	11.6	11.0	9.4	6.6	5.4
Service	9.0	9.6	7.8	9.8	11.7	10.5	11.8
Private household	5.4	5.0	3.3	4.1	4.7	2.6	2.8
Other service	3.6	4.6	4.5	5.7	7.1	7.9	9.0
Farm	37.5	30.9	27.0	21.2	17.4	11.8	6.3
Farmers and farm managers	19.9	16.5	15.3	12.4	10.4	7.4	3.9
Farm laborers and foremen	17.7	14.4	11.7	8.8	7.0	4.4	2.4

Source: *Occupational Trends in the United States, 1900 to 1950* (U.S. Department of Commerce, Bureau of the Census, Working Paper No. 5); U.S. Census of Population, 1960, PC (1)-1C.

quadrupled the number of teachers; the advancing frontiers of science have lifted the job total for physicists, mathematicians, chemists, biologists, and the like well into the six-figure category, in contrast to the relative handful at work in 1900; increasing income and levels of living, advances in life expectancy, breakthroughs in medicine have all combined to create a new demand for health services, with a corresponding impact on doctors, dentists, and nurses.

More recently, the *semiprofessional* or paraprofessional workers, or, as they are more commonly called, the technicians, have seen an upward surge in employment as the demand grows for technically trained workers to assist professional personnel and to take over some of their more routine duties.

No other group, however, moved up as did the *clerical* occupations with a fivefold upturn in their proportion of the total job picture. They are the fastest-growing major category.

Lewis Mumford once said that we were a paper economy. It is certainly true that the amount of paper used in our record-keeping and communication systems in business and government is staggering. In 1960 we had about 2.2 million secretaries, stenographers, and typists alone—more than fifteen times the number in 1900. Bookkeepers, cashiers and office machine operators, bank tellers and ticket agents, telephone operators and shipping and receiving clerks are included in this vastly expanded group.

The two other groups within the white-collar category also went up, as Table 11-3A shows. The *sales* group's increase in part reflects the uptrend in trade discussed earlier in this chapter. But other occupations are also involved. For example, the number of insurance agents and brokers has quintupled since 1900. There are also many more real estate agents and manufacturing sales personnel.

The *managers, officials,* and *proprietors* group reflects crosscurrents. Proprietors have actually declined in the retail field, for example, in the face of competition from discount houses, supermarkets, and such. The managerial group has grown in response to the changing size, scope, and organization of the business and industrial community.

Blue-Collar Trends

Within the blue-collar sector, too, the three major occupational groups have moved in significantly different fashion. Among the *craftsmen,* the general trend has been upward since 1900, but the numbers have been relatively stable for the more recent decades. This group includes the skilled sector of the nation's manpower resources, including the skilled construction workers; the mechanics and repairmen who install, maintain, and repair the constantly increasing amount of complex equipment used in industry and in the home; the metal craftsmen who make models, dies, tools, and patterns that form the basis of countless industrial processes; the production workers in such industries as printing and machinery; the locomotive engineers and firemen; and, of course, the one million foremen who supervise and train a substantial proportion of industrial workers.

The relative stability for the craftsmen group underscores the continued importance of this group over the long run, in peace and war, in prosperity and depression. But, as is true in all major occupational groups, it masks some very great changes that took place within the overall total.

For instance: In 1900 there were six skilled occupations—engravers, locomotive engineers, brickmasons, blacksmiths, metal molders, and shoemakers—that were so important in the industrial scheme that they accounted for one out of every four of the skilled work force in this country. Today they account for barely one in twenty.

Also in 1900, there were another six skilled occupations—carpenters, mechanics and repairmen, cranemen and stationary engineers, plumbers, electricians, and telegraph and telephone linemen—that made up fewer than two out of every five skilled workers. Today the figure for these six skilled occupations is closer to two out of every three.

Among the major occupational groups, the semiskilled sector of our working population, *operatives,* is the largest. The growth of this group, typified by the assembly-line worker in manufacturing, symbolizes the industrialization of the United States during the twentieth century. With increasing factory mechanization, the breakdown of many skilled hand trades into a series of routine operations, and the development of mass production industries such as automobiles and steel, there was bound to come an upturn in semiskilled jobs. In addition to assembly-line workers, the operatives classification includes the various jobs that involve drivers (bus, taxi, and truck) that obviously had no practitioners in 1900 but now number more than two million.

Finally, there is the *laborer* group among the blue-collar workers. In the nonfarm sector of the American economy, this is the only occupational group, aside from domestic or private household service workers, that has shown a decline since 1900. And the decline has been enormous. Among the top few occupational groups in 1900, it now accounts for a smaller proportion of workers, including farm, than any other except private household service. Only about one in twenty workers is classified as an unskilled laborer. Here again, this century has seen the substitution of mechanical and other power for the unskilled manual efforts involved in handling and moving heavy objects, loading, unloading, and excavating. In the place of the unskilled laborer, who used to account for about one out of every eight workers, we find conveyor systems, industrial trucks, earth-moving machinery, and the like.

Service Occupation Trends

The service field demonstrates again the importance of looking behind the overall figure. While domestic service has been cut in half as a proportion of the working population, the other service fields have moved up two and a half times.

Private household service work took its big drop during the period 1940–50, when better-paying jobs siphoned off older and newer workers from this type of job. The number and percent in this occupational group went up somewhat during the 1950s—but this happened in good part because of a large increase in the number of baby sitters, who are included in this category.

Other service jobs have been increasing for some time. Included are jobs associated with eating out (waiters, waitresses, bartenders, counter and fountain workers, cooks), protective services (firemen, guards, policemen, detectives, marshals, constables, sheriffs), and health services (attendants in hospitals and other institutions, practical nurses).

Farm Trends

Finally, on the farm sector, *farmers and farm managers* as well as *farm laborers and foremen* shared in the dramatic decline that has taken place since 1900.

Occupational Trends Among Men and Women

We move now to one further level of disaggregation, as we did in studying other facets of the labor force. The materials are found in parts B and C of Table 11-3, showing occupational trends for men and women separately. We can be relatively brief in summarizing the major points.

Male White- and Blue-Collar Workers

For men, the blue-collar field is still the largest. In fact, about half of all male workers are in this sector—up from one-third in 1900. This increase has been concentrated in the skilled and semiskilled groups, identified with industrialization, the growth of mass production, and assembly-line techniques. The unskilled laborer group has fallen persistently and consistently as a proportion of the job total.

TABLE 11-3B
Distribution by Major Occupation Group of the Economically Active Civilian Population, Males, 1900–60

Major Occupation Group	1900	1910	1920	1930	1940	1950	1960
Total	100.0%	100.0%	100.0%	100.0%	100.0%	100.0%	100.0%
White-Collar	17.6	20.2	21.4	25.2	26.6	30.5	35.3
Professional, technical	3.4	3.5	3.8	4.8	5.8	7.2	10.4
Managers, officials, proprietors	6.8	7.7	7.8	8.8	8.6	10.5	10.7
Clerical	2.8	4.4	5.3	5.5	5.8	6.4	7.2
Sales	4.6	4.6	4.5	6.1	6.4	6.4	7.0
Blue-Collar	37.6	41.3	44.5	45.2	13.3	48.4	49.7
Craftsmen and foremen	12.6	14.1	16.0	16.2	45.6	19.0	20.7
Operatives	10.4	12.5	14.4	15.3	15.5	20.5	21.2
Laborers (except farm and mine)	14.7	14.6	14.0	13.6	18.0	8.8	7.8
Service	3.1	3.8	3.7	4.8	12.1	6.2	6.4
Private household	.2	.2	.2	.2	6.1	.2	.1
Other service	2.9	3.6	3.6	4.6	.3	6.0	6.3
Farm	41.7	34.7	30.4	24.8	5.7	14.9	8.6
Farmers and farm managers	23.0	19.7	18.4	15.2	21.7	10.0	5.6
Farm laborers and foremen	18.7	15.0	12.1	9.6	8.4	4.9	3.0

Source: See footnote, Table 11-3A.

The proportion of men in white-collar jobs doubled from 1900 to 1960. The rise in professional and technical fields was particularly marked—one in ten men now works in these fields. The upturn was also very strong in the clerical field, but this category is much less important for the men than for the women.

TABLE 11-3C
Distribution by Major Occupation Group of the Economically Active Civilian Population, Females, 1900–60

Major Occupation Group	1900	1910	1920	1930	1940	1950	1960
Total	100.0%	100.0%	100.0%	100.0%	100.0%	100.0%	100.0%
White-Collar	17.8	26.1	38.8	44.2	44.9	52.5	56.3
Professional, technical	8.2	9.8	11.7	13.8	12.8	12.2	13.3
Managers, officials, proprietors	1.4	2.0	2.2	2.7	3.3	4.3	3.8
Clerical	4.0	9.2	18.7	20.9	21.5	27.4	30.9
Sales	4.3	5.1	6.3	6.8	7.4	8.6	8.3
Blue-Collar	27.8	25.7	23.7	19.8	21.6	22.4	19.1
Craftsmen and foremen	1.4	1.4	1.2	1.0	1.1	1.5	1.3
Operatives	23.8	22.9	20.2	17.4	19.5	20.0	17.2
Laborers (except farm and mine)	2.6	1.4	2.3	1.5	1.1	.8	.6
Service	35.4	32.4	23.9	27.5	29.4	21.5	22.7
Private household	28.7	24.0	15.8	17.8	18.1	8.9	8.3
Other service	6.8	8.5	8.1	9.7	11.3	12.6	14.4
Farm	18.9	15.8	13.5	8.4	4.0	3.7	1.9
Farmers and farm managers	5.9	3.8	3.2	2.4	1.2	.7	.6
Farm laborers and foremen	13.1	12.0	10.3	6.0	2.8	2.9	1.3

Source: See footnote, Table 11-3A.

The rest of the data in Table 11-3B should be quite clear by now. Obviously, very few men work in private household service; the increase has come in the other service fields described. The familiar trend in farm employment is evident here, also.

Female White-Collar Workers

The occupational profile for women is quite different, although the basic trends generating the changes since 1900 are much the same.

Among the women, white-collar jobs account not only for a plurality, but for a majority, of all employment. By 1930 they represented the biggest occupational sector, and no other sector has been close since. One occupational group stands out: the clerical jobs. They now account for more than 30 percent of all women workers—up seven and a half times since 1900. Professional and technical work, such as teaching or nursing, is a very important field of work for women, but women still have a long way to go in the managerial jobs.

It always comes as a surprise to realize that at the turn of the century more than one out of every four women workers were in the blue-collar category, typically as semiskilled operatives in textile mills and the like. While this is still an important sector of work, the proportion of women workers doing this kind of work has declined in the face of the surge in white-collar employment opportunities.

Women in the Services Field

Similarly striking has been the reversal in the service sector. The decline in domestic or private household service work has been enormous—enough to cut down the proportion of women workers in the overall service field from about one-third to one-fifth, despite a marked increase in other service fields.

Finally, it is perhaps relatively little known that farm work was the field of economic activity for almost 20 percent of all women workers in 1900; now the proportion is comparatively insignificant at less than 2 percent.

Table 11-3C, in portraying the changing occupational status of women, helps explain their changing labor force participation, described in previous chapters. For women in 1900, the single biggest major occupational group among the eleven we have been reviewing was domestic service in private homes; today it is clerical work in business, industry, and government. In 1900, 13 percent of the employment opportunities for women were in farm work; now the same percentage of women work as professional and technical personnel. In 1900 the proportion of women working as semiskilled operatives was greater than the proportion in all the white-collar jobs put together; today the proportion in white-collar jobs is triple that in semiskilled occupations. Thus, women have been in the vanguard in moving into the increasingly service-oriented, white-collar American working world.

Rising Educational Requirements

The occupational trends reviewed so far indicate a decided shift towards jobs that require more and more education, training, and skill. An occupational pattern that shows (as it did in 1900) one out of every three male workers employed as a laborer on or off the farm requires a relatively low degree of educational attainment on the part of the labor force.

A job pattern that shows (as it did, in contrast, in 1960) one in three male workers engaged as either a professional and technical person or a skilled craftsman requires of the labor force a significantly higher degree of educational attainment.

This trend toward more education helps to explain the marked increase in the age of first entry into the labor force that has occurred during this century. An increasing proportion of young persons are going to school beyond the high school and college levels.

Some idea of the intergenerational differences in educational attainment can be seen from the following table:

Age	*Median Years of School Completed 1960*
25–29	12.3
30–34	12.2
35–44	12.1
45–54	10.3
55–64	8.8
65 and over	8.4

Source: Bureau of the Census.

A full four years of educational attainment separates the youngest and oldest groups in this table. Those under forty-five years of age show a median educational attainment beyond high school; those in the later years, whose education was completed a generation or two ago, show a median educational attainment only a little beyond grade school.

The trend toward more education continues. In the first place, a bigger proportion of the school-age population is in school. As can be seen from Table 11-4, the increase in enrollment since the end of

World War II has been substantial indeed. Nearly all persons fifteen and under are of course still in school. For those sixteen and seventeen years of age—where dropping out of school is quite marked—the proportion enrolled has gone up from 67.6 percent in 1947 to 83.6 percent in 1961. Similar significant increases show up in the other age groups as well. From 1947 to 1961, the proportion of persons aged five to thirty-four years enrolled in school went up by a third.

Increased numbers of Americans have also acquired college degrees since World War II. In the academic year 1947–48 about 272,000 persons received their baccalaureate or first professional degree (M.D., D.D.S., LL.B.); by the academic year 1959–60 the number was up to 395,000—and the Office of Education, which compiles and projects these figures, looks for a figure of about 720,000 by 1970. In the meantime the number of those earning master's and doctor's degrees has doubled.

TABLE 11-4

Proportion of Population Five to Thirty-Four Years Old Enrolled in School, 1947–61, by Age

Year	Total	5 Years*	6 Years*	7–9 Years	10–13 Years	14 and 15 Years	16 and 17 Years	18 and 19 Years	20–24 Years	25–29 Years	30–34 Years
1947	42.3%	53.4%	96.2%	98.4%	98.6%	91.6%	67.6%	24.3%	10.2%	3.0%	1.0%
1949	43.9	55.1	96.2	98.5	98.7	93.5	69.5	25.3	9.2	3.8	1.1
1951	45.4	53.8	96.0	99.0	99.2	94.8	75.1	26.3	8.3	2.5	.7
1953	48.8	58.4	97.7	99.4	99.4	96.5	74.7	31.2	11.1	2.9	1.7
1955	50.8	58.1	98.2	99.2	99.2	95.9	77.4	31.5	11.1	4.2	1.6
1957	53.6	60.2	97.4	99.5	99.5	97.1	80.5	34.9	14.0	5.5	1.8
1959	55.5	62.9	97.5	99.4	99.4	97.5	82.9	36.8	12.7	5.1	2.2
1961	56.8	66.3	97.4	99.4	99.3	97.6	83.6	38.0	13.7	4.4	2.0

*Includes kindergarten.

Source: *School Enrollment: October 1961* (U.S. Department of Commerce, Bureau of the Census, Series P-20, No. 117, July 11, 1962).

Thus, the relation between our changing industrial and occupational structure, on the one hand, and the educational and training prerequisites for employment in this changing structure, on the other, has become a major dimension of labor force patterns and trends. Nothing promises to change this evolution.

Occupational Projections

As part of its overall program of labor force projections, the Labor Department has prepared estimates of occupational employment for the years ahead.

Table 11-5 shows the most recent predictions prepared for the decade 1960–70.

TABLE 11-5
Projected Changes in Employment, by Major Occupational Group, 1960–70

	1960		1970		
Occupational Group	Number (Millions)	Percent Distribution	Number (Millions)	Percent Distribution	Percent Change 1960–70
Total	66.7	100.0	80.5	100.0	21
White-Collar	28.8	43.1	37.5	46.6	30
Professional and technical	7.5	11.2	10.7	13.3	43
Managers, officials, proprietors	7.1	10.6	8.6	10.7	21
Clerical	9.8	14.7	12.8	15.9	31
Sales	4.4	6.6	5.4	6.7	23
Blue-Collar	24.2	36.3	27.6	34.3	14
Craftsmen and foremen	8.5	12.8	10.3	12.8	20
Operatives	12.0	18.0	13.6	16.9	13
Laborers (except farm and mine)	3.7	5.5	3.7	4.6	0
Service	8.3	12.5	11.1	13.8	34
Farm	5.4	8.1	4.2	5.3	–22

Source: 1960 data from MRLF (annual averages); 1970 data from *Employment Projections, by Industry and Occupation, 1960–75* (U.S. Department of Labor, Bureau of Labor Statistics, Special Labor Force Report No. 28, March 1963).

This projection utilizes the occupational returns from the MRLF for 1960 as a base and carries forward past trends on the basis of expectations during the 1960s. It anticipates a continued shift toward the white-collar and service job categories and away from the farm and unskilled industrial classifications.

Emphasis on Technology

If these projections hold up during the decade, we will have more than a 40 percent increase in professional and technical jobs. This is the biggest expected upturn, double the projected increase in employment as a whole. Underlying these projections are anticipated increases in the engineering and scientific professions because of rising expenditures for research and development, both civilian and military. A similar impact is expected on the technicians who work with the engineers and scientists. An expansion in the teaching profession is also expected to help raise professional work activity in view of the continuing trend toward more schooling. The same is true for the health professions in view of the growing demand for health services.

In two other major occupational groups, the clerical and the service fields, expansion is expected to be well above the national average. The forces favoring this were described in our section on long-term trends.

Among blue-collar workers, the largest projected increase is for skilled craftsmen, especially in the building trades and for mechanics, repairmen, and machinists. In the semiskilled trades, in view of the expected technological advances and automation in this sector of work, the projections call for a less than national-average growth. And of course a continuation of the decline in the proportion of unskilled labor is also projected.

In the farm sector we have a projected decline, not only in the proportion of persons employed but also in their actual numbers. If this turns out to be the case, soon only 5 percent of the entire American labor force will be engaged in farming occupations. The figure stood at 8 percent in 1960.

Increasing Need for Education

We have already reviewed briefly the relation of education and training to the occupational story. We close this discussion by pointing out that the job fields that are expected to go up the most in the 1960s are those requiring the most education and training.

In Table 11-6 we show the educational background of persons employed in each of the major occupational groups in 1962. The table just about speaks for itself.

The median years of education for professional and technical occupations in 1962 were already beyond those required for a college degree. In fact, if one subtracts from this category people following such occupations as athletics and acting, who are classified as professionals, the average is about seventeen, or a master's degree.

In the clerical group the average is already beyond a high school education—as is the case for the sales group. Those in the lower part of the educational spectrum are in areas of work where the expectations are for relative declines in employment. Even in these fields—as, for example, farming, which is increasingly taking on the characteristics of industrial enterprises and is feeling more and more the impact of science—the push is toward more education and training.

TABLE 11-6
Educational Attainment of Workers, by Major Occupational Group, March 1962

Occupational Group	Median Years of Education
Professional and technical	16.2
Managers, officials, proprietors	12.5
Clerical	12.5
Sales	12.5
Craftsmen	11.2
Service workers other than private household	10.8
Operatives	10.1
Laborers (except farm and mine)	8.9
Farmers and farm managers	8.8
Private household workers	8.7
Farm laborers	8.5

Source: Bureau of Labor Statistics.

Reference Notes

1. Alba Edwards, *Comparative Occupation Statistics for the United States, 1870 to 1940* (Sixteenth Census of the Population; Washington, D.C.: Department of Commerce, Bureau of the Census, 1943).
2. *Op. cit.*
3. *Occupational Trends in the United States: 1900 to 1950* (Working Paper No. 5; Washington, D.C.: Department of Commerce, Bureau of the Census, 1958).

Readings

The background of our changing industrial distribution can be found in

WOLFBEIN, S. L. "Changing Patterns of Industrial Employment 1919-1955," *Monthly Labor Review,* Vol. 79 (March 1956).

Current data on the industrial distribution of workers are reported each month in the Bureau of Labor Statistics' *Employment and Earnings* bulletin. Materials on government employment presented in this chapter are from

WOLFBEIN, S. L. "Postwar Patterns in Public Employment," *Challenge,* Vol. 10 (February 1962).

A basic document in the field of occupational trends is

EDWARDS, ALBA. *Comparative Occupation Statistics for the United States, 1870 to 1940.* (Sixteenth Census of the Population.) Washington, D.C.: Department of Commerce, Bureau of the Census, 1943.

See also

Occupational Trends in the United States, 1900 to 1950. (Working Paper No. 5.) Washington, D.C.: Department of Commerce, Bureau of the Census, 1958.

Current occupational statistics, limited to a relatively small number of occupational groups, are available each month from the MRLF and are published in the BLS *Employment and Earnings.* Occupational projections to 1970 are discussed in the first

Manpower Report of the President. Washington, D.C.: Government Printing Office, 1963. (This is scheduled as an annual report sixty days after Congress convenes, from 1963 on.)

The interrelationships between industrial and occupational movements are analyzed in

PALMER, G. P., and RATNER, ANN. *Industrial and Occupational Trends in National Employment.* (Research Report No. 11.) Philadelphia: Univ. of Pennsylvania, Wharton School, Industrial Research Department, 1949.

———. "Occupational and Industrial Distribution of Employment, 1910–1950," *Manpower in the United States.* (Industrial Relations Research Association Series.) New York: Harper, 1954. (In the same volume, see Chapter VIII by H. Wood, "Trends in the Specialization of Occupational Requirements."

See also

WOLFBEIN, S. L. "The Outlook for Skilled Workers," Journal of the *American Personnel and Guidance Association,* Vol. 40 (December 1961).

Back data on the educational attainment of the population, as well as a look ahead, are contained in

Current Population Reports. (Series P-20, No. 91.) Washington, D.C.: Department of Commerce, Bureau of the Census, January 12, 1959.

School enrollment figures are available annually from special surveys conducted each October in connection with the MRLF. The latest in the series is

"School Enrollment: October 1960," *Current Population Reports.* (Series P-20, No. 117.) Washington, D.C.: Department of Commerce, Bureau of the Census, July 11, 1962.

Educational attainment of the working population is reported biennially, also in connection with the MRLF survey. See

Educational Attainment of Workers, 1959. (Special Labor Force Report No. 1.) Washington, D.C.: Department of Labor, Bureau of Labor Statistics, February 1960.

Educational Attainment of Workers. (Special Report Labor Force No. 30.) Washington, D.C.: Department of Labor, Bureau of Labor Statistics, May 1963.

The relations between education, training, skill development, and changing manpower requirements have been examined in many forms by both private and public agencies. For example, the occupational outlook program of the Department of Labor carries on a substantial program in this field. See

MUSHKIN, S. (ed.). *Economics of Higher Education.* Washington, D.C.: Department of Health, Education, and Welfare, Office of Education, 1962.

Occupational Outlook Handbook. (Bureau of Labor Statistics.) Washington, D.C.: Government Printing Office, 1963 edition.

Dr. Eli Ginzberg and his colleagues at the Conservation of Human Resources Project and National Manpower Council, both at Columbia University, have produced substantial literature highly relevant to this field. See

Education and Manpower. (National Manpower Council.) New York: Columbia Univ. Press, 1960.

Ginzberg, E., and Bray, D. *The Uneducated*. (National Manpower Council.) New York: Columbia Univ. Press, 1953.

Improving the Work Skills of the Nation. (National Manpower Council.) New York: Columbia Univ. Press, 1955.

A Policy for Scientific and Professional Manpower. (National Manpower Council.) New York: Columbia Univ. Press, 1953.

A Policy for Skilled Manpower. (National Manpower Council.) New York: Columbia Univ. Press, 1954.

The Utilization of Scientific and Professional Manpower. (National Manpower Council.) New York: Columbia Univ. Press, 1954.

PART FOUR

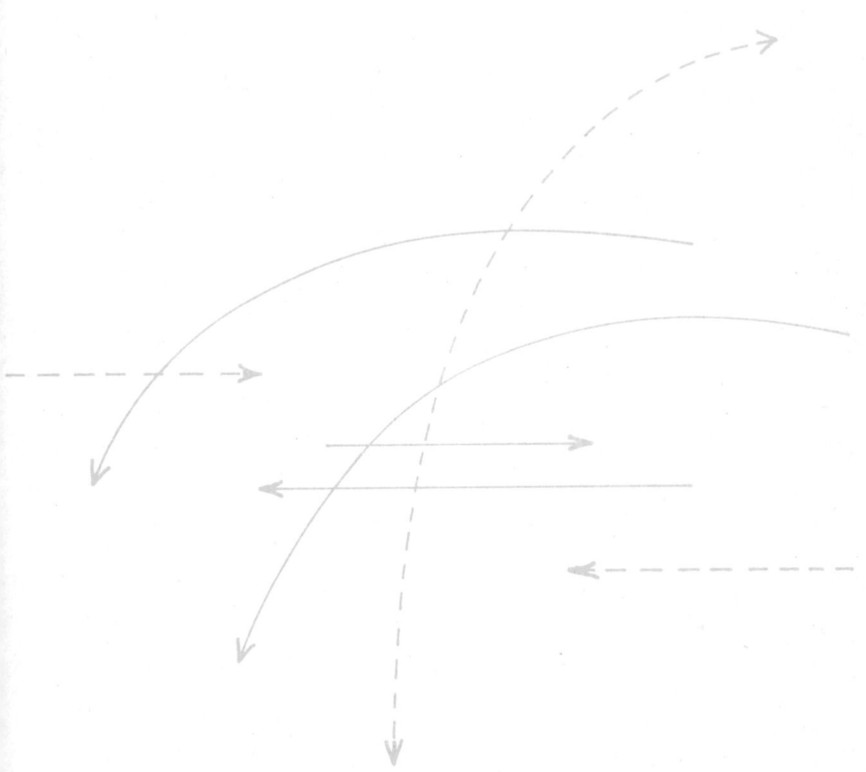

Migration, Mobility, and Movement

Introduction

IT IS AXIOMATIC THAT MIGRATION AND MOBILITY ARE A NECESSARY (ALTHOUGH not the only) condition for full employment. Without the geographic shifts that have occurred in the United States since its very beginnings, we would be a strange land indeed, with concentrations of jobs and manpower shortages in some places, lack of employment opportunity and manpower surpluses in other places. The internal migration and movement that take place within our national boundaries are one of the most effective mechanisms for matching people and jobs. This is of prime importance when the geographic shifts in employment opportunities themselves become very extensive, as they have in recent years.

The changing geography of our population and industry are relatively familiar, but with the development of current labor force measures such as the *Monthly Report on the Labor Force,* new dimensions of mobility began to be documented. It turns out that people not only move with considerable regularity from place to place but also exhibit a substantial amount of moving around, into, and out of the labor force. When in the labor force, they move into and out of employment and unemployment; and when in employment, into and out of jobs with different employers. Millions of persons change labor force, employment, and unemployment status each month. Over a year's time the number changing status is phenomenal, considering the fact that only a few decades ago the labor force was viewed as rather stable, changing slowly in response to population change. There is an enormous amount of shifting around in even a short time, reflecting changes in response to social, economic, and political change, cyclical ups and downs, and seasonal demands by industry, business, and agriculture. In addition, there are the regular departures and entries due to death, retirement, marriage and child bearing, on the one hand, and on the other, new graduations and reentries into the labor force by women and retired persons.

In the succeeding chapters, as we document the changing geography of employment opportunities we shall see that the shift is still persistently westward—although the years following World War II have seen a very substantial increase in nonagricultural employment in the South. We will review the dynamism of the labor force, showing the crosscurrents that make up a single month's or year's net change in the work force and its components.

When we talk about high migration and mobility rates, we should point out that there is a great deal of stability, too. The bulk of the adult male labor force, for example, remains in worker status (although there may be substantial shifts between employment and unemployment as cycles and seasons change). The image of ourselves as being practically nomadic is, of course, an exaggeration.

Migration and mobility can be an effective mechanism for matching people and jobs over space and time; they can be important to an individual's career development; they can make the difference in how effectively the labor force responds to geographic, industrial, and occupational changes with the minimum amount of hurt in the form of unemployment. The public employment services have as an important part of their mission to make these movements as efficient, responsive, and informed as possible.

Several aspects of migration and mobility are frequently discussed. These are:

First, there is the question of movement among the unemployed, especially the long-term unemployed in areas of substantial and persistent unemployment. Shall, for example, relocation allowances be provided to help these people move to areas of greater economic opportunity? Should not some provision be made for enhancing a person's employability in the area to which he might move? Should he not first be trained or retrained? Perhaps he should be assured of suitable employment before he is helped to move. Such a combination of training and relocation allowances is a feature of one recent government program, the Trade Expansion Act (1962), which makes these provisions for persons made jobless by foreign imports.

Second, how can new employment opportunities be brought into areas of high unemployment? It is felt that people with roots in the community, with children in school, with investment in homes, should have a better chance of finding gainful employment where they live. This viewpoint, too, is reflected in public policy. The Area Redevelopment Act of 1961, for instance, has provisions for helping areas endow themselves with facilities for becoming better work places as well as for training and retraining their workers. Similar public and private programs of area industrial development are common.

Third, an important factor is labor-management provisions that tie the worker more strongly to his employer, such as seniority systems, private pension plans, and severance pay plans that have developed since World War II. These have a very important role in affecting work-force mobility. Seniority systems have helped the older worker in each of the postwar recessions, as an analysis of the relevent data shows. Displacement is greatest among the younger workers with the least seniority. Seniority, of course, has not been an absolute shield against unemployment (as when layoffs are substantial or an establishment goes out of business) and it may create complex problems in cases of mergers.

Private pension plans (over and above government social security) have gone a long way to supplement income in older age. These plans have grown phenomenally since World War II—recent data show that one out of every two private wage and salary workers is covered by some such plan. Severance pay plans for terminated workers are also familiar these days.

It is often said that all these plans impede mobility. A laid-off worker is going to think twice, it is argued, before making a final break and moving elsewhere or taking another job in the same community—if it means giving up a role in a pension program in which he has participated for some time or giving up his position on the seniority list. The thinking goes that an unemployed person is going to hold on as long as possible before moving on and losing pension rights or a seniority position in his company. Even an employed person who might have the opportunity to move elsewhere will probably hesitate. Severance pay plans, it is felt, while potentially aiding mobility by providing resources to terminated workers, also can act as a brake to moving—employed persons do not like to give up this potential benefit in case of losing a job.

Whether these factors have notably impeded mobility has not been documented. As we will see, migration and mobility are greatest among the young, to whom these factors may be relatively unimportant.

Meanwhile three new factors involving private pension plans have developed: *vesting*, which guarantees to a worker little or no loss of his or her accrued retirement benefits for life, usually beginning at normal retirement age, regardless of whether he is still in the employ of the company at that time; *early retirement*, granting reduced monthly benefits payable for life to qualified workers beginning with the time of their termination of employment; and *portability of pension rights*, where full pension credit is given for service with any company belonging to a covered group. Even severance pay plans are beginning to take on some new aspects, being tied in some instances to retraining or transferring to another plant operated by the same firm.

CHAPTER TWELVE

Changing Geographic Patterns

MILLIONS OF AMERICANS MOVE ANNUALLY FROM ONE STATE TO ANOTHER, within the various states, from one county to another, and within the various local areas themselves. The so-called population explosion of recent years shows up in a large gross increase in total U.S. population. Internal migration has multiplied the population of some local areas—for example, Phoenix, Arizona; Hollywood, Florida; St. Clair Shores, Michigan; Park Forest, Illinois; Kettering, Ohio—at a rate far beyond that of the average U.S. population increase. Other areas have lagged behind the average growth—a few, including most central cities, have lost population.

Who are the movers and migrants? Typically, they are young people leaving home to find jobs, marry, and set up house. Whites migrate more frequently than nonwhites. Migration is higher among the unemployed.

Above all, migration correlates very closely with job opportunities. The largest growth in nonagricultural jobs has been around the western and southern rim of the country—plus several of the Rocky Mountain states. California, Texas, and Florida among the more heavily settled states have had the most marked growth.

Despite loss of agricultural employment and a heavy exodus of former agricultural workers from some Southern states, Southern nonagricultural employment has risen at a rate exceeding the national average.

The Northeastern, Middle Atlantic, and East North Central states, traditional manufacturing centers with over half of the nation's nonagricultural workers, have had a below-average job growth. Pennsylvania, West Virginia, and Rhode Island, which account for about half of the present areas of persistent and chronic unemployment, are far down the scale in new industrial jobs—West Virginia has had a considerable net loss in nonagricultural jobs.

Heavy increases in population in such areas as California, Texas, and Florida have brought with them increased emphasis on local government services, raising the total of service jobs in these areas. Defense industries in some of the fastest-growing states have also influenced the occupational geography of the United States. California, for example, now leads the nation in engineering employment.

The Mobile U.S. Society

Between any two periods of time, obviously, U.S. population totals will reflect how many people were born and how many died, and how many entered and left the country. When we measure population change among the different states, we observe the same factors—births, deaths, and migration—especially the last: the amount of moving from one state to another. This is also true when we look at the population change within a given state, and especially within a metropolitan area.

This kind of 'internal migration," as it is called, has enormous social, economic, and political ramifications. Under the Constitution and federal law, it can, for instance, change the size of the congressional delegation of any given state. Obviously, it affects the needs of different areas for housing, schools, and a vast array of other services. This movement is tied closely to the changing industrial and occupational base in the various states and the employment opportunities afforded.

It is well to present, therefore, a brief overview of the role that internal migration plays in population change. Table 12-1 will illustrate the impact internal migration had on the total U.S. population and on the population in a few selected states in the 1950s.

TABLE 12-1
Effect of Migration on Population Change, 1950–60

Regions* and Selected States	Net Change in Population 1950–60	Births	Deaths	Net Total Migration
Northeast	+5,200,000	9,254,000	4,390,000	+ 336,000
North Central	+7,158,000	11,990,000	4,711,000	— 121,000
South	+7,776,000	13,611,000	4,431,000	—1,404,000
West	+7,863,000	6,092,000	2,079,000	+3,850,000
Iowa	+ 136,000	640,000	271,000	— 233,000
Delaware	+ 128,000	101,000	37,000	+ 64,000
West Virginia	— 145,000	474,000	172,000	— 447,000
Mississippi	— 1,000	639,000	206,000	— 434,000
Arkansas	— 123,000	470,000	161,000	— 433,000
Florida	+2,180,000	915,000	351,000	+1,617,000
California	+5,131,000	3,142,000	1,156,000	+3,145,000
Arizona	+ 553,000	303,000	80,000	+ 330,000

Source: U.S. Department of Commerce, Bureau of the Census (Series P-25, No. 227, April, 26, 1961).

*States in these regions are: Northeast (New England and Middle Atlantic); North Central (East and West North Central); South (South Atlantic, East and West South Central); West (Mountain and Pacific).

Geographic Variations in Migration Rates

Among the four regions, the variations in migration totals were about as extreme as one could get. Between 1950 and 1960 the Northeast had a small net increase of about one-third of a million due to migration, while the West had a net total migration increase of more than ten times that size. The two other regions lost some of their population through migration—the North Central region lost on this score about 120,000, but the South lost more than ten times as many people. Thus, the persistent movement to the West that has characterized our history continues to the present time.

Now let us look at the selected states listed in our summary table. In Iowa a natural increase in the population (births minus deaths) of about 370,000 during the 1950s was offset somewhat by a net migration decline of about a quarter of a million persons; as a result, Iowa had a net population increase of only 136,000. Delaware, on the other hand, had a natural population increase of only 64,000—but its in-migration, stimulated by expanding job opportunities, matched that figure; as a result, it ended up the decade of the 1950s with almost as big a population increase as Iowa.

The next three states—West Virginia, Mississippi, and Arkansas—were the only ones (in addition to the District of Columbia) to have fewer people in 1960 than in 1950. As the reader can see, each had a very considerable excess of births over deaths, but each experienced a net migration decline of well over 400,000 during the past decade and this was enough to counterbalance the natural population increase. The result was an overall population decline.

In the final three states listed, the net population increase due to migration was bigger than the increase accounted for by the excess of births over deaths. In fact, in California and Florida, the population increase due to migration was about *triple* the increase due to births over deaths. These two states, incidentally, had a net increase in their population between 1950 and 1960 of about 7.3 million—more than 25 percent of the total U.S. population increase.

A study of the gains and losses in population generated by internal migration among the states during those past twenty years shows that the biggest migration losses were in the West North Central and Southern states; the biggest gains, in the West and Southwest plus some of the Rocky Mountain states and Florida. How does this dovetail with the changing geography of American industry?

Movers and Migrants

In addition to the questions discussed in Chapter 3, each *Monthly Report on the Labor Force* sample, as well as an additional quarterly sample panel, is asked a series of special questions. Since World War II, questions relating to mobility and migration have been added to the MRLF schedule in either March or April of each year. From these

TABLE 12-2
Mobility and Migration in the United States, 1947–61

	Percent of Civilian Population* One Year of Age and Over			Percent of Civilian Population* One Year of Age and Over	
Year	Mobility†	Migration‡	Year	Mobility†	Migration‡
1947–48	19.9	6.4	1954–55	19.9	6.6
1948–49	18.8	5.8	1955–56	20.5	6.8
1949–50	18.7	5.6	1956–57	19.4	6.2
1950–51	21.0	7.1	1957–58	19.8	6.7
1951–52	19.8	6.6	1958–59	19.2	6.1
1952–53	20.1	6.6	1959–60	19.4	6.4
1953–54	18.6	6.4	1960–61	20.0	6.3

*Includes members of armed forces living off post.
†Proportion who lived in a different house during year of reference.
‡Proportion who moved to different county during year of reference.
Source: *Mobility of Population of the United States, March 1960 to March 1961* (U.S. Department of Commerce, Bureau of the Census, Current Population Reports, Series P-20, No. 118, August 9, 1962).

answers, taken together with data currently available on the age, sex, color, and employment status of the respondents, we get a sizable fund of information on this subject.

Information on mobility is obtained by asking for all persons one year of age and over, "Was this person living in this house a year ago?" If the answer is "No," then the question is asked, "Was this person living in the same county a year ago?"; and if the answer is "No" again, the next question is, "What state (or foreign country) was this person living in a year ago?"

Anyone who makes one of the above moves during the year is called a "mover;" those movers who cross county lines are called "migrants." It is recognized that sometimes a move within a county can be for a longer distance and entail much more of a change than a move from one county to another or even one state to another; but the term migrant is confined to those who cross county lines.

Between March 1960 and March 1961 about 35.5 million of the 177.5 million persons one year old and over moved at least once. This is a mobility rate of 20 percent and confirms the considerable amount of movement, mobility, or "restlessness" (as the last census release on this subject called it) that prevails in this country. As Table 12-2 indicates, this 20 percent mobility rate has remained very stable during the fourteen-year period for which these data are available.

Table 12-2 also shows that the migration rate in this country has been running at about 6 percent during the postwar period. In other words, since 1945, about one out of every sixteen people one year and older moved across county lines each year.

Demographic Differences in Rate of Migration

There are distinct differences among the different sectors of the population when the total migration rate is broken down. Thus, while nonwhites are more *mobile* than whites, changing residences more than whites during a year, the white migration rates are higher.

In the period 1960–61, when the overall rate of migration was 6.3 percent, the rate was 6.6 percent for the whites and 4.3 percent for the nonwhites. This spread of about 2 percentage points between the two groups has prevailed for some years now.

As we break down the overall migration rate of 6.3 percent further, we find a number of additional differences among various population groups. For example, there is a very distinct age pattern to the migration rate that reflects both the pattern of career development and family formation in this country. Until about age thirty-five, the rate in 1960–61 was higher than 6.3 percent; after thirty-five, the rate was lower.

In the period 1960–61, for instance, migration rates varied with age in the following fashion. (See Fig. 12-1.)

The migration rate is relatively high for infants and children under five, whose parents tend to be on the younger side of the adult age scale. It drops somewhat for children of elementary and high school age, whose parents, now on a somewhat higher side of the adult age scale, generally try to minimize moving so as not to disrupt the children's schooling.

The migration rate picks up considerably once high school graduation age is reached. For people in their twenties it rises to double or more the overall rate. With advancing age it then moves consistently downward. The peak migration rates coincide with the process of marriage, family formation, and the beginning part of a person's working life. Migration in those years is spurred by more frequent job changing and changing housing needs.

Typically, in this country, we make our major moves in our twenties as we find our places in the world of work, get married, and have

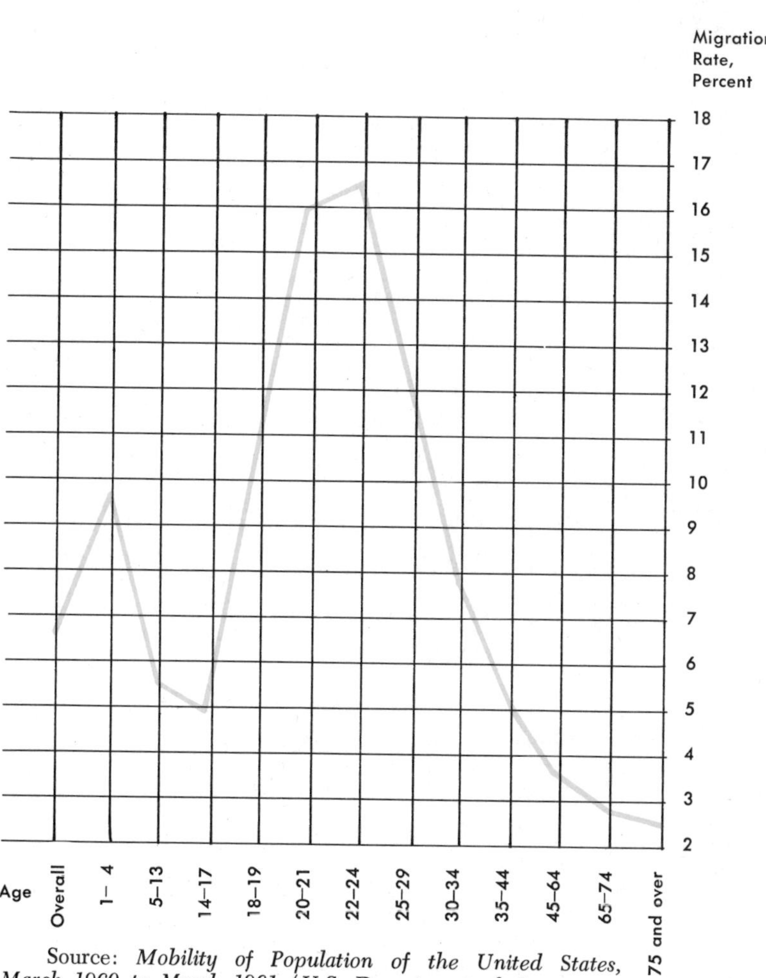

Source: *Mobility of Population of the United States, March 1960 to March 1961* (U.S. Department of Commerce, Bureau of the Census, Current Population Reports, Series P-20, No. 118, August 9, 1962).

FIG. *12-1 Migration rates by age, 1960–61.*

children. We tend to move around a little more as our families grow and our income goes up. Then we stay put as the homes we own, the schools our children go to, and the jobs we hold tie us more and more to the communities in which we live.

Relation to Economic Factors

Data from these surveys indicate a direct association between migration rates and economic level. Among the men, migration is substantially higher among the unemployed than the employed and among those toward the lower end than those toward the higher end of the economic scale.

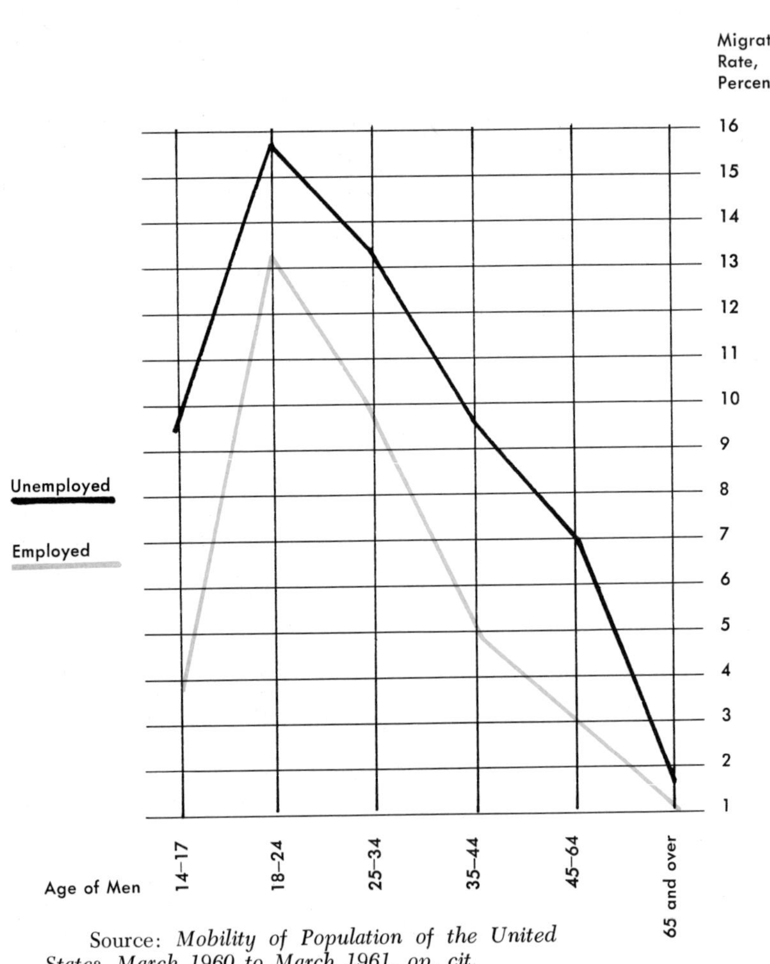

Source: *Mobility of Population of the United States, March 1960 to March 1961, op. cit.*

Fig. 12-2 *Migration rates by employment status, 1957–1961.*

In terms of the employment-status difference, for instance, an average for the five-year period 1957–61 is shown in Fig. 12-2.

On the income side, the figures show for the period 1960–61 for men with yearly incomes of $1000 to $1999, a migration rate of 11.7 percent; for men with total money income of between $2000 and $2999, the rate was 10.3 percent. As one goes up the income scale, the rate falls–for men with $15,000 or more it was 4.0 percent.

These tendencies seem to be confirmed by migration data classified by the man's work experience during the year. In the period 1960–61, men who were year-round workers (employed between 50 and 52 weeks) had a migration rate of 4.3 percent; those who worked between 27 and 49 weeks had a rate of 9.9 percent; and those who worked for a half year (26 weeks) or less had a rate of 13.4 percent.

These facts—the higher migration rate for the unemployed and the negative correlation between migration rates, income, and work experience—seem to confirm the association between economic opportunity and migration generally. What we cannot document at present is cause and effect. In other words, we do not know whether lower economic status spurs more migration or whether higher migration and movement affects economic status.

That the preponderant share of migration takes place in response to the economics of the labor market, however, seems quite certain—if only in terms of the fertility-migration-economic opportunity cycle we mentioned in the introduction to Part IV of this volume. This observation is underscored by a study of job mobility made by the Census Bureau in 1955. About 85 percent of those making a job change in 1955, a relatively prosperous year, did so to make more money or to get a more interesting job, or because of temporary layoff or complete termination of a job. (1)

It becomes important, therefore, to look at what has happened to the location of job opportunities in the United States.

The Changing Geography of U.S. Industry

As is well known, the center of U.S. population continues to move westward. And so does the center of job opportunities. A signifi-

TABLE 12-3
Nonagricultural Employment in the United States, by State

Geographic Divisions	1947	1962	Percent Change 1947–62
Continental U.S.	43,881.0	55,325.0	26.1
New England	3,333.3	3,790.8	13.7
Maine	262.8	280.4	6.7
New Hampshire	168.6	204.8	21.5
Vermont	99.0	109.3	10.4
Massachusetts	1,731.1	1,952.1	12.8
Rhode Island	298.0	295.4	−.9
Connecticut	773.8	948.8	22.6
Middle Atlantic	10,815.2	12,040.8	11.3
New York	5,518.2	6,270.7	13.6
New Jersey	1,622.6	2,080.5	28.2
Pennsylvania	3,674.4	3,689.7	.4
East North Central	10,067.9	11,646.3	15.7
Ohio	2,709.3	3,093.9	14.2
Indiana	1,194.2	1,459.7	22.2
Illinois	3,164.8	3,561.3	12.5
Michigan	2,013.7	2,323.0	15.4
Wisconsin	985.9	1,208.4	22.6
West North Central	3,413.6	4,261.2	24.8
Minnesota	765.8	982.3	28.3
Iowa	576.7	683.3	18.5
Missouri	1,136.0	1,354.6	19.2
North Dakota	92.4	127.2	30.6
South Dakota	109.5	150.5	37.4
Nebraska	301.4	392.9	30.4
Kansas	426.8	570.4	33.6
South Atlantic	5,268.7	7,532.7	43.0
Delaware	110.5	154.3	39.6
Maryland	673.3	948.3	40.8
District of Columbia	476.6	566.8	18.9

Source: Bureau of Labor Statistics.

cant and substantial transformation in the geography of jobs can be documented by data from the Bureau of Labor Statistics establishment reports, which give the number of payroll workers in nonagricultural establishments by state.

Geographic employment trends between 1947 and 1962 can be seen in Table 12-3 and in Fig. 12-3, the accompanying map. (2)

In those years U.S. nonagricultural employment increased more than 11 million, or 26 percent,, but the state and regional variations.

and Region, 1947–62 (In Thousands)

Geographic Divisions	1947	1962	Percent Change 1947-62
South Atlantic (cont.)			
Virginia	772.1	1,080.1	39.9
West Virginia	519.7	445.6	− 14.3
North Carolina	879.6	1,251.1	42.2
South Carolina	436.0	607.2	39.3
Georgia	759.4	1,096.7	44.4
Florida	641.4	1,382.6	115.6
East South Central	2,148.0	2,848.9	32.6
Kentucky	529.6	669.4	26.4
Tennessee	716.8	964.2	34.5
Alabama	610.4	790.8	29.6
Mississippi	291.2	424.5	45.8
West South Central	3,049.8	4,423.5	45.0
Arkansas	286.1	396.1	38.4
Louisiana	592.4	794.7	34.1
Oklahoma	437.3	602.0	37.7
Texas	1,734.0	2,630.7	51.7
Mountain	1,169.5	1,993.9	70.5
Montana	138.2	170.0	23.0
Idaho	122.6	162.7	32.7
Wyoming	73.2	96.2	31.4
Colorado	325.0	548.8	63.8
New Mexico	122.7	241.8	97.1
Arizona	145.7	363.2	149.3
Utah	178.5	287.4	61.0
Nevada	53.6	123.8	131.0
Pacific	4,170.5	6,842.4	64.1
Washington	670.9	856.0	27.6
Oregon	419.6	523.7	24.8
California	3,080.0	5,209.4	69.1

The map of job trends from 1947 to 1962 shows that the biggest increases are concentrated (as are the net migration increases) along the west coast, through the southwest to Florida.

There was a group of eight states where nonagricultural employment rose at double or more the national average. This happened in California, Texas, Florida, and five Rocky Mountain States—Colorado, New Mexico, Arizona, Utah, and Nevada.

In 1962 one out of every six nonfarm jobs was in California, Texas, and Florida. The Rocky Mountain states, while still relatively small in population, now account for close to two million wage and salary jobs in the nonagricultural sector.

What were some of the underlying reasons for this great geographic shift in jobs? They include the rise of certain service industries, such as style centers in Dallas and San Francisco; the upsurge in importance of petroleum products; the growth of recreational and leisure-time activities, as in Florida, California, and some of the Rocky Mountain states; and the development of centers related to national security, such as Cape Canaveral, Florida, and Los Alamos, New Mexico.

One of the most interesting developments has been the relatively good showing of the Southern states, even aside from Florida. Nonagricultural employment has been broadening gradually in that region, and the entire Southern tier of states has scored increases in nonfarm jobs *above* the national average. If this trend continues, we may see a greater evening out of nonfarm growth heralded by the growth in industrial and business employment in the South. We might then see nonfarm activity growing in areas of formerly predominantly farm activity. We may begin to get some changes in the classic westward pattern of migration as the areas of economic opportunity change.

Areas of Below-Average Job Growth

Below-average job growth (see Table 12-3 and the map) occurred in the New England, Middle Atlantic, and East North Central regions. Of considerable interest is the fact that this last group includes the five important Great Lakes states of Ohio, Indiana, Illinois, Michigan, and Wisconsin. For some time before and after World War II, the East North Central region experienced sizable, above-average job growth, took the lead in factory jobs from the Middle Atlantic states, and came very close to first place in all nonagricultural employment. These states have heavy concentrations of metalworking industries, such as steel, autos, and machinery. In the 1940s these industries burgeoned under the impact of war demands and immediate postwar pent-up demand for their peacetime products. In more recent years, however, their job growth has slowed down considerably under the impact of automation, technological change, and changing patterns of demand. The region grew 16 percent in the period 1947–62, compared with the national average of 26 percent.

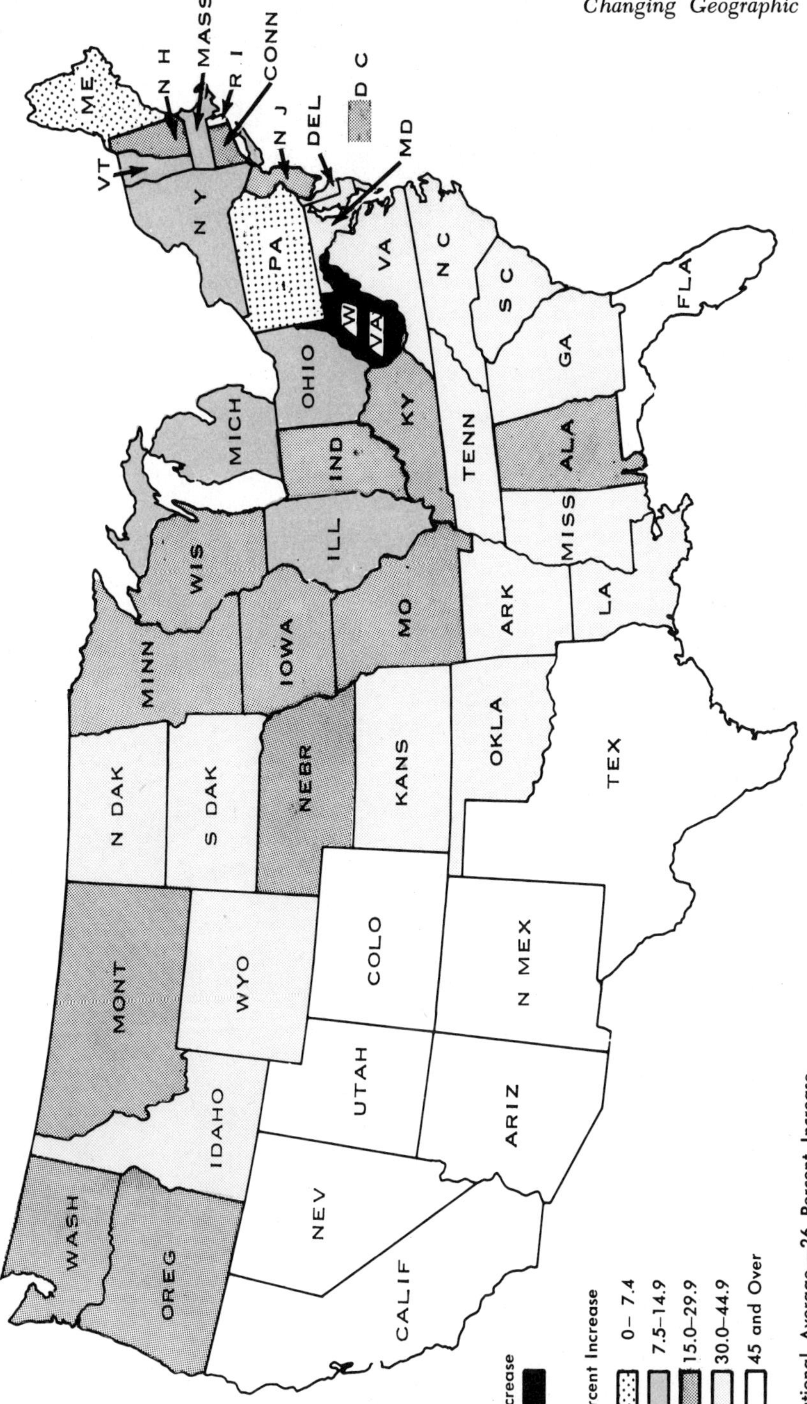

Source: Table 12-3.

FIG. 12-3 *Percent change in nonagricultural employment, by state, 1947–62.*

The New England region's growth (13.7 percent) during the period 1947–62 was only about half that of the national average; one of its states (Rhode Island) was one of two states to experience an actual decline in nonagricultural jobs over these years. The region, however, has maintained strength in such sectors as finance, insurance, electrical machinery, electronics, and educational services and continues to operate a vigorous program of industrial development.

The Middle Atlantic region has also shown job increases well below average. It still is the largest single region in terms of number of jobs and still maintains hegemony in finance and manufacturing. New York State alone, in 1962, had nearly as many nonfarm jobs as the whole Pacific region. However, one other state in this region —Pennsylvania—had the smallest advance in the nation in nonfarm jobs between 1947 and 1962. The decline in coal mining, the replacement of steam locomotives by diesel locomotives, and the general decline in railroad employment as a whole have had an important impact on that state's employment profile. Pennsylvania and West Virginia (the other state besides Rhode Island to show an actual decline in employment between 1947 and 1962) together account for half of the areas listed in a previous chapter as "areas of substantial and persistent unemployment."

Relation to Changes in Occupational Structure

The changes in industrial and occupational structure already described tie in with the geographic changes in employment opportunities just summarized. Some obvious ones are the declines in mining, which is geographically concentrated to begin with, and the relatively small growth or decline in some sectors of manufacturing, such as cotton textile manufacturing (New England) and metalworking (East North Central).

Increased Needs for Local Government Services

On the other hand, the states with the biggest increases in employment have also shown marked upturns in the service sectors. It will be recalled that eight states (California, Texas, Florida, and five of the Rocky Mountain states) led the job growth during the 1947–62 interval. These states showed far-above-average growth in state and local government employment—a sector that we described in the last chapter as a major source of new jobs. Employment in state and local government rose by 137 percent in Florida, 119 percent in California, 90 percent in Texas, and 100 percent in the five Rocky Mountain states between 1947 and 1962. The states with the lowest rates of overall employment growth were also those with the lowest growth in state and local government employment.

Influence of Defense Procurement

One important factor affecting the geography of jobs is represented by the economic effects of defense spending. This can be shown by what has happened to the location of engineering jobs during the last decade. (3)

As indicated in Chapter 11, engineering employment has been one of the occupations showing major growth in this country. Between 1950 and 1960 the census reported a 64 percent increase in the number of male engineers—from 520,000 in 1950 to almost 854,000 in 1960.

This increase in engineers appeared among the four major regions as follows:

Major Region	*Percent Increase in Male Engineers 1950–60*
West	129
South	69
North Central	49
Northeast	47

California's increase was 147 percent, Florida's 203 percent, Arizona's 187 percent. Another statistic: in 1950 New York had the single biggest block of engineers, 10,000 more than California; in 1960 California was in first place, with almost 40,000 more engineers than New York.

Behind these shifts lies the changing nature of defense procurement in the United States. In 1953, the last year of the Korean conflict, 50 percent of all military hard-goods contracts were for such items as tanks, ammunition, and weapons; by 1961 these items accounted for only 12 percent of all prime contract awards. On the other hand, missiles and electronics accounted for only 12 percent of all these in contracts in 1953 and 50 percent in 1961. Thus in eight years we have witnessed a complete reversal in military goods demands.

This change in defense goods has brought more emphasis on research and development and the advent of very complex and sophisticated manufacturing methods in the place of traditional fabricating techniques. Increased research and changed factory methods have generated substantial increases in engineering employment.

Coincidentally, the West has increased its share of defense prime contract awards from 19 percent during the Korean conflict to 33 percent in 1961. California's share of prime contract awards during this period has gone up from 14 to 24 percent. Add to this the fact that about one of every four engineers works in the electrical equipment and aircraft and related parts industries and that these, in turn, have major geographic concentrations, and the picture is clear.

Implications of Mobility

The problem of matching people and jobs is bound to be acute in view of the manpower supply profile for the current decade described in Chapter 10, the shifting industrial and occupational patterns reviewed in Chapter 11, and the changing geography of employment opportunities summarized in Chapter 12. While uttering our own warning about predicting future changes in labor force geography, we foresee nothing in the offing—barring a major economic decline—that will halt the mobility of industry, business, and commerce. To the contrary, industry already has come a long way in freeing itself from rigid locational ties as advance after advance has occurred in transportation, power, and techniques.

The development of energy sources has meant that fewer and fewer plants have to be near coal or water power; new power sources such as atomic energy would seem to foreshadow an acceleration of that trend.

Similarly, developments in transportation no longer make it so necessary for plants to be in close propinquity to their markets. A generation ago, a prime advantage of cotton textile mills in New Bedford, Massachusetts, was overnight boat service to the style center of New York City; today a jet airliner gets there faster from Los Angeles, California.

More and more, manpower cost factors have an added importance. Also more and more, an areas's suitability for industrial development depends on the availability and skills of its manpower. With industry becoming more mobile, these manpower factors seem almost certain to take on even added importance.

This already has been the case for many years, and, accordingly the responsiveness and adaptability of the manpower supply become of prime importance. We will underscore this in our chapter on unemployment. But before we do, we will move on to a review of occupational and job mobility within the labor force itself.

Reference Notes

1. *Job Mobility of Workers in 1955* (U.S. Department of Commerce, Bureau of the Census, Series P-50, No. 70, February 1957).
2. See also Seymour Wolfbein, "The Changing Geography of American Industry," *Monthly Labor Review,* Vol. 77 (July 1954), covering the period 1939–53.
3. See *The Growth of Engineering Employment in the United States, 1950–1960* (U.S. Department of Labor, Office of Manpower, Automation, and Training, Manpower Report No. 1, August 10, 1962).

Readings

An annotated bibliography of materials on migration can be found in Section VII, Part B, of

ELDRIDGE, H. T. *The Materials of Demography.* International Union for the Scientific Study of Population and Population Association of America, 1959.

An early landmark study is

GOODRICH, C., *et al. Migration and Economic Opportunity.* Philadelphia: Univ. of Pennsylvania Press, 1936.

See also

Population Redistribution and Economic Growth: United States 1870–1950. Philadelphia: American Philosophical Society, 1957.

WOLFBEIN, S. L., and JAFFE, A. J. "Internal Migration and Full Employment in the United States," *Journal of the American Statistical Association,* September 1945.

Recent data and analysis of internal migration from decennial census returns are in

Components of Population Change, 1950 to 1960, for Counties, Standard Metropolitan Statistical Areas, State Economic Areas and Economic Subgroups. (Current Population Reports, Series P-23, No. 7.) Washington, D.C.: Department of Commerce, Bureau of the Census, November 1962.

Current Population Reports. (Series P-25, No. 227.) Washington, D.C.: Department of Commerce, Bureau of the Census, April 26, 1961.

Information on movers and migrants is produced annually from a special survey in connection with the MRLF, the lastest of which is

Mobility of the Population of the United States, March 1960 to March 1961. (Series P-20, No. 118.) Washington, D.C.: Department of Commerce, Bureau of the Census, August 9, 1962.

Data on industrial employment by states are available monthly from establishment reports and published in the U.S. Bureau of Labor Statistics' *Employment and Earnings.* These have been analyzed in

WOLFBEIN, S. L. "The Changing Geography of American Industry," *Monthly Labor Review,* Vol. 77 (July 1954).

See also

FUCHS, V. R. "America's Changing Industrial Map," *Challenge,* Vol. 10 (February 1962).

Decennial census data on this subject are analyzed in

MANOR, S. P. "Geographic Changes in U.S. Employment from 1950 to 1960," *Monthly Labor Review,* Vol. 86 (January 1963).

The article above also describes corresponding geographic changes among occupational groups. Geographic changes among engineers are discussed in

The Growth of Engineering Employment in the United States, 1950–60. (Manpower Report No. 1.) Washington, D.C.: Department of Labor, Office of Manpower, Automation, and Training, 1962.

CHAPTER THIRTEEN

The Dynamics of the American Labor Force

WE NOW TURN TO AN EXAMINATION OF WHAT LIES BEHIND THE CHANGES THAT take place each year in the U.S. labor force.

Some of the causes we have already discussed—regular entries into the labor force of new young workers and exits by the old due to death and retirement; changing work patterns among women and other population groups; alterations in the industrial structure and in technology. There are, however, shorter-range phenomena, such as fluctuations due to the ups and downs of the business cycle and changes in the seasons.

In this chapter we shall discuss the volatility of labor force changes, especially among the young and among women workers —what was once thought to be a World War II phenomenon has persisted till now. We shall also review studies that cover "work experience" during a year's time rather than a one-month period—and discover that many more people in the United States work during a year's time than in any single month. We shall discuss labor turnover rates—a matter of particular concern to personnel managers as well as economists.

Of particular interest to many is so-called moonlighting—multiple jobholding. Who does most of the moonlighting, and does it take potential jobs away from the unemployed?

Finally, we shall discuss job tenure and job mobility. What influence does seniority have on unemployment among older and younger workers? It will be seen that stability, as well as mobility, is an important feature of the U.S. labor force. Job changing reaches its peak among men in their early twenties, for as men take on family responsibilities, unemployment becomes the principal reason for job shifts.

For a long time it was assumed that the labor force grew slowly and steadily from year to year in association with such long-range movements as population growth. In fact, during the thirties, one of the favorite ways of estimating unemployment was to get a figure on the labor force for any given year (projected from the 1930 decennial census base) and subtract from it a figure on employment. Basically this residual method of estimating the jobless was founded on the proposition that the labor force figure was a pretty steady one and that the changes that did occur were those involving shifts between employment and unemployment.

As we will see later in this chapter, the opposite is true: Millions of persons annually move into employment or unemployment from outside the labor force; millions more move from employment or unemployment right out of the labor force altogether each year.

Effects of the Business Cycle

A major factor remains to be discussed—one which goes more directly to the matter of year-to-year fluctuations in labor force size. It involves the question of how the labor force responds to changes in the business cycle.

This problem first became of some importance during the depression of the 1930s, when there was considerable argument as to whether the long depression caused an increase or a contraction in the labor force.

Business Turns and Labor Force Participation

At that time, some argued that a prolonged period of low levels of economic activity and high levels of unemployment typically forced additional family members into the labor force when the main breadwinner suffered from long-term joblessness. As a result, the labor force would tend to rise during these periods. Others took a contrary view, pointing to the sheer lack of job opportunities as a factor discouraging labor market participation by secondary family workers.

More recently—especially against the background of some apparent slowing-down of labor force growth juxtaposed against projected trends—there has been renewed interest in how the labor force acts in different periods of economic activity.

On an a priori basis it is possible to argue a number of propositions. One is that when economic activity ebbs and unemployment rises, there does ensue a sizable influx of so-called secondary workers who are forced in by the necessity of helping the family when the main breadwinner loses his job. When times are good and family incomes are relatively high, such secondary workers might withdraw from the labor force—or at least stay out of the labor force longer, for example, as students.

Others maintain that the lack of job opportunities during recession periods discourages new entrants. This proposition is closely allied with the idea that many of the unemployed—especially the long-term unemployed—get discouraged, too, about their reemployment opportunities, give up their active search for jobs, and thus get reported as out of the labor force. Another proposition is that the existence of good employment opportunities can itself attract people into the labor force. They may actively seek work if they know that they can get jobs, particularly if the jobs pay relatively well and involve skills that they have.

The available documentary evidence on year-to-year change in the labor force as shown in Table 13-1, or by an analysis of seasonally adjusted monthly or quarterly labor force changes, is by no means clear-cut in supporting any of these propositions. Much more information is needed, for instance, on the labor force activity of secondary workers, the factor of total family income, and differences between families in depressed and nondepressed areas. The Gordon Committee Report contains a discussion of this subject; it recommends that studies be made "to investigate the relationship between the rate of growth in the labor force and economic developments." (p. 72)

TABLE 13-1
Annual Changes in the Labor Force of the United States 1940–62 (In Thousands)*

Year	Total Labor Force	Change from Preceding Year	Year	Total Labor Force	Change from Preceding Year
1940	56,180	—	1952	66,560	577
1941	57,530	1,350	1953	67,362	802
1942	60,380	2,850	1954	67,818	456
1943	64,560	4,180	1955	68,896	1,077
1944	66,040	1,480	1956	70,387	1,491
1945	65,300	−740	1957	70,744	357
1946	60,970	−4,330	1958	71,284	540
1947	61,758	788	1959	71,946	662
1948	62,898	1,140	1960	72,820	874
1949	63,721	823	1961	74,175	1,049
1950	64,749	1,028	1962	74,681	506
1951	65,983	1,234			

Source: Bureau of Labor Statistics.

*About 150,000 members of the armed forces stationed outside the United States are included in figures for 1940–52. Beginning in 1953, figures are up by about 350,000 because of adjustments generated by introduction of 1950 census population levels. The 1961 and 1962 data include Alaska and Hawaii, and the change in labor force 1960–61 is calculated on the basis of a 1960 labor force figure of 73,126,000, which includes those two states. In 1962 the introduction of 1960 census population figures reduced labor force totals by about 200,000. Thus, the 1961–62 change was actually about 700,000. Data are annual averages.

The few data available on some of these factors are really not enough to permit any firm generalization on this subject. We do know that each of the propositions mentioned so far has some validity. Some secondary workers do enter the labor force when the primary breadwinner loses his job; some workers do get discouraged after repeated rebuffs and exit from the labor force under long periods of unemployment. Also, rising job opportunities have certainly elicited increased labor market participation by women.

The author's opinion is that in the first decade and a half after World War II, labor force reaction to the business cycle was relatively less important than such forces as growing job opportunities for women. For an example, an April 1962 special survey showed that 4.75 million family heads with wives or relatives eighteen years of age and over first became unemployed in 1961. In only 12 percent of the cases did a secondary worker enter the labor force because of the family head's unemployment.

Moreover, a study of fluctuations in women's worker rates since 1947 shows little correlation with the business cycle. In times of extreme economic change, as for example, during the depression of the 1930s or the period of World War II, the labor force reaction was perhaps easier to assess. In times of more moderate economic swings, like the ones we have had since 1947, chances are that the business cycle played a relatively small role in short-term labor force change.

Working Wives

There is some relevant information on the labor market experiences of married women in relation to their husbands' employment and income status. We have the following data, for example, for March 1962 for husband-wife families:

	Employed Family Heads	*Unemployed Family Heads*	*All Family Heads*
Total	100.0%	100.0%	100.0%
No other family member in labor force	55.3	49.0	55.0
Family member in the labor force	44.7	50.9	45.0
Family member employed	41.9	42.6	42.0
Family member unemployed	2.8	8.3	3.0

Source: Bureau of Labor Statistics, Special Labor Force Report No. 26, January 1963.

This evidence seems to indicate that employed husbands (family heads) have a somewhat lower proportion of secondary workers in their families than do unemployed husbands. The difference seems to be in the relatively high proportion (8.3 percent) of unemployment among secondary workers where the husband is also unemployed. This may be due to the fact that some of the same conditions causing unemployment among heads of families—for example, location in an area of relatively high joblessness—would also affect the employment status of the secondary family workers.

TABLE 13-2
Occupational Distribution of Employed Wives Classified by Employment Status and Occupation Group of Their Husbands March 1961

Status and Occupation of Husband	Occupation of Employed Wives										
	Total	Professional, Technical	Managers, Proprietors	Clerical	Sales	Craftsmen	Operatives	Laborers	Services	Farmers	Farm Laborers
Unemployed	100.0%	7.8	3.6	21.4	7.0	.9	24.0	.9	33.4	—	1.0
Employed	100.0	13.1	5.0	30.4	9.5	1.1	16.4	.4	19.2	.4	3.9
Professional, technical	100.0	41.3	3.3	35.1	7.4	.4	4.9	—	7.3	—	.3
Managers, proprietors	100.0	13.8	15.8	35.2	5.4	1.3	6.6	.1	11.8	.1	—
Clerical	100.0	14.7	1.9	45.1	8.3	.8	12.2	.5	16.2	—	.4
Sales	100.0	15.4	7.9	45.2	13.5	2.1	9.2	—	6.7	—	.1
Craftsmen	100.0	8.8	3.7	33.9	10.7	1.0	22.0	.4	18.7	.2	.5
Operatives	100.0	5.5	2.9	25.6	7.7	1.3	30.8	.7	24.5	.4	.6
Laborers	100.0	4.7	3.4	17.0	4.5	1.1	24.3	.9	42.7	.6	.9
Services	100.0	6.0	4.7	20.3	7.6	1.3	16.3	1.6	42.2	.5	—
Farmers	100.0	9.5	2.2	8.2	4.1	1.2	10.2	.3	13.9	2.8	47.7
Farm laborers	100.0	2.2	—	11.6	4.4	—	12.2	—	40.9	1.1	27.6

Source: Bureau of Labor Statistics, Special Labor Force Report No. 20, January 1962.

The evidence is rather strong that secondary workers tend to fall roughly into the same broad skill categories as the heads of their families—white-collar, blue-collar, and service jobs. Table 13-2 shows the occupational distribution of husbands' occupations and those of their working wives.

Note that fully two out of overy five employed wives of husbands who are professional or technical personnel are also in that occupational category; in fact, 80 percent are in white-collar jobs. Similarly, 75 percent of the wives of managerial, clerical, and sales workers are engaged in the white-collar occupations. Among the working wives of industrial and farm workers, the concentrations are much heavier in the blue-collar and service jobs.

What it all adds up to is that when wives do work for a living, the preponderant majority work in the same broad occupational sector as their husbands.

The relation of labor market participation by wives to family income is also of some interest here, although again the evidence really does not speak directly to the point of their response to changes in economic activity. As one would expect, until one reaches the very high income groups, the higher the income of the family, the higher the proportion of wives working in 1960.

Work Experience of Wife, 1960

Family Income	Total	Worked During Year	Worked: Full Time, Year Round	Worked: Other	Did Not Work During Year	Percent of Family Income Contributed by Wife
Total	100.0%	43.3%	14.1%	29.2%	56.7%	20.2%
Under $2,000	100.0	39.5	5.8	33.7	60.5	4.7
$2,000–2,999	100.0	36.2	5.5	30.7	63.8	9.8
3,000–4,999	100.0	39.5	8.9	30.6	60.5	13.8
5,000–6,999	100.0	39.8	10.8	29.0	60.2	17.4
7,000–9,999	100.0	50.6	21.1	29.5	49.4	27.4
10,000–14,000	100.0	55.1	29.8	25.3	44.9	29.7
15,000 and over	100.0	35.1	16.3	18.8	64.9	16.7

Source: Bureau of Labor Statistics, Special Labor Force Report No. 20 (January 1962).

In the typical husband-wife family in which the wife works, she makes a very substantial contribution to the total family income —and the higher the total family income, the higher hers is—again, with the exception of the group with family incomes of $15,000 and over.

Says the Bureau of Labor Statistics:

"The bearing of a husband's income on the wife's propensity to work . . . has been long recognized. Generally, wives of men with higher-than-average income are less likely to work than other wives. However, the importance of the husband's income is not as great as in former years, and the participation rate of married women appears to have risen somewhat faster among those married to men in higher income brackets. While economic necessity probably continues to be the major reason married women work, many in middle- and upper-income families today work to raise the family's standard of living or for personal satisfaction." (1)

Such a comment ties in with what we have been pointing out about rising educational attainment among women and their ability to get jobs during the postwar period in the growing service-producing, white-collar occupations.

The tendency for the more highly educated married women to enter the labor force in much greater proportions than their less educated counterparts can be seen from the following few figures:

LABOR FORCE PARTICIPATION RATES OF MARRIED WOMEN, HUSBAND PRESENT

Years of School Completed	*18–34 Years*		*35 Years of Age and Over*	
	1959	*1962*	*1959*	*1962*
Under 5	22.3%	21.7%	17.5%	20.1%
8	25.0	24.1	28.4	27.6
12	30.8	30.4	35.8	38.4
16	36.9	44.6	46.0	52.3

Source: Bureau of Labor Statistics, Special Labor Force Report No. 30, May 1963.

Labor market participation rates rise with educational attainment for married women; in fact, the rates for college graduates are more than double those of women with less than five years of schooling. This is true for all ages, and, significantly, the more highly educated women have increased their labor market participation since 1959, while the less educated married women have not.

Under these circumstances it would not be surprising to find that many married women are joining the labor force, perhaps not so much because of sheer financial necessity as to take advantage of their previous training and the job opportunities that are available, in order to derive the satisfactions that come from gainful work activity outside the home and the status that is attained by following an occupation, and to raise their family's level of living by their income.

Seasonal Changes

There is a further dimension of labor force change, represented by seasonal forces. Almost all the labor force components show some degree of seasonality. Perhaps the most obvious example is agriculture, with its employment changes running from spring sowing and planting to autumn harvest. Many manufacturing activities based on the flow of agricultural produce, such as food processing, show marked seasonal employment fluctuations. Similarly, construction employment obviously follows the course of the seasons, rising in the spring and the good-weather months that follow and falling in the wintertime.

The seasonal influence is clear in the apparel industry's spring and fall style changes; the annual model changeover time in autos; the rise in Thanksgiving- and Christmas-trade employment; the spurt in federal government employment in the post offices to meet the Christmas rush.

Seasonal Changes in Labor Force

Seasonal movements are so ingrained in labor force, employment, and unemployment patterns that we must take them into account in order to make a reasoned analysis of month-to-month overall changes. When unemployment goes up between May and June, for example, it may reflect only the fact that every year—in peace or war, in prosperity or recession—hundreds of thousands of students leave school (either as graduates or for the summer vacation); some of them get jobs and swell the employment total; some of them look for work but do not find jobs and add to the jobless figure. The reverse is true in September, which sees an exodus of the young from the labor force back to school, with a consequent expected reduction in both employment and unemployment.

Table 13-3 uses the course of unemployment in 1962 as an example. Note that between March and April 1962 unemployment fell from 4,381,000 to 3,047,000 persons; the rate of unemployment (number of unemployed divided by the civilian labor force) fell correspondingly from 6.2 to 5.6 percent. Unemployment, however, is always expected to fall between March and April, as spring begins and agriculture, construction, trade, and apparel manufacturing begin to move up. In 1962, on the basis of seasonal expectations, unemployment actually did not fall enough. The Labor Department, therefore, reported that the *seasonally adjusted* unemployment rate actually moved from 5.5 to 5.6 percent.

TABLE 13-3
Unemployment in 1962, Actual and Seasonally Adjusted

Month	Actual (In Thousands)	Unemployment Rate (Unadjusted)	Unemployment Rate (Seasonally Adjusted)
January	4,663	6.7%	5.8%
February	4,544	6.5	5.7
March	4,381	6.2	5.5
April	3,947	5.6	5.6
May	3,719	5.2	5.5
June	4,464	6.0	5.5
July	4,018	5.5	5.4
August	3,932	5.3	5.7
September	3,512	4.9	5.6
October	3,293	4.6	5.3
November	3,801	5.3	5.8
December	3,817	5.3	5.5

Source: Bureau of Labor Statistics.

Unemployment rose between May and June 1962 from 3,719,000 to 4,464,000, with a corresponding rise in the unadjusted rate from 5.2 to 6.0 percent. As we have already noted, an upturn in unemployment is usual for this time of the year, when schools close. On the basis of past experience for this season, the observed drop in unemployment was actually just about what was expected; consequently, the Labor Department reported no change in the seasonally adjusted unemployment rate.

As Table 13-3 shows, unemployment in 1962 fell by about 850,-000 between January and December, with a corresponding decline in the unadjusted unemployment rate from 6.7 to 5.3 percent. A good part of that drop was the seasonal drop between a month like January and a month like December. Part was a more-than-seasonal improvement, shown by the decline in the seasonally adjusted unemployment rate from 5.8 to 5.5 percent between January and December 1962.

For every month, therefore, we have available government-collected data on changes in the various components of the labor force, employment, and unemployment and the seasonally expected changes for each. How similar or different they are helps us discern the underlying forces of change that may or may not be present.

Seasonal factors have been calculated for many of the components of the labor force, including the wage and salary worker figures from establishment reporting and hours of work. The methodology of calculating these seasonal factors is complex and there are differences of opinion on the concepts and techniques that should be used. In any case, the idea is always the same: to take a series of data on any labor force component and to extract from it the nonseasonal changes—those due to secular, long-term influences, the cyclical ebb and flow of economic activity and any irregular movements caused by such factors as strikes. Remaining are changes caused by seasonal fluctuations. Currently, the practice is to go through this process for each of the labor force components on the basis of how they performed during the past five years. The seasonal pattern that emerges from this examination is then considered the pattern of expectation for the ensuing year. Annual recomputations are made to keep the patterns up to date.

At best, of course, this exercise is an approximation. Even if the seasonal factors were perfect, care still would have to be exercised in their application. In any given year the pattern itself can be off the mark for such reasons as changes in industrial practice—for example changing the time of annual model changeovers in the auto industry. The pattern may reflect even the way the calendar falls, sometimes giving us an early, and at other times a late, Easter. These seasonal factors, however, help to provide some standard of expectations against which we can match what actually happens.

Age and Sex Factors in Seasonal Changes

Tables 13-4 and 13-5 show some of the recent seasonal patterns in labor force components by age and sex. They make clear that a major part of the seasonal moving in and out of employment and unemployment status (and, of course, the labor force) can be traced to younger persons.

The unemployment picture shown in Table 13-4 is particularly instructive. The amplitude of change among boys and girls in their teens is enormous during the year, not only much bigger than among adults but quite different in pattern. Seasonally, teen-age unemployment tends to be relatively low in the winter months, when the bulk of these young people are not in the labor force. Contrariwise, it is very high during the summer months. Among teen-age boys, June, the month of graduation and school closings, shows an unemployment figure about 100 points above that for the month of September, when schools reopen. Among teen-age girls, for whom the labor market participation rate is generally lower, the amplitude of change is even greater, reaching a factor well above 200 in June and falling back to about 75 in winter.

Among the post-teen groups the pattern is nearly the reverse.

TABLE 13-4
Seasonal Adjustment Factors for Unemployment in 1963, by Age and Sex*

Month	Males 14–19 Years	Males 20 Years and Over	Females 14–19 Years	Females 20 Years and Over
January	90.2	124.9	75.4	108.7
February	91.0	124.8	77.8	107.0
March	93.8	123.4	81.3	105.8
April	87.4	104.0	84.8	97.7
May	96.0	91.2	105.4	94.0
June	181.7	90.0	205.9	101.6
July	130.9	91.0	140.5	101.8
August	100.4	91.7	101.2	100.3
September	79.6	80.8	90.7	96.4
October	80.3	80.5	80.3	98.1
November	78.3	92.2	87.8	98.5
December	90.2	104.5	69.4	90.2

Source: Bureau of Labor Statistics.
*Monthly variations about annual average of 100.

Among men, seasonal unemployment is lowest in the summer, when activities ranging from agriculture to construction are high, and highest in the wintertime, when these activities fall off. The amplitude of change is quite significant, too, the winter months unemployment rising 25 to 30 percent higher than the average for the year. Among women the seasonal variations over the year are relatively small.

TABLE 13-5
1963 Seasonal Adjustment Factors for Selected Labor Force Components

Labor Force Component	Jan.	Feb.	Mar.	Apr.	May	Jun.	Jul.	Aug.	Sept.	Oct.	Nov.	Dec.
Nonagricultural employment												
Men 20 years and over	98.6	98.6	98.7	99.4	100.3	100.8	100.6	100.8	100.8	100.9	100.7	100.0
Women 20 years and over	99.2	100.4	101.0	101.3	101.7	98.7	96.5	97.4	99.9	101.1	101.5	101.8
Boys 14–19 years	85.2	88.5	85.6	90.2	98.9	118.9	132.0	129.8	94.9	92.8	92.6	91.0
Girls 14–19 years	90.3	90.0	91.8	89.5	90.9	108.1	120.5	120.3	93.8	99.7	99.8	105.5
Agricultural employment												
Men 20 years and over	91.4	92.8	94.9	99.8	103.5	106.0	104.7	104.1	105.0	103.8	100.4	93.4
Women 20 years and over	61.2	65.1	69.2	81.1	110.9	142.4	131.6	114.5	125.2	132.3	100.9	65.7
Boys 14–19 years	59.9	62.0	71.2	81.4	94.7	167.9	164.3	148.5	103.0	99.0	82.9	64.7
Girls 14–19 years	24.3	30.7	34.1	44.3	77.7	212.3	209.9	188.3	136.7	143.5	69.2	29.1
Unemployment rate												
Married men	128.5	125.4	126.8	105.1	89.0	86.1	88.6	90.2	79.1	80.1	94.0	107.4
Experienced wage and salary workers	119.7	118.5	116.2	101.8	92.6	97.9	94.4	93.3	86.8	85.9	93.5	98.6
Percent of labor force time lost	112.6	113.3	110.5	99.9	92.2	108.6	102.0	97.8	86.5	84.6	94.5	97.2
Unemployed												
Less than 5 weeks	112.8	93.1	89.2	86.7	88.4	147.1	103.5	93.0	94.4	91.5	99.1	101.2
5 to 14 weeks	125.6	140.9	129.4	83.7	81.8	80.4	110.1	107.4	77.3	76.0	89.7	97.2
15 weeks and over	99.1	113.2	129.0	134.2	113.1	94.9	92.5	87.5	81.8	85.0	83.0	86.7

Source: Bureau of Labor Statistics.

Table 13-5 shows the picture for a number of other labor force components, and the reader can compare the seasonal variations in these components among the teen-agers and adults and see some of the same striking differences in the unemployment picture.

Here, then, is another dimension of U.S. labor force movement. Demands for workers do follow seasonal patterns; they generate seasonal variations in economic activity; they do elicit a labor force response with corresponding seasonal patterns in employment and unemployment. Obviously, these seasonal swings are not immutable; they change with the changing composition of employment (imagine the seasonal shifts when one out of every three workers was in farming) and changing industrial and business practice and technology (for example, changes in building materials, enabling their use in cold and even freezing weather). Because some of these seasonal variations do generate a considerable amount of corresponding unemployment, governments and labor and management groups have undertaken steps to reduce the amplitude of these changes. These may range from a shift by an enterprise in its basic activity with the changing seasons (a classic example is the company engaged in both the coal and the ice business) to provision of certain kinds of public-work activity during the off-season months.

Gross Changes in the Labor Force

The ebb and flow of labor force activity involved in the various long-term forces of change (described earlier) and the short-term forces (described in this (chapter add up to a significant and substantial amount of in-and-out movements from the work force itself, as well as within the employment and unemployment components. A large body of evidence on the basic patterns of work activity that the U.S. population follows has been developed in recent years. It is to this subject that we now turn.

In our discussion of the technical aspects of labor force measurement, we indicated that the *Monthly Report on the Labor Force* sample is rotated so that a household is enumerated for four months, dropped for eight months, and then returned to the sample for another four. We noted that the operation is so phased that for any two adjacent months 75 percent of the sample households are the same. In an examination of the labor force changes that occur from one month to the next, it is thus possible to follow through those households that were common to the sample of both months and find out what happened to the individuals involved. This month-to-month match or follow-up is a potential mine of information on labor force patterns and change.

Thus, if a person is classified as a student one month, what happens to him the following month? Does he stay as a student? Or does he move into the labor force? If the latter, is he employed or not?

TABLE 13-6
Average Number of Persons Moving into and out of Labor Force, Employment, and Unemployment July–November 1945

	Percent Shifting into*			Percent Shifting out of†		
Age and Sex	Civilian Labor Force	Employment	Unemployment	Civilian Labor Force	Employment	Unemployment
Total	5.1	5.5	61.1	6.0	6.9	54.5
14–19	10.4	11.6	64.7	19.5	20.4	66.7
20–24	6.8	7.3	60.9	6.2	7.7	50.3
25–44	4.8	5.2	62.1	4.4	5.8	52.5
45–64	3.2	3.7	56.5	3.5	4.2	52.7
65 and over	3.5	5.6	64.4	6.2	6.8	45.7
Male	3.0	3.4	63.0	3.1	4.1	52.5
14–19	10.1	10.9	70.8	20.9	21.8	67.6
20–24	7.9	8.0	69.4	4.0	6.5	47.7
25–44	2.7	3.1	64.2	1.0	2.1	50.3
45–64	1.1	1.6	55.2	1.1	1.9	49.0
65 and over	3.8	4.0	65.7	4.2	4.6	55.6
Female	8.9	9.5	58.3	11.2	11.9	57.1
14–19	10.8	12.2	59.2	17.9	18.9	65.8
20–24	6.3	6.9	55.0	7.2	8.2	51.5
25–44	8.6	9.1	58.8	10.4	11.1	55.2
45–64	9.7	10.1	61.5	10.7	11.0	64.6
65 and over	14.0	14.1	60.0	16.5	17.6	12.5

Source: *Shifts in the Labor Force, July–November 1945* (U.S. Department of Commerce, Bureau of the Census, Labor Force Memorandum No. 2, June 11, 1947).

*Persons classified in a status group who were classified in a different status the preceding month—average, August–November 1945.

†Persons classified in a status group who were classified in a different status the following month—average, July–October 1945.

If a person is recorded as unemployed one month, what happens to him the following month? Does he stay jobless? Or does he leave the ranks of the unemployed? If the latter, is it to employment because he got a job, or is it to a status outside the labor force altogether?

Another person is employed; what happens to him the following month? Does he stay employed? Or does he leave employment status? If the latter, is it because he becomes unemployed or because he exits from the labor force altogether?

When all these actions, all these crosscurrents, are summarized, we begin to get some idea of the size of the gross changes that lie behind the net changes in labor force, employment, and unemployment that are announced each month.

1945 Study of Gross Changes

The potentialities of this approach were recognized in the 1940s, early in the development of the MRLF, and one of the first published sets of materials on this subject covered the months immediately following the end of World War II. Analyzed for the months July to November 1945, the data showed very extensive shifts into and out of the labor force, into and out of employment and unemployment status.

For the few months covered, a monthly average of about 2.75 million, or 5 percent of the civilian labor force, were newcomers to the work force; an average of about 3.33 million, or 6 percent of the civilian labor force, shifted out of the work force each month. As can be seen from Table 13-6, these movements were disproportionately concentrated among the younger boys and girls and older women. The turnover in employment was extensive too, but nothing like the shifting into and out of unemployment, where an average of more than 60 percent of any month's jobless were newcomers to that status and about 55 percent shifted out of that category each month. Both sexes and just about every age group exhibited this substantial moving in and out of unemployment status.

1952 Study

It was thought during this time that these extensive shifts were generated by the moving out of the labor force of hundreds of thousands of women at the war's end and the reverse shift by former members of the armed forces back to the civilian work force. But subsequent months and years have shown emphatically that these massive monthly personal labor force shifts are par for the course.

During any given year, literally millions of persons customarily move into and out of the labor force and the employment and unemployment categories.

Here, for example, are some of the results for 1952:

Between December 1951 and December 1952 the civilian labor force rose from 62,688,000 to 62,921,000—up about 230,000 over the year. This net change was the result of about 38,316,000 separate additions to the labor force and about 38,088,000 separate exits from the labor force—just during the calendar year 1952. As can be seen, there was a total of more than 76 million ins and outs during the year—all producing a small separate net change in the labor force over the year.

Needless to say, these figures do not represent a count of separate individuals, but include many students who come in and out during the summer vacation and who may even enter again during the school term for a part-time job; included, too, are many housewives who move into and out of the labor force during the agricultural season or for part-time Christmas jobs. For 1952 the figures showed an average addition to the labor force of about 3,200,000 each month, and an average reduction from the work force of about the same number. However these figures are interpreted, they indicate an enormous amount of labor force movement.

Unemployment fell between December 1951 and December 1952 from 1,674,000 to 1,412,000, or about 260,000 over the year. This net change was the result of about 12.3 million entries to unemployment and about 12.6 million exits from unemployment—representing an enormous amount of turnover in the jobless group. In an average month in 1952 about a million persons became newly unemployed and about the same number exited from unemployment.

Of the million people becoming unemployed each month, more than half (650,000 a month) lost jobs; the remainder entered the jobless ranks from outside the labor force altogether. Of the million or so who left unemployment each month of 1952, almost three-fourths (700,000) got jobs; the remainder left the labor force altogether.

During 1952 an average of about 3.1 million persons a month entered nonagricultural employment. Some of them (about 650,000 a month) were unemployed people and slightly more than a million a month entered nonagricultural employment directly from outside the labor force. Interestingly, during this period about a third of a million persons moved from agricultural to nonagricultural employment each month. But the reverse movement was also there each month. During 1952 an average of almost 300,000 persons a month left nonagricultural employment to move into agricultural jobs.

Continued Volatility of Labor Force Changes

Because of technical difficulties beyond the scope of our discussion here, gross change data have not been available on a regular basis since 1952. The Census Bureau hopes eventually to solve these difficulties; in the meantime these data are made available from time to time for special analyses. Gross changes are still averaging about 5 percent of the civilian labor force each month, and the largest numbers still involve the women and teen-age boys and girls. Thus, the American labor force as a whole—especially through its young, but also through many of its women and older workers—is a flexible work force, responding to seasonal and other demands of economic activity. All of this adds up, we repeat, to strikingly large gross changes in monthly labor force status.

There is a good deal of interest in the kind of volatile gross changes that lie behind the unemployment figures. In April 1958, when unemployment was on the increase, the following situation was found:

	Millions
Unemployed in March 1958	5.2
Found employment in April	−1.5
Left labor force in April	− .6
Reductions in unemployment, March–April 1958	−2.1
Remaining unemployed in March–April 1958	3.1
Lost employment in April	+1.2
Entered labor force and unemployment in April	+ .8
Additions to unemployment, March–April 1958	+2.0
Unemployed in April 1958	5.1

Note that the net change in unemployment during that month was only 100,000. Behind that small net decline was a very substantial number of persons finding and losing jobs, coming into and leaving the labor force. Even though this was a recession year, 1.5

million jobless persons did find jobs between March and April; but about 1.2 million became unemployed at the same time.

One year later, when unemployment was on the decline, the MRLF reported as follows:

	Millions
Unemployed in March 1959	4.4
Found employment in April	−1.6
Left labor force in April	− .7
Reductions in unemployment, March to April 1959	−2.3
Remaining unemployed in March–April 1959	2.1
Lost employment in April	+ .8
Entered labor force and unemployment in April	+ .7
Additions to unemployment, March–April 1959	+1.5
Unemployed in April 1959	3.6

In a month of declining unemployment, 800,000 persons still lost jobs and entered the jobless ranks and another 700,000 were newcomers to unemployment from outside the labor force. In fact, about 40 percent of April 1959's unemployed (1.5 million out of 3.6 million) were newly jobless that month.

During any one month, the unemployment figure is the result of the activities of three groups—those who are still unemployed from the previous month; those who left unemployment by finding jobs or leaving the labor force; and the newly jobless, those who lost employment or came from outside the labor force. If we add all three and divide by the current month's unemployment figure, we get a rate of gross change in unemployment. Similar rates, of course, can be calculated for labor force and employment.

For example, those who left unemployment (2.3 million) in April 1959 plus those who remained unemployed from the previous month (2.1 million) plus those who became unemployed (1.5 million) equaled 5.9 million; dividing by the April unemployment figure of 3.6 million and multiplying by 100 to get a rate gives us a figure of 160—the rate of gross change in unemployment. A figure of 160, in this case, means that it took 160 different people to produce a net change of 100 in the number of persons unemployed.

During the period 1957-59 the rate fluctuated between about 140 and 160; was higher for women than for men; and seemed to show a cyclical pattern, going down in the recession and rising in the years of higher economic activity.(2) It may be that these changes, large as they are, do vary inversely with the business cycle, slowing down in a downturn and accelerating during an upturn. But we need more data before we can prove such a conclusion.

All these movements add up to a considerable number of unemployment experiences. In 1957, a relatively good year, there were 18 million unemployment experiences—18 million entries into unemployment status, either because of loss of a job or entry from outside the labor force. Some of these were "repeaters" with two or more spells of new unemployment. The Bureau of Labor Statistics estimates, however, that 10.6 million different persons were involved, and this is an enormous figure for a year when unemployment averaged just below 3 million.

Thus, the data on gross changes are of general interest not only in terms of labor force mobility, flexibility, and change but also as indicators of the sheer impact unemployment has on people: 18 million new unemployment experiences in 1957 (or 22.5 million new unemployment experiences in 1960) are social, economic, and political matters to be reckoned with. These very large gross changes also have a heavy impact on local employment-service offices and on personnel offices in business and industry. They are also relevant to programs and policies relating to unemployment.

Work-Experience Studies

As we all know by now, the labor force data made available currently through the MRLF yield information on the work status of the noninstitutional civilian population fourteen years of age and over as of a very specific period of time each month: the week containing the 12th. This specificity of time reference is critically important for current estimates and is one of the keystones of the conceptual structure that we described earlier. These extremely valuable data add up to twelve snapshots a year that give us an excellent picture of the labor force and related matters for each of those dozen exposures.

The need for a bigger time exposure, for an observation that permits us to see what happens to an individual's labor force activity over a longer time, has led to annual surveys of the work experience of the population covering a full year's time. Thus, each year (in February) the regular monthly survey of the labor force includes additional questions on an individual's labor force activity for the full previous calendar year. In other words, all persons fourteen years of age and over who were in the civilian noninstitutional population in February 1962, for example, were asked a series of questions concerning their activities in the calendar year 1961.

Annual Employment Patterns

One of the first things revealed by such surveys is that there are many more individuals in the labor force during a calendar year than are reported in any given month. Thus, in 1961, the average size of the civilian labor force was 71,603,000; the range went from 69,837,000 in January to 74,286,000, the seasonal high, in June. Actually, the work-experience survey that year showed there were 81,963,000 different individuals in the civilian labor force during the calendar year 1961. It was their combined activities, their movements into and out of the labor force throughout the year, that were caught (enumerated) during each of the twelve monthly observations yielded by the MRLF.

From these data we can calculate an employment rate, not as of a month or as an annual average of twelve monthly figures, but on an annual basis. This annual rate would represent the proportion of the noninstitutional civilian population fourteen years of age and over (or any separate age or sex or other group within that total) that had some work experience. Obviously, these rates will be higher than those computed on a monthly basis, since any work experience during the year counts. Table 13-7 shows some of these figures for 1950, 1955, and 1961.

Approximately two-thirds of the civilian noninstitutional population fourteen years and over put in some work during 1961. The proportion among men runs over four out of five and it is noteworthy that almost half of all the females put in some work during the year. The age and sex differentials are the familiar ones we learned when reviewing labor market participation levels and trends. Note the declines in annual work experience among the young and older men and the rise among women since 1950.

Work experience on an annual basis continues relatively high for teen-agers, however. Almost half of the fourteen- to seventeen-year-old boys and 80 percent of the eighteen- to nineteen-year-old boys did some work during 1961; the corresponding proportions among the girls were about one-third and two-thirds, respectively. A good part of this, of course, represents seasonal ins and outs during the summer vacations from school.

Proportion of Part-Time Work

One very important dimension of work experience revealed by these surveys is the information on how long people work during the year—whether they are year-round workers or not, whether they are part-time or full-time workers. A year-round worker is one who

TABLE 13-7
Percent of the Population Who Worked During the Year, by Age and Sex, 1950, 1959, 1961

Age and Sex	1961	1955	1950
Total	63.5	65.4	63.1
Male	83.1	86.8	86.8
14–17	46.1	54.5	52.2
18–19	80.9	90.5	84.0
20–24	92.5	92.0	92.7
25–34	97.7	98.0	97.5
35–44	97.7	98.4	97.9
45–54	95.9	97.4	96.6
55–64	89.7	90.4	89.6
65 and over	41.0	48.1	49.3
Female	45.8	46.0	41.1
14–17	33.2	36.3	33.3
18–19	64.7	70.3	61.6
20–24	59.4	63.4	58.7
25–34	46.6	46.9	43.7
35–44	52.8	52.6	47.2
45–54	57.0	53.5	44.9
55–64	45.6	41.3	32.3
65 and over	15.2	15.9	11.8

Source: C. Rosenfeld, *Work Experience of the Population in 1961* (Bureau of Labor Statistics, Special Labor Force Report No. 25, December 1962).

worked for fifty weeks or more; a part-year worker is one who was employed for less than fifty weeks. A full-time worker is one who was employed thirty-five or more hours a week for most of the weeks in which he worked during the year; a part-time worker is one who worked at jobs that provided less than thirty-five hours a week of work in most of the weeks in which he worked during the year. Table 13-8 shows the data for 1961, some of which are portrayed in Fig. 13-1.

In 1961 (and these overall percentages have not changed significantly in recent years) about two-thirds of the men were year-round, full-time workers—that is, about as fully employed as one can get. For all women, the corresponding proportion was a little over one-third; considering the fact that married women are such a large percentage of the female work force, this is a rather high proportion

TABLE 13-8
Percent of Persons with Work Experience in 1961, by Age and Sex

Work Experience and Sex	14–17	18–19	20–24	25–34	35–44	45–54	55–59	60–64	65–69	70 and Over	Total
Male	100.0	100.0	100.0	100.0	100.0	100.0	100.0	100.0	100.0	100.0	100.0
Worked full-time jobs	22.6	63.2	87.7	95.9	96.3	95.3	93.1	91.6	73.5	51.7	87.2
50–52 weeks	3.1	15.3	47.3	72.3	77.6	75.6	73.6	70.2	46.8	34.2	63.7
Less than 50 weeks	19.5	47.9	40.4	23.6	18.7	19.7	19.5	21.4	26.7	17.5	23.5
Worked part-time jobs	77.4	36.8	12.3	4.1	3.7	4.7	6.9	8.4	26.5	48.3	12.8
50–52 weeks	24.1	26.1	4.0	1.4	1.3	1.9	3.3	3.6	9.9	21.4	4.5
Less than 50 weeks	53.3	10.7	8.3	2.7	2.4	2.8	3.6	4.8	16.6	26.9	8.3
Female	100.0	100.0	100.0	100.0	100.0	100.0	100.0	100.0	100.0	100.0	100.0
Worked full-time jobs	19.1	68.9	81.9	72.9	70.7	72.8	71.0	67.5	53.3	45.4	68.2
50–52 weeks	.9	15.1	33.5	36.1	43.3	47.8	46.3	43.8	29.9	26.9	36.9
Less than 50 weeks	18.2	53.8	48.4	36.8	27.4	25.0	24.7	23.7	23.4	18.5	31.3
Worked part-time jobs	80.9	31.1	18.1	27.1	29.3	27.2	29.0	32.5	46.7	54.6	31.8
50–52 weeks	10.7	6.2	3.4	7.4	10.2	11.4	12.9	13.8	18.0	17.2	9.7
Less than 50 weeks	70.2	24.9	14.7	19.7	19.1	15.8	16.1	18.7	28.7	37.4	22.1

Source: *Work Experience of the Population in 1961* (Bureau of Labor Statistics, Special Labor Force Report No. 25, December 1962).

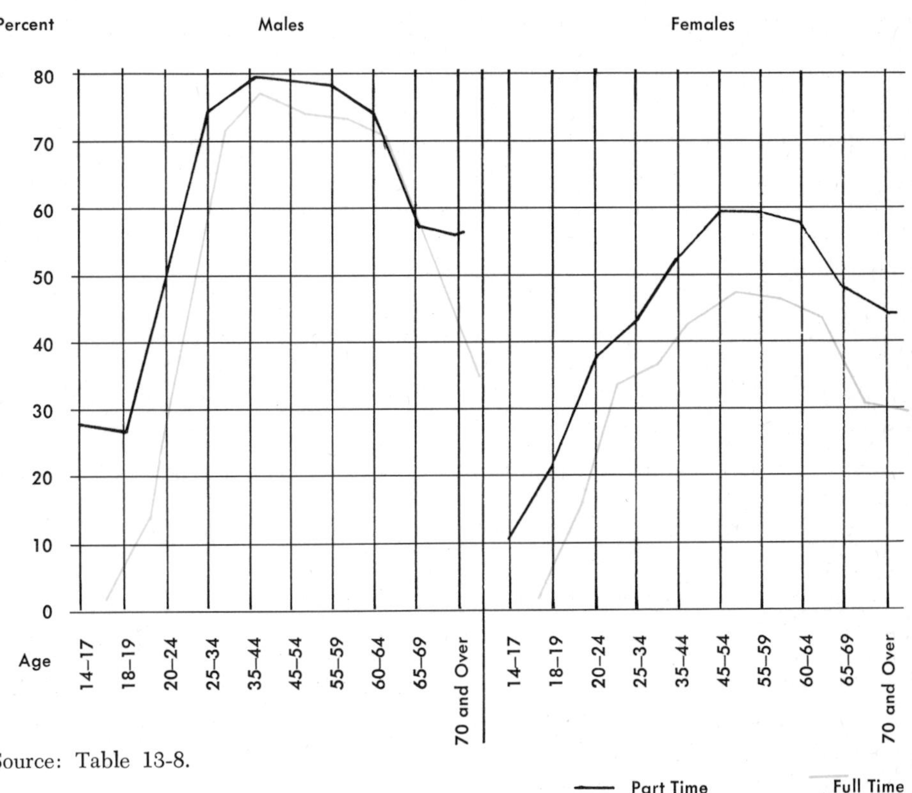

Source: Table 13-8.

FIG. *13-1 Persons with work experience in 1961; proportion working year round at full- and part-time jobs.*

spending full time on year-round jobs. Another 30 percent, in fact, were full-time workers, but for less than fifty weeks of the year.

These proportions, as we would expect, vary significantly with age. Thus, full-time year-round work goes up—for both men and women—as we go past the teen-agers, remains higher in the adult years, and then tapers off in the older age brackets. For women, year-round work, but at part-time jobs, is a significant dimension of their work patterns, accounting for increasing proportions of women workers the higher one goes up the age scale. About one in four boys fourteen to seventeen years old worked the year round in 1961 at part-time jobs—generally at service-type jobs.

The reader will want to examine in more detail the age-sex patterns in these different levels of work experience during a year. At this point we will only add that these annual work-experience data taken together with trends in labor-market participation, throw much more light on what has been happening to the labor force. Observe, for example, this additional detail for men sixty-five years of age and over:

	1950	*1960*	*1961*
Percent who work during the year	49.3	43.1	41.0
Percent working	100.0	100.0	100.0
Full-time year-round jobs	52.3	39.1	41.1
Full-time jobs less than 50 weeks	24.2	22.5	22.7
Part-time year-round jobs	7.9	15.6	15.2
Part-time jobs less than 50 weeks	15.7	22.9	21.2

Source: Bureau of Labor Statistics, Special Labor Force Report No. 25.

Not only have labor market participation rates for these men fallen substantially, as we already have noted, but their annual work-experience rates have come down considerably as well. About one of two men sixty-five years of age and over did some work in 1950; the proportion in 1961 was closer to two in five. The pattern of their working lives has changed even more. The proportion engaged as year-round workers has gone down more than 10 percentage points in ten years—a very significant downturn for such a short time. The proportion working part time, however, has gone up considerably, doubling, for example, for those at year-round part-time jobs.

The pattern of annual work experience also changes with other demographic variables. For example, in 1961 one-third of the married women twenty-five to forty-four years of age who worked that year held only part-time jobs—four times the proportion for single women in that age group. Also, nonwhite men were much more likely to work mostly at part-time jobs than white men. In fact, two-thirds of the white men held year-round full-time jobs in 1961; only half of the nonwhite males fell in that category. Many of the latter work at jobs with the highest rates of part-time employment.

Detailed data that are available on annual work experience by occupation(3) verify the substantial differences that exist between general socioeconomic occupation groups. Overall, it will be recalled, almost two-thirds of the men who worked in 1961 had year-round, full-time jobs. But professional personnel and managerial and proprietory personnel had rates well above the average—closer to three-fourths, as a matter of fact. On the other side of the spectrum were unskilled workers (laborers), of whom the proportion of men working at full-time, year-round jobs was only half the overall average. In many occupational groups these ratios varied widely with the industry in which the man was employed. Thus, skilled workers (craftsmen) employed in a seasonal industry such as construction had lower rates of full-time, year-round employment; for example, the rate for carpenters was only 35 percent in 1961. Mechanics and repairmen or metal craftsmen, on the other hand, had rates more than double that of the carpenters.

Unemployment Viewed from Annual Basis

The gross-change information indicated the substantial number of persons experiencing some unemployment during a year—an observation that the data from these annual work-experience studies confirm. During 1961, 15.1 million of the almost 82 million persons with some labor force activity experienced unemployment. This is a ratio of 18.4 percent—or almost one in five. Here is a brief summary of the 1961 picture:

(In Thousands)

All persons who were in civilian labor force in 1961	81,963	100.0%		
With no unemployment	66,867	81.6		
With some unemployment	15,096	18.4	100.0%	
With no work experience in 1961	1,676		11.1	
With work experience in 1961	13,420		88.9	100.0%
One spell of unemployment	8,477			63.1
Two spells of unemployment	2,299			19.8
Three or more spells of unemployment	2,644			17.1

About 1.7 million—or 11 percent—of those who had some unemployment experience did not find any work at all during 1961. About one-third of these were teen-agers, most of whom were looking for some temporary or part-time work.

It is also of some interest, with respect to labor force dynamics, that a substantial number and proportion had more than one spell of unemployment during the year; in fact, 20 percent of all those who combined some work and some unemployment experienced three or more spells of unemployment during 1961.

We note also that unemployment was a major reason why many of the workers in 1961 did not work the year round—confirming again the shifting in and out of employment-unemployment status that takes place during a year. About one out of every two males who were part-year workers in 1961 gave as the reason for not working the year round the fact that they were unemployed. The proportion was actually very much higher for the men, since reasons among the young for not being year-round workers include going to school, summer vacations, and serving in the armed forces.

Labor Turnover

The movements we have described obviously generate numerous entries into and exits from industrial and business payrolls. We have available a significant amount of information on this industrial labor turnover.

Interest in this particular aspect of job changes is strong among personnel managers. Employers have considerable interest in the rate with which their staffs turn over, in terms of plant performance, efficiency of operations, staff morale, and labor-management relations. Turnover is also clearly related to recruitment and maintenance of an adequate manpower supply.

Current Data

A statistical series on labor turnover was started by the Metropolitan Life Insurance Company in 1926; on July 1, 1929, the company transferred the responsibility for the collection and publication of these labor-turnover rates to the Bureau of Labor Statistics.(4) The bureau currently publishes the information monthly for the manufacturing sector, each of the twenty-one major industry groups and almost 200 individual manufacturing industries. Some data are also available in mining and communications. Similar data collection is being developed among the various states.

Table 13-9 presents factory labor-turnover rates for the period following World War II. These data closely follow changes in the business cycle.

TABLE 13-9
Factory Labor-Turnover Rates: Annual Averages, 1947–62 (Per Thousand Employees)

Year	Total Accessions*	New Hires	Total Separations*	Quits	Layoffs
1947	62	—	57	41	11
1948	54	—	54	34	16
1949	43	—	50	19	29
1950	53	—	41	23	13
1951	53	41	53	29	14
1952	54	41	49	28	14
1953	48	36	51	28	16
1954	36	19	41	14	23
1955	45	30	39	19	15
1956	42	28	42	19	17
1957	36	22	42	16	21
1958	36	17	41	11	26
1959	42	26	41	15	20
1960	38	22	43	13	24
1961	41	22	40	12	22
1962	40	25	41	14	20

Source: Bureau of Labor Statistics.
*Total accessions and separations include transfers from one establishment to another of the same company beginning in 1959.

The rates shown in the table are based on data collected from establishments on a separately provided schedule (Form 1219) in a manner similar to that described in an earlier chapter. For any given month, a rate for a given turnover item is calculated by dividing the total number of turnover items occurring in a given industry by the total number of employees in that industry's establishments during the payroll period ending nearest the 15th of the month.

For example, in Industry A we might find a total of 865 layoffs in establishments having a total employment of 41,700 during the payroll period nearest the 15th. We would calculate the layoff rate as follows:

$$\frac{865}{41,700} = .021$$

Multiplying by 100, we get a figure of 2.1, which is the layoff rate per 100 employees (the way the Bureau of Labor Statistics publishes these rates); or multiplying by 1000, we get a figure of 21, the layoff rate per 1000 employees (the way Table 13-9 is presented). The industry group rates can then be calculated by weighting the rates for the individual industries according to their importance in the overall employment picture, and these in turn can be weighted up to give us an all-manufacturing figure of the kind presented in Table 13-9.

Turnover Rates as Cyclical Indicators

Here is a brief description of each of the turnover items listed:

Total accessions represent all the additions to the payroll during the month, permanent or temporary, from whatever source they may come.

New hires, figures for which began to be collected in 1951, are that part of the total accessions represented by people who have not before been in the employ of the establishment. As Table 13-9 shows, they represent a significant proportion of the additions to establishment payrolls.

Total separations represent terminations of employment, and therefore exits from payrolls of firms. They include not only quits and layoffs, which are shown in Table 13-9, but also exits because of retirement, death, military service, and physical disability.

Quits, as the term implies, represent voluntary terminations on the part of the worker of his association with the establishment.

Layoffs, on the other hand, represent removals from pay status initiated by the employer, for such reasons as lack of work, model changeover, inventory taking, end of season, shortage of materials, or introduction of a new machine.

What makes these rates such important lead economic indicators is their record of sensitivity to the ups and downs of the business cycle. Note, for example, the clear-cut drops in the accession rate in the recession years of 1949, 1954, 1958, and 1960 and the rebounds they take in more prosperous years.

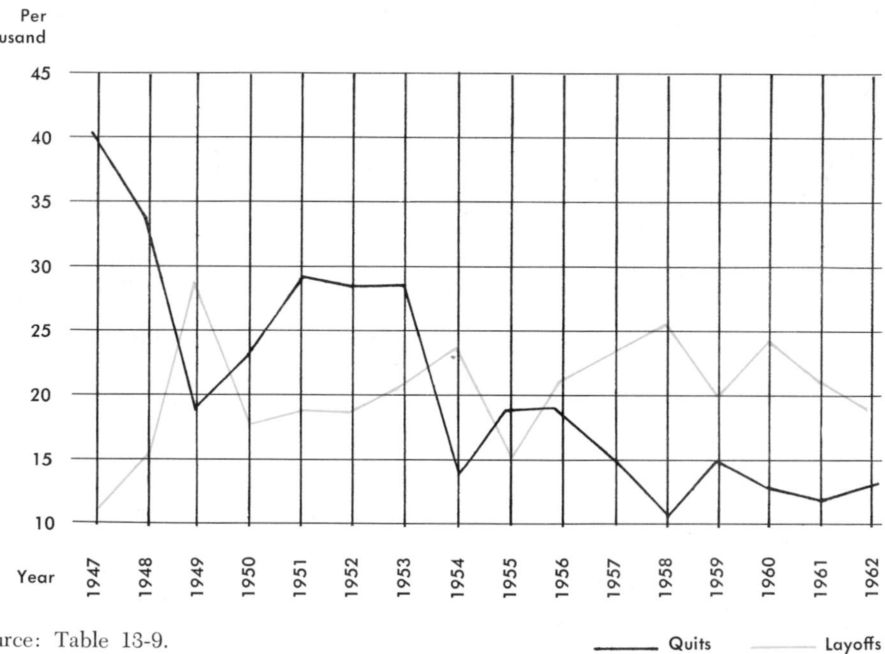

ource: Table 13-9.

FIG. 13-2 *Quit and layoff rates in manufacturing, 1947–62.*

As might be expected, the "quits" and "layoffs" categories behave in opposite directions with changes in economic conditions (Fig. 13-2). Voluntary exits from the payrolls rise in periods of prosperity, fall off in recessions; while involuntary exits (layoffs) do the contrary—fall off in prosperous years, rise in periods of economic decline.

Whatever the turnover action, whatever the general level of the economy, this kind of labor turnover underscores again the substantial amount of moving about that occurs among the employed. As an example, an average month in 1961 saw forty-one additions to factory employment for every 1000 persons on the payroll, while forty exits for every 1000 on the payroll took place. With employment in manufacturing running over 16 million, this turnover rate represented an enormous amount of shifting onto and off the employment rolls for just one major industry division.(5)

Multiple Jobholding

The holding of more than one job at the same time by the employed part of the working population, commonly known as moonlighting, is a subject that is often related to the problem of unemployment, since multiple jobholders might be considered to be filling some jobs that might otherwise go to the unemployed. However, the relatively stable nature of multiple jobholding in good times and bad and the kind of employment involved indicate that it is not competitive with the unemployed. So we prefer to discuss it as a part of the general pattern of jobholding.

It will be recalled that in household enumeration surveys (as distinguished from establishment reporting) a person is counted once and only once, and if he has more than one job during the week of reference, he is counted in the one where he put in more hours. With supplementary questions, however, it is possible to explore the matter of multiple jobholding in some detail. Several of these supplementary surveys have been conducted during the past decade and they are beginning to produce some hard evidence on the nature and extent of this phenomenon.

Extent of Moonlighting

The proportion of employed persons who hold down more than one job has been relatively stable, averaging about 5 percent and showing little change with differing levels of economic activity:

	July 1956	*July 1957*	*July 1958*	*Dec. 1959*	*Dec. 1960*	*May 1962*
Percent employed with more than one job	5.5	5.3	4.8	4.5	4.6	4.9
Seasonally adjusted unemployment rate	4.4	4.2	7.5	5.4	6.6	5.5

As the evidence comes in on multiple jobholding, it tends to belie a number of ideas about this phenomenon. A rate of multiple jobholding of 4.9 percent in May 1962 was the equivalent of about 3.33 million workers, and while not an insignificant amount, it does not indicate that it is a pervasive characteristic of the American labor force. Neither has it shown, so far at least, any significant correlation with changes in the business cycle. The highest rates of multiple jobholding have shown up in July of 1956 and 1957, when agricultural dual jobholders were considerably higher than in other periods. Actually, manufacturing is the industry most subject to the impact of business cycles; yet the rate of multiple jobholding in that sector did not vary by more than three-fourths of one percentage point from 1957 through 1962.

Even the term "moonlighting" isn't quite apropos. The December 1960 survey asked for the first time a question on what part of the day that work on the secondary job was performed. About one in three (34 percent) did do this kind of work mostly at night, but most (42 percent) held their secondary jobs during the weekday working hours (6 A.M. to 6 P.M. Monday through Friday); and interestingly, about one in four (24 percent) worked on their other jobs during the weekends. The May 1962 survey showed almost exactly the same proportions: 32 percent, 44 percent, and 24 percent for night work, work during weekday morning hours, and weekend work respectively.

The average workweek for multiple jobholders in May 1962 was fifty-two hours. Typically, 69 percent of the multiple jobholders worked full time on their primary job and part time on their secondary job. Most of the rest (25 percent) worked part time on both jobs, and only 6 percent reported working full time (thirty-five hours or more) on both jobs.

Who Are the Multiple Jobholders?

The pattern of multiple jobholding is quite set in terms of who these jobholders are and what they do for a living. Holding more than one job is typically a man's, and particularly a married man's, lot. In May 1962, men had a rate of multiple holding that was more than triple that of women. Married men were multiple jobholders at a rate almost double that of single men. This is a likely bit of evidence on financial necessity as one factor in the matter of holding down more than one job.

Table 13-10 shows the occupational distribution of multiple jobholders and shows where this phenomenon is concentrated. Here again, the popular idea of moonlighting concentrated among the blue-collar worker is belied. Thus, professional personnel generally have a higher-than-average multiple-jobholding rate, with by far the heaviest concentration among teachers, where almost one out of every five was in this category.

TABLE 13-10
Rate of Multiple Jobholding Among Men, by Occupational Group, May 1962

Occupations	Rate of Multiple Jobholding*
Total	6.4%
Professional and technical	9.6
Medical and other health service	8.9
Teachers (except college)	17.4
Other	8.5
Farmers and farm managers	7.7
Managers, officials, proprietors	4.1
Clerical	8.0
Sales	5.5
Craftsmen, foremen	5.7
Carpenters and construction craftsmen	6.1
Mechanics, repairmen	5.7
Other	5.3
Operatives	6.2
Private household workers	—
Other service workers	7.6
Protective service	14.8
Waiters, cooks, bartenders	4.5
Other	5.4
Farm laborers	7.0
Laborers (except farm and mine)	5.2

Source: J. Shiffman, "Multiple Job Holders in May 1962," *Monthly Labor Review,* May 1963.

*Multiple jobholders are employed persons who, during the survey week, had jobs as wage and salary workers with two or more employers, or were self-employed and also had a wage or salary job, or were unpaid family workers with a secondary wage or salary job. Excluded are persons with more than one job in private household work (maids, baby sitters, gardeners), self-employed persons with additional farms or businesses, and persons with more than one unpaid family-work employment.

The farm sector, too, contains a high proportion of persons with more than one job. Actually, in May 1962 double jobholders with one or more of their jobs in agriculture accounted for one-fourth of all multiple jobholders, even though farm employment represented only one-thirteenth of total employment at that date.

Other higher-than-average rates are found among clerical personnel, but this is, in good part, a reflection of the high rate for postal clerks who are included in this category. Protective-service workers (firemen, policemen, guards) also have a relatively high rate. Significantly, industrial workers—skilled, semiskilled, and unskilled—have a relatively modest rate of multiple jobholding.

Additional data are available on multiple jobholding by industry and on the relation between the primary and the secondary job. They emphasize several major facts concerning U.S. job patterns and mobility. Financial necessity must certainly be a spur: we have already indicated the concentration among married men, teachers below the college level, and the farm workers and owners who are finding it more and more necessary to find employment both in and out of agriculture. But the availability of secondary work and being in a position to do it are also to be reckoned with: the teacher does have a work schedule that makes it possible to take on another job; the same is true for persons in protective-service occupations. The smaller rate of multiple jobholding among industrial workers is also relevant. A significant proportion of the secondary jobs were in trade and service, where part-time work is prevalent.

Finally, one must have the necessary skills and experience to get another job, and this is no doubt a major reason why professional personnel, for example, have a relatively high rate of multiple jobholding.

Job Tenure and Job Mobility

Moving from job to job is one factor of labor force dynamics that has been studied for a relatively long time. Interest has centered, particularly, on the pattern and extent of job mobility, the characteristics of those workers who change jobs, and their reasons for doing so.

Stability Also a Characteristic of U.S. Labor Force

We begin by recalling our previous comments on the stability as well as the mobility that characterizes U.S. employment. The data on this matter are comparatively rare for the labor force as a whole, but the Bureau of the Census did make one very instructive survey in 1951. All civilian workers were asked during the regular MRLF survey in January 1951 whether or not they were still working on the same jobs they had just before Pearl Harbor and U.S. entry into World War II (that is, in November 1941, a time most were likely to remember). Thus, a period of just a little over nine years was covered. It was found that 13 million of the 59 million civilian workers employed in January 1951—more than a fifth of all the workers involved—were still employed at the same jobs or businesses they had at the time of Pearl Harbor.

This is a large number to have remained with the same employer or business—considering the years involved, which covered a period of enormous dislocation during World War II and part of the Korean episode; the mass movement of men into and then out of the armed forces (this was considered a break in jobholding, even though the person retained reemployment rights to the job); the normal entries and exits from the labor force on account of youth and age plus the growing work activity of women; the extensive changes in industrial and occupational demands of that period.

Workers with long, continuous job tenure naturally tended to be concentrated in the older age groups and the male sector. Two out of every three of the 13 million workers still employed in January 1951 in jobs or businesses acquired before our entry into World War II (6), for example, were forty-five years of age and over. In fact, for both men and women, the average number of years in continuous employment went up consistently with age.

As might be expected, there was a big difference in this regard between the sexes, since jobholding by women is affected by marriage and childbearing. Married women with no children, for example, spent twice as much time continuously on the same job as married women with children of preschool age. Continuous job tenure was also consistently longer for whites than for nonwhites, mostly because of the latter being concentrated in occupations and industries more subject to unemployment.

Occupational differentials were, in fact, most important in affecting the length of job tenure among American workers—as can be

TABLE 13-11
Experience of Workers at Their Current Jobs, by Major Occupation Group, January 1951

Occupation	Percent with Jobs Acquired Before World War II	Median Years on Current Job
Total	22.0	3.4
Farmers, farm managers	50.0	9.4
Managers, officials	33.0	5.1
Craftsmen, foremen	27.9	4.3
Professional, technical	24.9	3.7
Clerical	17.4	2.9
Operatives	16.9	2.9
Farm laborers, foremen	18.2	2.7
Sales	14.0	2.2
Service (except household)	14.1	2.0
Laborers (except farm)	11.6	1.6
Private household service	10.2	1.2

Source: S. L. Wolfbein, "Job Tenure of American Workers," *Monthly Labor Review*, September 1952.

seen from Table 13-11. Farmers especially stood out in the 1951 data in this respect; their average stay on the job or business was almost double that of the next-highest group; and the managerial group, too, had a relatively high level of job tenure. In general, continuity of jobs varied with the skill level of the employed, ranking relatively high for professional and skilled personnel, relatively low for the less skilled workers.

Other factors that seemed to affect job tenure were employment in industries where seniority played a major role (for example, railroads, where the average skilled worker had spent ten years or more on the same job) and the stability or intermittency of industrial jobs (the average for skilled workers in utilities was almost six years; for those in construction, only two years).

1963 Study of Job Tenure

Twelve years after the 1951 study was made, another survey reconfirmed the large amount of job stability in the United States.

Out of the 66 million people employed in January 1963, no less than 19.5 million—three out of every ten—had been continuously with the same job or business for more than ten years. In fact, 6.5 million of these were found to be in the same job or business they had at least twenty-one years before—that is, before January 1942, right after America's entry into World War II:

LENGTH OF EMPLOYMENT OF WORKERS AT THEIR CURRENT JOB—JANUARY 1963

Date Current Job Started	*Number (In Thousands)*	*Percent*
Total	65,935	100.0
Jan. 1962–Jan. 1963	16,168	24.5
Jan. 1960–Dec. 1961	10,357	15.7
Jan. 1953–Dec. 1959	17,906	27.2
July 1950–Dec. 1952	4,265	6.5
Oct. 1945–June 1950	6,285	9.5
Jan. 1942–Sept. 1945	2,619	4.0
Before Jan. 1942	6,491	9.8
Date not reported	1,844	2.8

Source: "Job Tenure of American Workers, January 1963," *Monthly Labor Review,* October 1963.

The average time spent on the same job or business for all workers in January 1963 was 4.6 years, as against the average of 3.4 years shown by the 1951 survey, which was affected by the dislocations of World War II. Otherwise the general pattern of job tenure was pretty much the same, with continuous jobholding higher among the older age groups, the men, single women in contrast to married women, and whites for the reasons we have cited.

As was also true in 1951, one of the most important factors affecting job tenure was the occupation of the employed. As can be seen from the tabulation on the next page, the farm group has by far the highest rate of job stability. For the rest, the proportion of steady jobholders varies with training, education, and skill.

Who Are the Job Changers?

In more recent years, special questions attached to the MRLF schedule have yielded additional information on the magnitude and pattern of job changing and the characteristics concerning those persons who make these changes.

Supplemental information available in 1955 and 1961 tells a very significant story as shown in the table on the next page.

Average Years on Current Job by Major Occupation Group—January 1963

Occupation	*Male*	*Female*
Total	5.7	3.0
Farmers, farm managers	18.0	—
Managers, officials	8.4	5.8
Craftsmen, foremen	6.9	4.8
Professional, technical	5.4	3.7
Clerical	5.3	3.0
Operatives	5.1	4.1
Sales	3.5	2.9
Service (except household)	3.5	1.9
Laborers (except farm)	2.5	—
Private household work	—	1.7

Source: "Job Tenure of American Workers, January 1963," *Monthly Labor Review*, October 1963.

As can be seen from Table 13-12, in both 1955 and 1961 about one out of every ten people who had some work experience could be called a "job changer," that is, changed jobs one or more times during the given year. The rate at which these persons changed jobs, however, varied substantially with age. Here we find confirming evidence again of the concentration of job changing among those early in their career development.

These age differentials hold for both sexes, although the rate of job changing itself is somewhat smaller for women, as is shown by Fig. 13-3.

Another confirming piece of evidence on the magnitude and pattern of mobility is shown when these results are classified by occupation and industry. As Table 13-12 shows, the overall rate of job changing for males in 1961 was 11.0 percent. It was only 1.9 percent for farmers and farm managers, and only 4.7 percent for managers, officials, and proprietors. It was also lower than the overall average for men in such white-collar jobs as professional and clerical work. It was highest for the less skilled men, working, for example, as laborers. In fact, the latter groups had rates of job changing about double that of professional personnel in 1961. One group that had a relatively substantial rate of job changing was the skilled (craftsman) category; this was apparently associated with the fact that a

TABLE 13-12
Percent of Persons with Work Experience Who Changed Jobs One or More Times, by Age and Sex, 1955 and 1961

Age and Sex	1955	1961
Total	11.1	10.1
Male	12.5	11.0
14–17	12.9	8.9
18–19	27.4	23.5
20–24	27.8	24.4
25–54	12.2	10.8
55–64	5.6	4.0
65 and over	3.4	3.4
Female	8.7	3.0
14–17	10.8	5.8
18–19	20.8	22.2
20–24	14.9	16.3
25–54	7.5	7.5
55–64	4.3	4.1
65 and over	1.9	1.9

Sources: *Job Mobility of Workers in 1955* (U.S. Department of Commerce, Bureau of the Census, Current Population Reports, Series P-50, No. 70); G. Bancroft and S. Garfinkle, *Job Mobility in 1961* (Bureau of Labor Statistics, Special Labor Force Report No. 35, August 1963).

large proportion of these men are engaged in the construction industry, where the character of production (the typically small unit working on specific projects, the seasonality inherent in its operations) generates a considerable amount of job changing.

In 1961 the construction industry led all the rest in its rate of job changing: 25 percent of all the men with work experience in

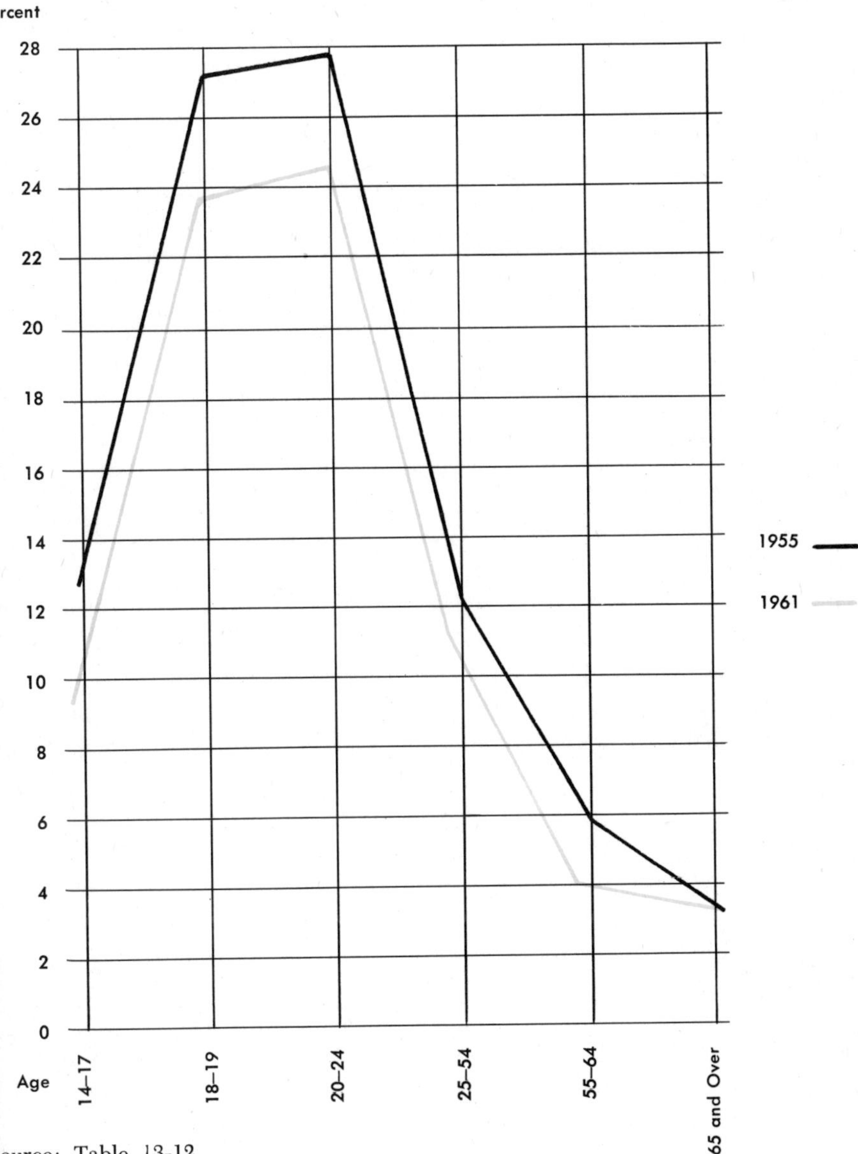

Source: Table 13-12.

FIG. 13-3 *Proportion of men who changed jobs one or more times, by age, 1955–61*

that field changed jobs during the year. The occupational picture for 1961 appeared as follows:

Percent of Persons with Work Experience Changing Jobs in 1961

Occupation	*Men*	*Women*
Total	11.0	8.6
Professional, technical	8.5	8.3
Farmers, farm managers	1.9	1.9
Managers, proprietors, officials	4.7	5.5
Clerical	9.1	10.1
Sales	13.0	8.6
Craftsmen	13.3	4.4
Operatives	13.8	8.8
Private household workers	5.1	3.6
Other service workers	12.1	12.0
Farm laborers	15.2	5.3
Laborers (except farm)	16.4	10.6

Source: Bureau of Labor Statistics, Special Labor Force Report No. 35.

As the data build up in this field, a clearer picture of the patterns of job mobility begins to emerge. Additional queries added to MRLF surveys have yielded information on such factors as the reasons for making these job changes and the amount of joblessness that is associated with job shifting.

Job Changing by Age Groups

Among the young (fourteen to seventeen years of age) job changing and job seeking are obviously a much more marginal dimension of total activities; many are students substantially supported by their parents. Almost seven out of ten boys in this age group who did change jobs changed only once—in 1961—and 40 percent of these went directly from one employer to the next, without any loss of working time. Even when they did lose time in changing jobs, about 50 percent did not look for work at all between jobs. When asked the reason for leaving their jobs, the majority reported the termination of a temporary job or some reason such as going back to school.

For eighteen- and nineteen-year-olds in the job-change category, the picture is quite different. Many here are making their first full-time entry into the labor force. Almost 60 percent of the males in this group gave as their reason for shifting out of a job either a direct job loss or a move on their part to improve their job status. These figures clearly reflect the difficulties new entrants into the work force face as inexperienced workers, and their lack of seniority. They reflect the expectations and aspirations that lead about one-third of them to leave jobs to improve their status.

Job changes reach a peak among twenty- to twenty-four-year-old men, and here, too, job-related reasons for shifting predominate: 65 percent left jobs in 1961 either because of a job loss or their own leaving to improve their job status. Unlike the early teen-age boys, the bulk of those who lost work actively sought another job.

As Fig. 13-3 shows, the rate of job changing moves down in adult and later years, as family responsibilities and longer job tenure stabilize employment patterns. Among those men, job shifting not only is primarily economic but is generated in very substantial part by the loss of work. Thus, more than 40 percent of the core of the adult male labor force (twenty-five to fifty-four years of age) who changed jobs in 1961 were involved in a job loss.

Beyond the age of fifty-five, job changing falls drastically. What job changes do occur are mostly job-related, and substantial proportions (two out of three) of the persons involved lose work between jobs. At age sixty-five and over, however, one out of every four men leaves a job for reasons that are basically not job-related—for example, to retire.

Job Changing by Women

The situation among women is the same in its age contour, but the forces associated with job changing are different: marriage, child-bearing, the predominance of part-time work. Much greater proportions of the women do not look for work between jobs (the proportion in the age group twenty-five to fifty-four not looking for work was quintuple that of the men in 1961); and the proportion of women job changers who leave work for non-job-related reasons (such as household responsibilities) is, of course, much larger than for the men. Again, for the big group twenty-five to fifty-four years of age, the proportion of women leaving a job because of a direct job loss was half that of men; the proportion of women leaving because of termination of a temporary job was twice that of men; and the proportion of women leaving a job because of such other reasons as health or household responsibilities was three times the corresponding proportion of men of that age group.

All in all, these data on the specifics of job mobility of American workers confirm the patterns of work revealed by the overall information we reviewed in previous chapters.

Reference Notes

1. J. Shiffman, *Marital and Family Characteristics of Workers, March 1960* (U.S. Department of Labor, Bureau of Labor Statistics, Special Labor Force Report No. 13, April 1961), p. 7.
2. See S. L. Wolfbein, "Some Aspects of Unemployment Change," *Proceedings of Social Statistics Section, American Statistical Association,* 1957.
3. C. Rosenfeld, *Work Experience of the Population in 1961* (U.S. Department of Labor, Bureau of Labor Statistics, Special Labor Force Report No. 25, December 1962).
4. The Metropolitan Life Insurance Company series on labor turnover, 1919–29, can be found in the *Monthly Labor Review,* July 1929, p. 62.
5. Each turnover action recorded in the statistics does not necessarily represent a separate person; the same individual may be recorded as a separation and an accession during any given month or year.
6. For wage and salary workers, a job was defined as a "continuous period of employment with a single employer"; for the self-employed, as a "continuous period of employment in a particular type of business in the same locality."

Readings

An early discussion of some of the facets of the subject of this chapter will be found in

Myers, H. B. "Dynamics of Labor Supply," *Journal of the American Statistical Association,* Vol. 36 (June 1941).

Discussions on the relation between labor force size and the business cycle as it pertained to the depression decade of the 1930s were highlighted in

Woytinsky, W. S. *Additional Workers and the Volume of Unemployment in the Depression.* (Pamphlet Series 1, Social Science Research Council.) New York: the Council, 1940.

and in

Humphrey, D. D. "Alleged 'Additional Workers' in the Measurement of Unemployment," *Journal of Political Economy,* June 1940.

Woytinsky's reply to Humphrey appeared in the October 1940 issue of this journal. Some more recent discussions of this topic can be found in

Hansen, W. Lee. "The Cyclical Sensitivity of the Labor Supply," *Journal of the American Economic Association,* June 1962.

Long, C. D. *The Labor Force Under Changing Income and Employ-*

ment, Princeton, N.J.: National Bureau of Economic Research, 1958.

Measuring Employment and Unemployment. (Gordon Committee Report.) Washington, D.C.: President's Committee to Appraise Employment and Unemployment Statistics, 1962. Pp. 67–72.

Data relating to labor market participation by women in relation to their husbands' labor market and occupational status as well as to family income are from

Shiffman, J. *Marital and Family Characteristics of Workers, March 1961.* (Special Labor Force Report No. 20.) Washington, D.C.: Department of Labor, Bureau of Labor Statistics. (Additional data can be found in Special Labor Force Report No. 26, January 1963.)

These data are reported annually on the basis of surveys conducted in connection with the ongoing MRLF. See also

Meredith, J. L. "Labor Force and Employment, 1960–62," *Monthly Labor Review,* Vol. 86 (May 1963).

Seasonal factors used in labor force, employment, and unemployment series are available from the Bureau of Labor Statistics. The seasonally adjusted data are reported and analyzed monthly in the ongoing reports on the employment situation by the U.S. Department of Labor. The technical aspects of seasonal adjustments are discussed in Chapter VI of the Gordon Committee Report. See also

Brittain, J. A. "A Bias in the Seasonally Adjusted Unemployment Series and a Suggested Alternative," *Review of Economic Statistics,* Vol. 41 (November 1959).

Gordon Committee Report, Appendix G, "The Bureau of Labor Statistics Seasonal Factor Method."

New Seasonal Adjustment Factors for Labor Force Components. (Special Labor Force Report No. 8.) Washington, D.C.: Department of Labor, Bureau of Labor Statistics, 1960.

Raff, M. S. "The BLS Seasonal Factor Method," *Employment and Earnings.* Washington, D.C.: Department of Labor, Bureau of Labor Statistics, March 1963.

Shiskin, J. "Seasonal Adjustments of Economic Indicators: A Progress Report," *Proceedings of the Business and Economic Statistics Section, American Statistical Association,* 1957.

Data and analyses of gross changes in the labor force for earlier periods can be found in

Gross Changes in the Labor Force: May 1948 to January 1949. (Current Population Reports, Labor Force Series P-50, No. 16.) Washington, D.C.: Department of Commerce, Bureau of the Census, October 10, 1949.

Shifts in the Labor Force, July-November 1945. (Labor Force Memorandum No. 2.) Washington, D.C.: Department of Commerce, Bureau of the Census, June 11, 1947.

More recent data and discussion will be found in

The Extent and Nature of Frictional Unemployment. (Study Paper No. 6, Joint Economic Committee of the Congress, 86th Congress, First Session.) Washington, D.C.: Government Printing Office, November 1959.

PEARL, R. B. "Gross Changes in the Labor Force: A Problem in Statistical Measurement," *Employment and Earnings* (Bureau of Labor Statistics), April 1963.

WOLFBEIN, S. L. "Some Aspects of Unemployment Change," *Proceedings of Social Statistics Section, American Statistical Association,* 1957.

Work experience data are from annual surveys conducted in connection with the MRLF. See

ROSENFELD, C. *Work Experience of the Population in 1961.* (Special Labor Force Report No. 25.) Washington, D.C.: Department of Labor, Bureau of Labor Statistics, December 1962.

The Metropolitan Life Insurance Company series on labor turnover, 1919–29, can be found in the *Monthly Labor Review,* July 1929. An explanation of the Bureau of Labor Statistics labor turnover series is given in a BLS document entitled *Measurement of Labor Turnover* (November 1961). Labor turnover data are reported monthly in a brief release and are carried in the monthly detailed report *Employment and Earnings.*

Data on multiple jobholding are derived from special surveys in connection with the MRLF. See also

Monthly Labor Review. (Special Labor Force Reports Nos. 9 and 18.) Washington, D.C.: Department of Labor, Bureau of Labor Statistics, October 1960, October 1961.

SHIFFMAN, J. *Multiple Job Holders in May 1962.* (Special Labor Force Report No. 29.) Washington, D.C.: Department of Labor, Bureau of Labor Statistics.

There is extensive literature in the field of labor mobility, much of it relating to experience within one or more labor markets. For relevant materials of the immediate postwar period, see

SHULTZ, G. P. "Recent Research on Labor Mobility," *Proceedings of the Fourth Annual Meeting of the Industrial Relations Research Association* (Massachusetts Institute of Technology Publications in Social Science, Series 2, No. 34), December 1951.

Good examples of such works during the 1950s are

JEFFERYS, M. *Mobility in the Labor Market.* London: Routlidge & Kegan Park Ltd., 1954.

Labor Mobility and Economic Opportunity. Cambridge, Mass.: M.I.T. Press; and New York: John Wiley & Sons, 1954.

MIERNYK, W. H. *Inter-Industry Labor Mobility,* Boston: Northeastern Univ., 1955.

Palmer, G. L. *Labor Mobility in Six Cities.* New York: Social Science Research Council, 1954.

Studies of an overall national kind stem from surveys made in connection with the MRLF and include

Hamel, H. R. "Job Tenure of American Workers," *Monthly Labor Review,* Vol. 86 (October 1963).

Wolfbein, S. L. "Job Tenure of American Workers," *Monthly Labor Review,* Vol. 75 (September 1952).

The job mobility studies of 1955 and 1961 are reported in

Bancroft, G., and Garfinkle, S. *Job Mobility of Workers in 1961.* (Special Labor Force Report No. 35.) Washington, D.C.: Department of Labor, Bureau of Labor Statistics, August 1963.

Job Mobility of Workers in 1955. (Current Population Reports, Series P-50, No. 70.) Washington, D.C.: Department of Commerce, Bureau of the Census.

PART FIVE

The Anatomy of Unemployment

Introduction

IN 1933, AT THE LOW POINT OF THE GREAT DEPRESSION, 25 PERCENT OF ALL workers in the United States were unemployed; a decade later, the rate of joblessness had dropped below 2 percent under the impact of World War II. Thus, the living memory of many people who are still relatively young encompasses enormous swings in the unemployment situtation and the conditions that accompanied them.

These two points in our history represent extreme situations. They nevertheless constitute important stages in our country's evolution, if only because they put the unemployment problem toward the forefront in social and economic policy and in political programs. Against this background, it is not surprising that in the first full peacetime year after World War II, in the Employment Act of 1946, the Congress declared it to be public policy that all persons able and wanting to work should be afforded the opportunity to do so.

In the years following World War II the levels of U.S. economic activity and employment moved at a relatively fast pace. This postwar activity came partly in response to an enormous demand for goods and services built up during ten years of depression and four years of war. Added to this were (1) a perseveringly high birthrate (one out of every three persons enumerated in the census of 1960 was not yet born at the end of World War II) and (2) the demands in the 1940s, 1950s, and 1960s growing out of our defense and international posture.

Nevertheless, the two decades since World War II have witnessed four business cycles. Each has been relatively shallow, but each has left us with a somewhat higher level and rate of unemployment. The swings in unemployment obviously have not been as wide as in the 1933–45 era that we have referred to, but the seasonally adjusted unemployment rate has been as low as 2.5 percent and as high as a little over 7.5 percent in the decade 1953–62 inclusive.

Of particular concern have been the persistence of the unemployment rate at 5 percent or more for six consecutive years, 1958–63; the need for accelerated economic growth and more job opportunities; and the concentrations of joblessness among particular sectors of the population, such as the young—especially dropouts from school—older people with obsolete skills, Negroes, workers generally at the lower levels of skill development, and people in depressed areas.

In these circumstances it is not surprising to find that there has been a considerable demand for more information on the various aspects of the unemployment problem. In the next chapter we shall review what the data reveal about our unemployment problem. We shall try to look beyond the overall global figures for a better perception of the anatomy of unemployment. We shall then analyze how we have fared in comparison with other countries of the free world.

CHAPTER FOURTEEN

The Nature and Conditions of Unemployment

In the first chapter we briefly sketched the kinds of attitudes toward unemployment found in England during the past several centuries and how they were reflected in the treatment of and provision for those without work. This evolution has come a long way to the point where, in twentieth century America as well as the rest of the free world, public policy has as its aim the minimization—if not prevention—of unemployment and its amelioration wherever it exists.

The provision of adequate information and intelligence about unemployment therefore ranks high as a public goal, and a significant proportion of the work done in the field of labor force statistics in the past quarter of a century has focused on this task. Modern labor force studies, born during the depression of the 1930s, gave this subject considerable attention. While only a minimal problem during World War II, it has occupied an important place since then.

Unemployment as a National Problem

In this chapter we shall discuss four categories of unemployment—frictional, seasonal, cyclical, and structural. It will be seen that each presents a different problem. The fact that any unemployed person may be out of work for only a month or so because it may take that long to get a new job in his trade is not as significant, obviously, as the fact that another person is chronically unemployed because he has spent his life in an industry or at a job that is now technologically obsolete.

We shall learn that a substantial proportion of the jobless in this country experience relatively short periods of unemployment. We shall also see that the average duration of unemployment in the United States has steadily grown in recent years.

Who are the unemployed? More than others, they are young people, especially high school dropouts; they are more often nonwhites, especially nonwhite dropouts; they are—more than other groups—unskilled or semiskilled workers; they work in certain industries, such as construction, agriculture, coal mining, and manufacturing; they frequently live in certain chronically depressed areas.

Of special interest are unemployed heads of families. Just as society must meet the problem of youth unemployment, it must pay particular attention to family breadwinners out of work.

Another group of special interest are the self-employed and those employed in family enterprises, who may not show up in unemployment figures when their farms or businesses are in trouble—they may keep working and hope for a business improvement.

Many people work part time—to what extent is this by choice? A substantial amount of part-time work is involuntary, especially among males twenty-five to sixty-four years old. About three million Americans in recent years have worked part time because they could not obtain full-time work.

How much total work time is lost in the United States by unemployed workers and involuntary part-time workers? We shall try to answer this question, too.

How does U.S. employment compare with that of other countries? Among eight industrialized nations, Canada had the highest unemployment rate (7 percent) in 1960; the United States was in second place, with 5.6 percent. Italy had about 4 percent, Great Britain 2.5 percent, France 2 percent, Sweden 1.5 percent, Japan 1 percent, and West Germany 1 percent.

Special factors, such as the existence of widespread paternalism in Japanese industry, in which workers and employers lose social status if there is a break in employment, played some role in these differences. The fact that some countries have yet to go through the same industrial evolution as the United States may be another factor.

The Categories of Unemployment

In a recent study undertaken for the Joint Economic Committee of the Congress of the United States (1), more than fifty different terms or labels applied to unemployment were identified. "Disguised," "short-term," "volitional," "cultural," "vicarious," "secondary" illustrate types of unemployment referred to by writers.

The attempt to identify different kinds of unemployment is quite important, if only because it may point to different remedial programs, policies, and solutions. The unemployment problem of a college student seeking a job during the summer vacation between school terms differs from that of the married family breadwinner; the problem of an older worker whose skill has become obsolescent under the impact of technological change can have quite different implications from that of the skilled construction craftsman who is regularly employed except during the winter; similarly, the prognosis for an unemployed school dropout is overwhelmingly different from that of an engineer who is between jobs.

For our purposes here, it will suffice to identify four categories of unemployment. They are selected because they appear often in professional literature and they point up some major problems.

Let us note at the start that it is well-nigh impossible to definitely classify most individual workers according to these categories. How can we really tell whether a man has been laid off because of the turn of the business cycle or because of dislocations such as automation? In some cases we may not be able to tell much at all until after the fact—for example, until the business cycle turns again, recovery ensues, and production in his industry or plant comes back or even surpasses its previous mark.

Frictional Unemployment

The term "frictional" unemployment (more recently called by some "transitional" unemployment) connotes joblessness generated by the imperfect working of the labor market itself. Even with the availability of enough employment, it takes a while before workers show up at the right time, in the right place, with the needed skills to fill the jobs.

If people voluntarily quit their jobs, for instance, it takes some time for them to catch up with the right kind of job. While they are out seeking employment they are counted as unemployed.

Enterprises go out of business, and the same thing happens to many of the employees. Migration and mobility are substantial, and many of these movers may also be enumerated as unemployed while temporarily between jobs.

Some new entrants into the labor force, whether they be brand-new college graduates or housewives returning after many years to the job market, also may take a little time before matching their skills and needs with those of the labor market.

This type of short-term and transitory unemployment is caused by the normal frictions that exist in a free labor market. In the typical case of this kind of unemployment some time lag is almost bound to interpose itself before the worker and the job get together. Part of this unemployment is thus practically unavoidable under current conditions.

Assigning part of unemployment to frictional causes, however, does not mean that all of it is inevitable and nothing can be done about it. To the contrary, better job information and more effective use of employment services would help avoid at least some of it and cut down its duration, brief as it is.

The evidence on the existence of frictional unemployment is twofold. First, there is always some unemployment, even during peak periods of employment. Even during 1944, at the height of our war effort—with millions of men in the armed forces, with the civilian economy at full strain, and with the demand for workers at unprecedented levels—unemployment averaged a little more than 1 percent of the labor force. The unemployment rate was 1.9, 1.2, and 1.9

percent in 1943, 1944, and 1945, respectively. These were, of course, completely abnormal years and are not relevant to a peacetime economy—but they do show that joblessness, while minimal, existed even in times of extremity. As can be seen from Table 14-1, on an annual average basis, the only other time the unemployment rate was below 3 percent was in the Korean war year of 1953, when the rate was 2.9 percent.

The second type of evidence equates frictional unemployment with very-short-term unemployment. As we shall see, detailed data are available on the duration of unemployment among those reported as jobless each month. One category includes those out of work less than five weeks.

For any given month this group of newly unemployed workers will include some who get right back to jobs and others who will stay unemployed for longer periods; that is, next month they will show up as unemployed for two months (five to eight weeks). It is possible to derive from the MRLF data a figure on the number and proportion of people who are unemployed less than five weeks during any given month and who do *not* show up as unemployed five to eight weeks the next month. Table 14-2 presents these data for the post-war period.

It should be noted that these data do not speak unequivocally to the point of frictional unemployment as we have defined it. Persons may exit from unemployment after a brief stay because of seasonal influences—a separate category that we shall discuss. Note, too, that exits from unemployment not only may take the form of getting a job but also can be effected by leaving the labor force altogether. At any rate, these are the very-short-term unemployed, and the figures give us some concept of that part of the unemployment total that is the least serious in economic terms and that represents in part what we have termed frictional unemployment.

As Table 14-2 shows, the short-term jobless account for anywhere from a fourth to a half of all the unemployed. It is therefore fair to say that at any given time some important part of the unemployment total does represent very short, transitory joblessness.

The reader will note that there are cyclical variations in the proportion of total unemployment represented by these very-short-term jobless persons. In the recession year 1949 this proportion was down to around one-third; in the boom year 1953 it was close to one-half—followed by a drop to a little over 30 percent in the recession year 1954 and an increase in 1955. With higher overall rates of

TABLE 14-1
Employment Status of the Noninstitutional Population Annual Averages,

Year	Total Noninstitutional Population	Total Labor Force Including Armed Forces		Civilian Labor Force						
					Employed*			Unemployed*		
		Number	Percent of Noninstitutional Population	Total	Total	Agriculture	Nonagricultural Industries	Number	Percent of Labor Force	Not in Labor Force
1929	†	49,440	†	49,180	47,630	10,450	37,180	1,550	3.2	†
1930	†	50,080	†	49,820	45,480	10,340	35,140	4,340	8.7	†
1931	†	50,680	†	50,420	42,400	10,290	32,110	8,020	15.9	†
1932	†	51,250	†	51,000	38,940	10,170	28,770	12,060	23.6	†
1933	†	51,840	†	51,590	38,760	10,090	28,670	12,830	24.9	†
1934	†	52,490	†	52,230	40,890	9,900	30,990	11,340	21.7	†
1935	†	53,140	†	52,870	42,260	10,110	32,150	10,610	20.1	†
1936	†	53,740	†	53,440	44,410	10,000	34,410	9,030	16.9	†
1937	†	54,320	†	54,000	46,300	9,820	36,480	7,700	14.3	†
1938	†	54,950	†	54,610	44,220	9,690	34,530	10,390	19.0	†
1939	†	55,600	†	55,230	45,750	9,610	36,140	9,480	17.2	†
1940	100,380	56,180	56.0	55,640	47,520	9,540	37,980	8,120	14.6	44,200
1941	101,520	57,530	56.7	55,910	50,350	9,100	41,250	5,560	9.9	43,990
1942	102,610	60,380	58.8	56,410	53,750	9,250	44,500	2,660	4.7	42,230
1943	103,660	64,560	62.3	55,540	54,470	9,080	45,390	1,070	1.9	39,100
1944	104,630	66,040	63.1	54,630	53,960	8,950	45,010	670	1.2	38,590
1945	105,520	65,290	61.9	53,860	52,820	8,580	44,240	1,040	1.9	40,230

*Data for 1947–56 adjusted to reflect changes in the definition of employment and unemployment adopted in January 1957. Two groups averaging about one-quarter million workers who were formerly classified as employed (with a job but not at work)—those on temporary layoff and those waiting to start new wage and salary jobs within thirty days—were assigned to different classifications, mostly to the unemployed.

†Not available.

‡Beginning with 1953, labor force and employment figures are not strictly comparable with those of previous years as a result of the introduction of material from the 1950 census into the estimating procedure. Population levels were

unemployment in more recent years, the proportion of very-short-term unemployed has been running on the low side, although here again cyclical variations are always quite evident. When we express these very-short-term unemployed as a percent of the labor force, of course, the proportion tends to go the other way—up in recession, down in more prosperous years.

What is impressive is the relative stability in the numbers in this

1929–62 (Thousands of Persons Fourteen Years of Age and Over)

Year	Total Non-institutional Population	Total Labor Force Including Armed Forces.		Civilian Labor Force						
					Employed*			Unemployed*		
		Number	Percent of Non-institutional Population	Total	Total	Agriculture	Non-agricultural Industries	Number	Percent of Labor Force	Not in Labor Force
1946	106,520	60,970	57.2	57,520	55,250	8,320	46,930	2,270	3.9	45,550
1947	107,608	61,758	57.4	60,168	57,812	8,256	49,557	2,356	3.9	45,850
1948	108,632	62,898	57.9	61,442	59,117	7,960	51,156	2,325	3.8	45,733
1949	109,773	63,721	58.0	62,105	58,423	8,017	50,406	3,682	5.9	46,051
1950	110,929	64,749	58.4	63,099	59,748	7,497	52,251	3,351	5.3	46,181
1951	112,075	65,983	58.9	62,884	60,784	7,048	53,736	2,099	3.3	46,092
1952	113,270	66,560	58.8	62,966	61,035	6,792	54,243	1,932	3.1	46,710
1953‡	115,094	67,362	58.5	63,815	61,945	6,555	55,390	1,870	2.9	47,732
1954	116,219	67,818	58.4	64,468	60,890	6,495	54,395	3,578	5.6	48,401
1955	117,388	68,896	58.7	65,848	62,944	6,718	56,225	2,904	4.4	48,492
1956	118,734	70,387	59.3	67,530	64,708	6,572	58,135	2,822	4.2	48,348
1957	120,445	70,744	58.7	67,946	65,011	6,222	58,789	2,936	4.3	49,699
1958	121,950	71,284	58.5	68,647	63,966	5,844	58,122	4,681	6.8	50,666
1959	123,366	71,946	58.3	69,394	65,581	5,836	59,745	3,813	5.5	51,420
1960§	125,368	73,126	58.3	70,612	66,681	5,723	60,958	3,931	5.6	52,242
1961	127,852	74,175	58.0	71,603	66,796	5,463	61,333	4,806	6.7	53,677
1962	130,081	74,681	57.4	71,854	67,846	5,190	62,657	4,007	5.6	55,400

raised by about 600,000; labor force, total employment, and agricultural employment by about 350,000.

§Beginning with 1960, data include Alaska and Hawaii and are therefore not strictly comparable with those of previous years. This inclusion has resulted in an increase of about half a million in the noninstitutional population fourteen years of age and over, and about 300,000 in the labor force, four-fifths of this in nonagricultural employment. The levels of other labor force categories were not appreciably changed.

Source: U.S. Department of Labor.

category, hovering very near the million mark during the period following World War II. Because it is a relatively stable group, its proportion would vary inversely with the movement of the total unemployment figure, which varies much more sharply up and down with the business cycle.

The figure for the short-term unemployed, perhaps, moves up a little during recessionary periods, accounting for its slightly rising

TABLE 14-2
Short-Term Unemployment in the United States, 1948–62
(In Thousands)

Year	Civilian Labor Force	Total Unemployed	Unemployed Less than Five Weeks in One Month, and Not Unemployed Next Month			Year	Civilian Labor Force	Total Unemployed	Unemployed Less than Five Weeks in One Month, and Not Unemployed Next Month		
			Total	As a Percent of Unemployed	As a Percent of Labor Force				Total	As a Percent of Unemployed	As a Percent of Labor Force
1948	61,442	2,325	1,002	43.1	1.6	1956	67,530	2,822	1,083	38.4	1.6
1949	62,105	3,682	1,200	32.6	1.9	1957	67,946	2,936	1,030	35.1	1.5
1950	63,099	3,351	1,040	31.0	1.6	1958	68,647	4,681	1,202	25.7	1.8
1951	62,884	2,099	948	45.2	1.5	1959	69,394	3,813	1,145	30.0	1.6
1952	62,966	1,932	929	48.1	1.5	1960	70,612	3,931	1,231	31.3	1.7
1953	63,815	1,870	912	48.8	1.4	1961	71,603	4,806	1,245	25.9	1.7
1954	64,468	3,578	1,114	31.1	1.7	1962	71,854	4,007	1,208	30.1	1.7
1955	65,848	2,904	1,000	34.4	1.5						

Source: Bureau of Labor Statistics.

proportion of the labor force in those intervals. A greater number may experience very-short-term unemployment during recession years. On the other hand, the interval between jobs may increase somewhat during these periods, placing some individuals in a longer-term category of unemployment.

Seasonal Unemployment

A second category usually differentiated from other kinds of joblessness is seasonal unemployment. Not all seasonal fluctuations in production, of course, generate unemployment, since the labor force expands and contracts seasonally too. Some persons may join the work force to meet seasonal demands of certain industries and then voluntarily leave the labor force altogether when the seasonal demands end. Where seasonality is quite marked, however, and where adult males make up the bulk of the work force, as in the construction industry, relatively high unemployment can result. A good part of the unemployment associated with seasonality tends to be of short duration. Seasonal unemployment extending over the winter months, however, can go on for some time and no doubt contributes to the observed seasonal upswing in long-term unemployment during the first several months of each year.

As is the case with any category of unemployment, measuring the extent of seasonal unemployment with precision is difficult. A general idea of its magnitude can be seen from the tables and charts presented in the Chapter 13. The Bureau of Labor Statistics did make an estimate of the magnitude of seasonal unemployment in 1957, which looked like this:

Industry Division	*Seasonal as a Percent of Total Unemployment in 1957*
Total	26
Wage and salary workers in	
Agriculture	41
Construction	43
Manufacturing	30
Trade	14
Transportation	8
Service	29

Here, again, we have a not inconsiderable proportion of the unemployed. According to these estimates, joblessness due to seasonal influences accounted for one-fourth of total U.S. unemployment in 1957. Not suprisingly, this proportion was about 40 percent in such outdoor activities as agriculture and construction.

Cyclical Unemployment

As the name implies, this kind of joblessness is generated by periodic changes in the business cycle.

These changes are prominent in the figures presented in Table 14-1, showing the unemployment rate during the period 1929–62 on an annual average basis. They can also be seen from Fig. 14-1, depicting the course of the seasonally adjusted unemployment rate, by month, since 1948.

Between 1945 and 1962, economists recognize four business cycles with their resultant impact on employment and unemployment. The National Bureau of Economic Research has pinpointed the peaks and troughs of each of these cycles and the intervening recession and recovery periods on the basis of a large number of economic indicators, with the following results:

UNEMPLOYMENT IN FOUR POSTWAR BUSINESS CYCLES (SEASONALLY ADJUSTED DATA)

*Year and Month**	*Number of Unemployed (In Thousands)*	*Rate of Unemployment*	*Year and Month*	*Number of Unemployed (In Thousands)*	*Rate of Unemployment*
Nov. 1948	2,308	3.8%	July 1957	2,843	4.2%
Sept. 1949†	4,129	6.6	Apr. 1958	4,998	7.3
June 1950	3,441	5.4	Dec. 1958	4,318	6.3
July 1953	1,695	2.7	May 1960	3,567	5.1
Aug. 1954	3,863	6.0	Feb. 1961	4,891	6.8
Apr. 1955	3,028	4.6	Oct. 1961	4,831	6.8

*For each of the four cycles, the dates represent peak, trough, and eight months after trough.

†Trough was actually October 1949; September is shown instead because October figures were affected by coal and steel strikes.

As can be seen from this brief summary table and Fig. 14-1, the unemployment rate rises quite sharply as the peak of business activity is passed and the recession deepens; it usually reaches its high point near the trough of the cycle and stays high for some months after general improvement in the economy takes place. It then begins to fall as the recovery continues.

In the lexicon of the business-cycle analyst, unemployment is a "lag" economic indicator; that is, it begins to change in response to changes in underlying economic conditions later than do some other indicators. Economic indicators such as the factory workweek are called "lead" indicators, because they tend to turn earlier than others in portending a change in the business cycle—on the way up or down. Employers generally tend to reduce the workweek when demand for goods and services begins to decline, before they take the step of laying off workers. When the demand for goods and services begins to turn up, employers tend to increase the workweek rather than take on workers.

Since the causes of cyclical unemployment and the causes of the other two kinds of joblessness are quite different, obviously the

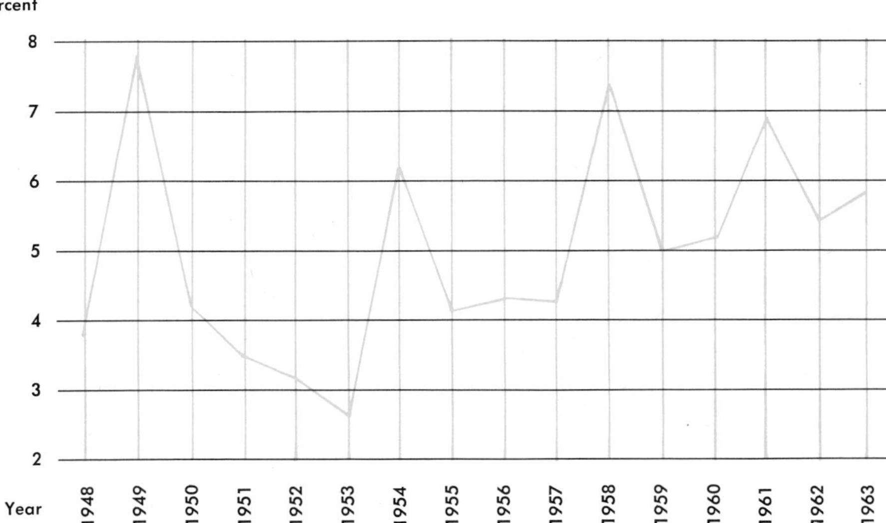

Source: Bureau of Labor Statistics.

FIG. *14-1 Seasonally adjusted unemployment rate of all civilian workers, July 1948–July 1963.*

amelioration of the cyclical type calls for different policies and programs. What these should be depends on the social, economic, and political view of the proponents, but generally they tend to concentrate on three approaches:

One, to stimulate investment and increase business profits—for example, by reducing corporate taxes or permitting more favorable depreciation allowances to stimulate purchases of capital equipment.

Two, to stimulate government spending at all levels for schools, highways, and public works, bringing about greater demands for goods and services of all kinds and inducing hiring and rehiring of workers.

Three, to stimulate more consumer spending, as, for example, through personal income tax reduction, which, of course, would have the same effect.

Students of business cycles differ quite extensively in what they consider to be the primary causes of these phenomena, and this difference of opinion brings about different kinds of suggested solutions. All three approaches (they are not, of course, mutually exclusive) have been used in this country during the period following World War II.

Structural Unemployment

In each of the three kinds of unemployment that have been briefly reviewed, the joblessness involved is considered to have some terminal point. Frictional unemployment, as we have defined it, is transitory by its very nature; seasonal unemployment, while of relatively long duration in some trades, changes with the seasons of the year; and cyclical unemployment again carries with it a connotation of up-down-up movement, a periodicity, an ebb and flow—all pointing to an anticipated improvement.

This is not to say that cyclical unemployment cannot be extensive, deep, and long-term; witness the situation in the 1930s. With the passage of the Employment Act of 1946 calling for government policy and action to sustain economic growth and stability, and with built-in stabilizers in the economy such as our social-insurance programs, the present outlook is hopefully for relatively short cycles in business activity and employment and unemployment.

The situation is different in our fourth category, most often referred to as structural unemployment. Here, joblessness is a function of deeper-seated changes in the economy and tends to be more intractable, more persistent, more long-term. As such, it is much more serious from a social, economic, and political point of view.

Structural unemployment is caused by the relocation of industry, leaving depressed areas in its wake; automation, and technological changes that make skills obsolescent; and shifts in occupational and industrial composition that aid the change in the character of labor demand.

Some well-known examples are the decline in the use of both bituminous and anthracite coal and its concomitant impact on scores of communities in Pennsylvania, West Virginia, and Kentucky; the shift from steam to diesel locomotives; the depletion of resources characteristic of the upper peninsula of Michigan and the Mesabi range in Minnesota; the geographical shift of cotton textiles; the upending of the agricultural economy under the impact of enormous increases in productivity; the effect of automation in some of the hard-goods industries; the shift from the goods-producing to the service-producing sectors; the precipitous decline in the demand for unskilled labor. Unemployment of this kind also shows up, partly at least, in the differentially high unemployment rates among certain sectors of the population—among school dropouts and the unskilled in the depressed areas.

We are involved here with the problem of matching the workers left behind geographically, occupationally, and industrially with new job opportunities. In a sense, we are dealing with the frictions involved in making this match (and this is why structural unemployment is sometimes included under frictional unemployment). But the frictions are much more powerful and the solutions are quite different. Generally, they involve

> trying to bring new job opportunities to the unemployed, as for example, through encouraging plant location in depressed areas—witness the Area Redevelopment Act of 1961 and the help it gives those areas to get the wherewithal (facilities, trained labor force) to attract enterprises;
>
> endowing workers with the skills required through training and retraining—witness the Manpower Development and Training Act of 1962; and
>
> providing relocation allowances for displaced workers—witness the Trade Expansion Act of 1962.

Structural unemployment tends to be of long duration—although it does not follow that all long-term unemployment is of the structural sort.

The Duration of Unemployment

A common thread that runs through the descriptions of the various kinds of unemployment is its duration. Monthly data on this factor are usually presented in a classification of the unemployed out of work short-term (less than five weeks), intermediate (five to fourteen weeks), long-term (fifteen to twenty-six weeks), and very-long-term (twenty-seven weeks and more).

These data bear on one of the major dimensions of our subject, for it is difficult indeed to derive a correct perception of the unemployment situation without knowledge of this factor. Conceivably, a U.S. unemployment total of five million with the preponderant majority in the short-term category could be a much less serious problem than, say, three million with most in the long-term category.

TABLE 14-3
Percent Distribution of the Unemployed, by Duration of Unemployment, 1947–62

Year	Total	Less than 5 Weeks	5–14 Weeks	15–26 Weeks	27 Weeks and Over
1947	100.0	53.3	29.9	9.9	7.0
1948	100.0	58.0	28.8	8.3	5.0
1949	100.0	49.0	31.5	11.6	7.0
1950	100.0	45.2	31.5	12.7	10.7
1951	100.0	58.3	27.4	7.9	6.5
1952	100.0	61.3	26.7	7.7	4.4
1953	100.0	63.0	25.8	7.1	4.2
1954	100.0	46.1	31.2	13.8	8.9
1955	100.0	47.8	28.1	12.6	11.6
1956	100.0	52.6	28.6	10.7	8.2
1957	100.0	50.6	30.4	10.9	8.1
1958	100.0	39.2	29.9	16.8	14.2
1959	100.0	43.5	29.2	12.3	15.0
1960	100.0	45.7	29.9	12.8	11.5
1961	100.0	39.5	28.6	15.1	16.7
1962	100.0	43.8	28.3	13.3	14.6

Source: Bureau of Labor Statistics.

The basic data on the duration of unemployment are presented in Table 14-3. The figures confirm what we already have indicated: The short-term unemployed, for example, at any given time represent a large proportion of the total jobless figures. In fact, those out of work for a month or less have represented the biggest category of the unemployed throughout the period following World War II.

That the duration of unemployment varies with the business cycle is also to be expected. The data for the four postwar business cycles presented in Table 14-4 parallel the data presented in Table 14-2 as part of the discussion of cyclical unemployment.

As we move from the peak to the trough of a cycle, the proportion of short-term jobless declines and the proportion of long-term jobless goes up. The reemployment of these long-term laid-off workers is one of the slower reactions during a business recovery: Note how the proportion stays high even after eight months past the trough of each recession.

TABLE 14-4
Duration of Unemployment During Four Postwar Business Cycles

	Short Term (Less than 5 Weeks)		Long Term (15 Weeks and Over)		Very Long Term (27 Weeks and Over)	
Year	As a Percent of Unemployment	As a Percent of Labor Force	As a Percent of Unemployment	As a Percent of Labor Force	As a Percent of Unemployment	As a Percent of Labor Force
4th quarter 1948	56.7	2.1	13.4	0.5	4.7	.2
4th quarter 1949	45.8	3.2	23.7	1.6	9.3	.6
2nd quarter 1950	43.5	2.4	25.1	1.4	11.9	.7
3rd quarter 1953	63.2	1.7	10.4	.3	4.0	.1
3rd quarter 1954	43.9	2.6	26.4	1.5	10.4	.6
1st quarter 1955	44.1	2.1	26.5	1.3	13.5	.6
3rd quarter 1957	51.4	2.2	18.8	.8	4.9	.3
2nd quarter 1958	38.1	2.8	30.9	2.2	12.0	.9
4th quarter 1958	38.7	2.5	36.0	2.3	18.9	1.2
2nd quarter 1960	48.7	2.6	22.9	1.2	11.3	.6
1st quarter 1961	41.9	2.8	28.8	2.0	14.0	1.0
3rd quarter 1961	38.8	2.7	33.7	2.3	18.5	1.3

Source: Bureau of Labor Statistics.

Table 14-4 also shows that since World War II each recession has left a higher plateau of long-term jobless. In a five-year period, 1957 through 1962, the following occurred:

Total unemployment rose from an average of 2.9
  to 4.0 million—up 40 percent
Short-term unemployment rose 20 percent
Long-term unemployment rose 100 percent

Very-long-term unemployment rose 150 percent

As a result, the average duration of unemployment has followed this course:

Year	*Average Duration of Unemployment (Weeks)*	*Year*	*Average Duration of Unemployment (Weeks)*
1947	9.8	1955	13.2
1948	8.6	1956	11.3
1949	10.0	1957	10.4
1950	12.1	1958	13.8
1951	9.7	1959	14.5
1952	8.3	1960	12.8
1953	8.1	1961	15.5
1954	11.7	1962	14.7

The data we have presented will take on additional significance when we move on to our next step, looking behind the global totals to such demographic factors as sex, age, and color.

The Characteristics of the Unemployed

Age, sex, color, marital condition, existence of youthful dependents, and other personal characteristics have, as might be expected, a direct bearing on employment and employment status.

Age

As Fig. 14-2 indicates, there is a marked variation in the rates of unemployment by age. Unemployment rates over the years have always been a good deal higher for younger persons than for adults. In 1962, for example, teen-agers (fourteen to nineteen years) had an unemployment rate double that of persons aged twenty years and over. Young people under twenty-five represented only one-fifth of the labor force in 1962 but contributed one-third of the unemployed.

Some concentration of unemployment among the young is to be

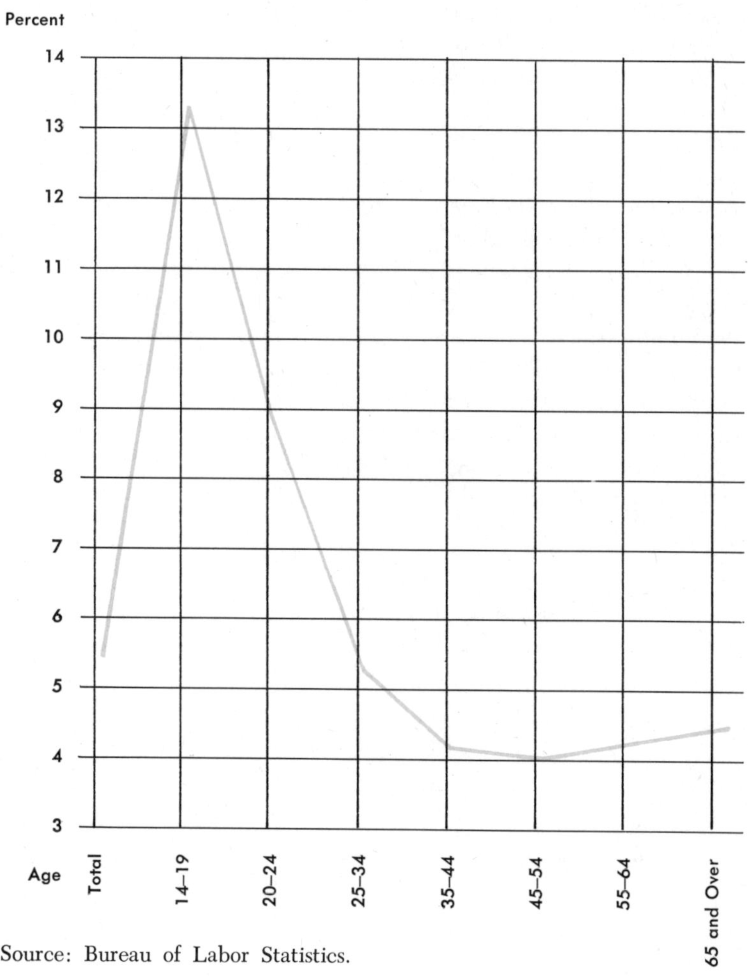

Source: Bureau of Labor Statistics.

FIG. *14-2 Unemployment rates, by age, 1962.*

expected. After all, they are at the beginning of their career development, have the least job seniority, engage in considerable moving around and job changing, and generally lack any considerable background of work experience and skill development.

But recent years have indicated that there is more to the differentially high rates of unemployment among the young than just these factors. Unemployment, particularly long-term joblessness, has moved up substantially among this group in the last half dozen years or so. The rate of long-term unemployment among twenty- to twenty-four-year-olds, for example, went up more than 100 percent between 1957 and 1962, double the corresponding rise among the labor force as a whole. One reason may be the continuing dramatic decline in unskilled and semiskilled jobs that once provided a good entry for newcomers into the labor market.

Of particular concern is the serious nature of joblessness among dropouts—the boys and girls who do not stay on in school to get their high school diplomas. More and more, employers are requesting evidence of high school completion as a prerequisite for employment. So it is not surprising to find that 27 percent of the dropouts who left school in 1961 were unemployed in October of that year—a rate almost 10 percentage points higher than that for high school

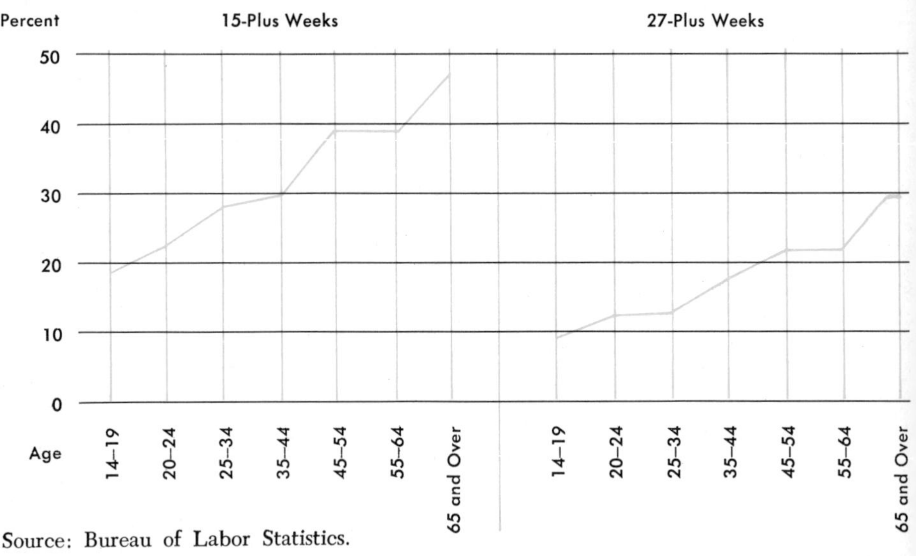

Source: Bureau of Labor Statistics.

FIG 14-3 *Long-term unemployment, by age, 1962 (as percent of unemployed in age group).*

graduates. Neither is it surprising to find that the unemployment rate for dropouts continues high even several years after they have left school. For example, those who left school in 1959 had an unemployment rate in October 1961 of almost 17 percent—double that of the high school graduates of 1959.

Even when employed, of course, the dropout is lodged characteristically in the lower-paying, less skilled jobs. In October 1961, one year after last attending school, about one out of every two dropouts found himself in an unskilled (laborer) job; the corresponding proportion among high school graduates was only one in five. Four out of every ten graduates held a white-collar clerical job; the corresponding proportion for the dropouts was only one in ten.

The serious nature of the problem is underscored by what we anticipate for the decade of the 1960s: 7.5 million dropouts among the 26 million new young workers expected to enter the labor force during the current decade.

As Fig. 14-2 also indicates, people at the upper end of the age scale have a somewhat higher unemployment rate than those in the middle years. Their problem lies more in the fact that, once out of a job, they have a much more difficult time becoming reemployed. The persistent uptrend in the duration of joblessness associated with age is clearly demonstrated in Fig. 14-3.

Color

Also among the more persistent patterns of unemployment in this country is the substantial differential that exists between whites and nonwhites (mainly Negroes). To put this point briefly: Nonwhite workers in 1962 accounted for 11 percent of the labor force, 22 percent of the unemployed, 26 percent of the long-term unemployed. In recent years, when there has been a generally higher unemployment rate among all groups, the differential between whites and nonwhites has actually been widening. In 1962, unemployment among nonwhites rose to two and a half times the corresponding rate for whites—about double the differential of a decade earlier.

One factor in this picture is the disproportionate concentration of dropouts among nonwhites. Thus, nonwhites accounted for 20 percent of the 1961 dropouts, but only 9 percent of the 1961 high school graduates and only 6 percent of those who went on to college. Nonwhite dropouts constitute one of the really intractable unemployment problems in this country, and they represent one big reason why nonwhite teen-agers have one of the highest unemployment rates of any part of our labor force. In 1962, nonwhite teen-age boys experienced an unemployment rate of 21 percent, while the girls' rate was 28 percent; for white boys and girls in this age group the rate was 12 percent.

Skill

One of the factors affecting unemployment among nonwhites is the concentration of nonwhite work opportunities, despite some progress in the World War II and postwar periods, among the less skilled jobs. The unskilled and semiskilled, of course, are more prone to attacks of unemployment. In fact, occupational differentials that are really skill differentials are a prime common denominator among the jobless. Table 14-5 speaks eloquently to this point.

Note that throughout the period following World War II, on an average annual basis, the unemployment rate has never gone above 2 percent for professional and technical personnel. In fact, for the entire white-collar group (professional, managerial, clerical, and sales) the rate has never gone much above 4 percent, the only real exception coming in 1961, when clerical and sales personnel experienced a rate closer to 4.5 percent.

Skill differentials are distinctly marked within the blue-collar group as well; witness the steady upward progression of the unemployment rate as one moves from the skilled (craftsmen) to the semiskilled (operatives) to the unskilled (laborers). For the five years 1958–62, the unemployment rate for nonfarm laborers was about two and a half times that for skilled craftsmen. The disproportionate concentration of unemployment among the less skilled can also be seen from the fact that during these same five years only three of the eleven major occupational groups listed in Table 14-5 had rates of unemployment above the national average. They were the semiskilled and unskilled industrial workers and the service workers (except private household workers). This last group includes persons employed in laundries, dry-cleaning establishments, shoe-repair stores, and the like.

The major differences in unemployment by skill-related categories have focused attention on the needs for more and better education, training, and retraining. This particularly applies to such groups as the dropouts, older workers whose skills have become obsolescent under the impact of technological change, and people in depressed areas whose basic sources of livelihood have disappeared. They represent a prime reason for the provisions for training and retraining in the Area Redevelopment Act of 1961, the Manpower Development and Training Act and Trade Expansion Act of 1962, and accelerated programs to increase the holding power of the high schools and reduce the potentially explosive numbers of dropouts.

What gives these programs added urgency is the persistent push

TABLE 14-5
Percent of Unemployment by Major Occupation Group, Annual Averages, 1947–62

Major Occupation Group	1947	1948	1949	1950	1951	1952	1953	1954	1955	1956	1957	1958	1959	1960	1961	1962
Total	3.6	3.4	5.5	5.0	3.0	2.7	2.5	5.0	4.0	3.8	4.3	6.8	5.5	5.6	6.7	5.6
Professional, technical, and kindred workers	1.9	1.7	1.9	2.2	1.5	1.0	.9	1.6	1.0	1.0	1.2	2.0	1.7	1.7	2.0	1.7
Farmers and farm managers	.2	.2	.2	.3	.3	.2	.2	.4	.4	.4	.3	.6	.3	.3	.4	.3
Managers, officials, and proprietors (except farm)	1.2	1.0	1.5	1.6	1.0	.7	.9	1.2	.9	.8	1.0	1.7	1.3	1.4	1.8	1.5
Clerical and kindred workers	2.9	2.3	3.8	3.4	2.1	1.8	1.7	3.1	2.6	2.4	2.8	4.4	3.7	3.8	4.6	3.9
Sales workers	2.6	3.4	3.5	4.0	2.8	2.5	2.1	3.7	2.4	2.7	2.6	4.0	3.7	3.7	4.7	4.1
Craftsmen, foremen, and kindred workers	3.8	2.9	5.9	5.6	2.6	2.4	2.6	4.9	4.0	3.2	3.8	6.8	5.3	5.3	6.3	5.1
Operatives and kindred workers	5.1	4.1	8.0	6.8	4.3	3.9	3.2	7.6	5.7	5.4	6.3	10.9	7.6	8.0	9.6	7.5
Private household workers	3.4	3.2	5.2	5.6	3.8	3.2	2.5	5.0	4.1	4.2	3.7	5.2	4.8	4.9	5.9	4.9
Service workers (except private household)	4.7	4.8	6.1	6.8	4.3	3.7	3.6	5.2	5.8	4.8	5.1	7.4	6.4	6.0	7.4	6.4
Farm laborers and foremen	2.7	2.3	3.9	5.0	2.1	2.3	2.5	4.2	3.7	3.7	3.7	6.2	5.1	5.2	5.7	4.3
Laborers (except farm and mine)	7.5	7.5	12.9	11.7	5.6	5.7	6.1	10.7	10.2	8.2	9.4	14.9	12.4	12.5	14.5	12.4

Source: Bureau of Labor Statistics.

toward the higher-skilled jobs which has characterized our economy, and for which we see no change in the offing.

Industry

As Table 14-6 shows, there are substantial industrial differentials in unemployment, particularly among those sectors that have been and are sensitive to seasonal and cyclical ups and downs as well as long-term declines in production.

Thus, there has not been a single year in the postwar period when, on an average annual basis, the construction industry did not have an unemployment rate at least twice as high as the overall figure. This is an industry that characteristically combines sharp sea-

TABLE 14-6
Percent of Unemployment, by Major Industry Group, Annual Averages, 1948–62

Major Industry Group	1948	1949	1950	1951	1952	1953	1954	1955	1956	1957	1958	1959	1960	1961	1962
Total	3.4	5.5	5.0	3.0	2.7	2.5	5.0	4.0	3.8	4.3	6.8	5.5	5.6	6.7	5.6
Experienced wage and salary workers	3.7	6.2	5.6	3.2	2.9	2.7	5.5	4.3	3.9	4.5	7.2	5.6	5.7	6.8	5.5
Agriculture	4.7	6.5	8.2	3.9	3.9	4.7	8.0	6.4	6.5	6.7	9.9	8.7	8.0	9.3	7.3
Nonagricultural industries	3.7	6.2	5.4	3.2	2.8	2.6	5.4	4.2	3.8	4.5	7.1	5.5	5.6	6.7	5.5
Mining, forestry, fisheries	2.9	8.5	6.6	3.8	3.4	4.9	12.3	8.2	6.4	6.3	10.6	9.7	9.5	11.6	8.6
Construction	7.6	11.9	10.7	6.0	5.5	6.1	10.5	9.2	8.3	9.8	13.7	12.0	12.2	14.1	12.0
Manufacturing	3.5	7.2	5.6	3.3	2.8	2.5	6.1	4.2	4.2	5.0	9.2	6.0	6.2	7.7	5.8
Durable goods	3.4	7.4	5.2	2.6	2.4	2.0	6.5	4.0	4.0	4.9	10.5	6.1	6.3	8.4	5.7
Nondurable goods	3.6	6.9	6.0	4.0	3.3	3.1	5.7	4.4	4.4	5.3	7.6	5.9	6.0	6.7	5.9
Transportation and public utilities	3.0	5.2	4.1	1.9	1.9	1.8	4.8	3.5	2.4	3.1	5.6	4.2	4.3	5.1	3.9
Wholesale and retail trade	4.3	5.8	5.8	3.7	3.1	3.0	5.2	4.3	4.1	4.5	6.7	5.8	5.9	7.2	6.3
Finance, insurance, and real estate	1.6	1.8	2.0	1.3	1.5	1.6	2.0	2.1	1.4	1.8	2.9	2.6	2.4	3.3	3.1
Service industries	3.5	5.1	5.0	3.1	2.6	2.4	4.0	3.8	3.2	3.4	4.6	4.3	4.1	4.9	4.3
Public administration	2.0	2.9	2.8	1.6	1.1	1.2	2.0	1.8	1.6	2.0	3.0	2.3	2.6	2.7	2.2

Source: Bureau of Labor Statistics.

sonal variations in activity, fluctuations associated with business cycles, and short-term projects that require workers to make more job changes than most.

The other differentials by industry can be noted from Table 14-6. Particularly noteworthy are the higher-than-average unemployment rates in agriculture, also highly seasonal as well as subject to a long-term decline; mining, where mechanization and competition from other sources of energy and power have created long-duration unemployment; and manufacturing, perhaps most sensitive to variations in the business cycle.

Within manufacturing, the variations by industry groups are enormous. Some of them, such as the automobile industry, experience very wide swings in unemployment as a result of technological change, cyclical variations, shutdown for model changeover, and so on. In some months, for example during 1961, the unemployment rate has moved as high as 27 percent among auto workers.

One will also note that the unemployment rate has been mostly above the national average in goods-producing industries and mostly lower than the national average in the service-producing sectors—tying in with our previous discussion of industrial trends.

Geography

In Chapter 12 we stressed the changing geography of American industry and some of the factors associated with it; here we discuss the geographic differences in unemployment, also substantial, and often a result of those locational changes.

We also listed in an earlier chapter (cf. Fig. 14-4) recent areas of substantial and of substantial and persistent unemployment. In recent years these areas have accounted for approximately one-fourth of the nation's nonfarm workers, but about one-third of the total jobless. The hardest hit are those that are centers of hard-core unemployment stemming from resource depletion, technological change, and basic locational shifts, such as cotton textiles in the North.

Most of them have been problem areas for a quarter of a century or more, and while conditions do change with the state of the overall economy, their problems are more deep-seated. These areas will require specific programs such as area redevelopment for any lasting solution of the disproportionate unemployment that they have experienced for so long.

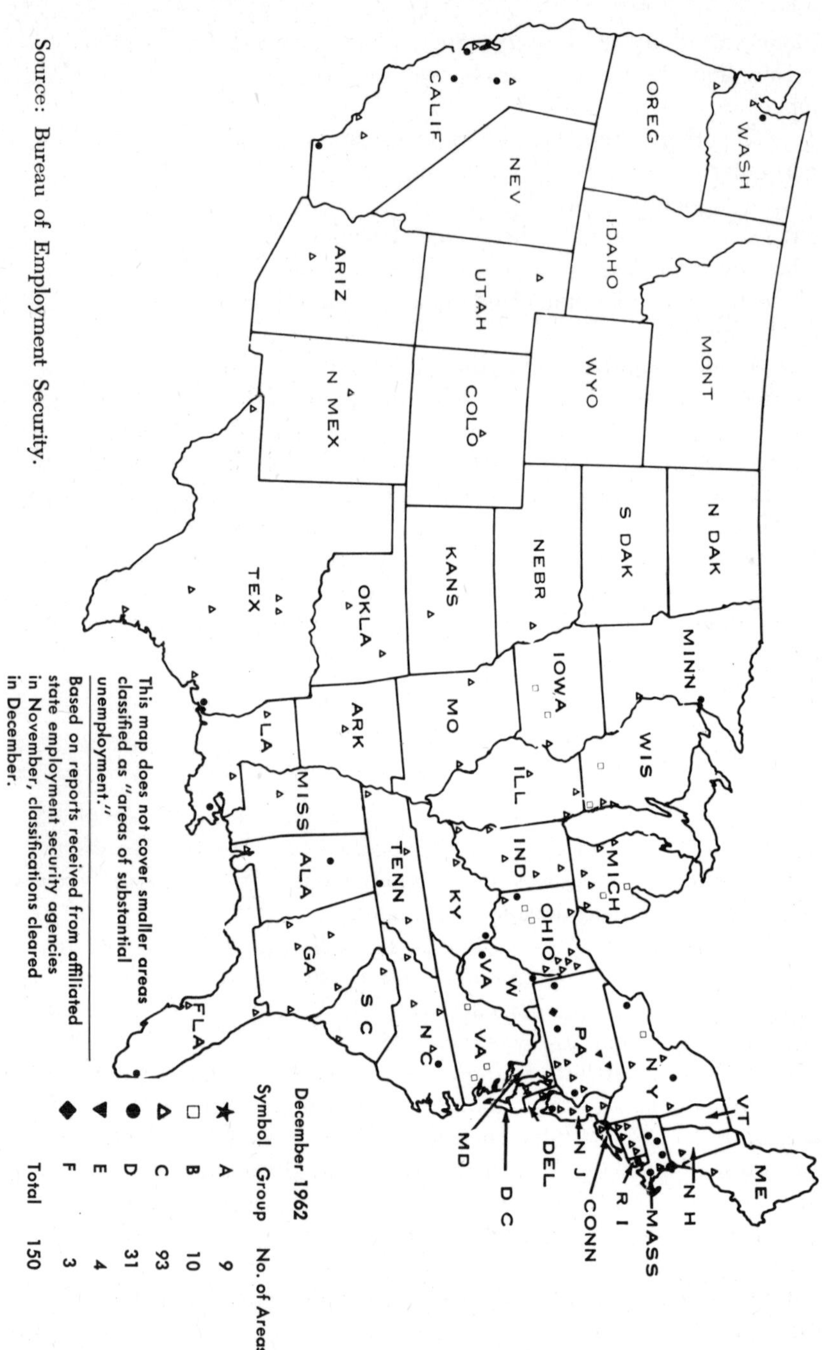

FIG. *14-4 Classification of 150 major labor market areas according to relative adequacy of labor supply.*

Unemployment Among Married Men and Experienced Wage Workers

Many more classifications of the unemployed are available each month, and greater detail is available to the student of the field who wishes to explore this subject further. There are two others to be noted here. In recent years these have been receiving more attention and more analysis.

The first is unemployment among married men. There has been considerable focus on these "male family breadwinners" because they are considered a critical group, where unemployment can be very serious because of family responsibilities.

Some insist that this is the most serious type of unemployment. This is a matter partly of point of view. Unemployment can also be serious, of course, among young dropouts or even young graduates who are finding it hard to break through the threshold of employment; among married women who may be in the labor market because of the unemployment or disability of their husbands; or of the elderly who may be seeking work because of compelling circumstances, such as illness in the family.

Table 14-7, presenting the data on unemployment among married men, shows that joblessness tends to be lower for them than for the labor force as a whole. This is to be expected, since married men are in the age group with the lowest unemployment rates to begin with; smaller proportions of them are in the very young age groups where boys are still single, and those men who are widowed and divorced tend to be in the older age groups; yet it is at both ends of the age scale that unemployment tends to be the highest.

Interestingly, recently available data indicate that married men living with their wives have lower unemployment rates and lower duration of unemployment than the other marital-status groups, age for age. Perhaps being married does exert more pressure on the man to find and to hold a job, and it could be that the personal characteristics of men who marry make them more employable (as we saw in an early chapter, they are more prone to be in the labor force in the first place).

While lower than the national average, unemployment rates for married men are quite sensitive to cyclical variations, since substantial proportions are engaged in such industries as manufacturing and construction.

The second group represents the experienced wage and salary

workers. The point has often been made that the self-employed (people who own their own business) and unpaid family workers engaged in a family enterprise are not as subject to the risk of unemployment as are wage and salary workers. Among the self-employed, including owners of family businesses, bad times often result in substantial losses but the owners stay in the count of employed by sticking with their business though operating at a loss.

Unemployment rates, therefore, have been calculated by excluding the self-employed and unpaid family workers. These figures are also shown in Table 14-7. Excluded also are those with no work experience at all—therefore the term "experienced wage and salary workers." As Table 14-7 shows, the differences between this rate and that for all workers are quite small; and perhaps just as important, they move very similarly over the months and years.

Another kind of unemployment rate is sometimes calculated by excluding the self-employed and unpaid family workers, but leaving in new workers—for example, those with no previous work experience.(3) The results—in terms of levels and trends over time—are

TABLE 14-7
Unemployment Rates for Selected Groups, 1948–62*

	Unemployment Rate		
Year	All Workers	Married Men†	Experienced Wage and Salary Workers
1948	3.8%	—	4.2%
1949	5.9	3.4%	6.7
1950	5.3	4.6	6.0
1951	3.3	1.5	3.7
1952	3.1	1.4	3.3
1953	2.9	1.7	3.2
1954	5.6	4.0	6.0
1955	4.4	2.6	4.8
1956	4.2	2.3	4.4
1957	4.3	2.8	4.5
1958	6.8	5.1	7.2
1959	5.5	3.6	5.6
1960	5.6	3.7	5.7
1961	6.7	4.6	6.8
1962	5.6	3.6	5.5

Source: Bureau of Labor Statistics.
†Married men living with their wives.
*Annual averages.

also quite similar. Basically, the reason for this similarity is that the proportion of the employed who are wage and salary workers is about 85 percent, and this is usually enough to swing the rate no matter how it is calculated.

It is important to know, however, that the concept of unemployment as applied to self-employed groups is rather different from that in the case of the wage and salary workers. The data that show the very low rates of unemployment for such groups as farm managers and proprietors and managers should be assessed accordingly.

Involuntary Part-Time Work

In the conceptual structure of the MRLF an unemployed person is one who is actively seeking employment and has no work at all. Just one hour of work during the week of reference puts him into the employed category. Employed persons involuntarily doing part-time work do represent an under utilization of our manpower resources, and some indication of the magnitudes involved seems worthwhile. This circumstance has generated requests for regularly published data on the extent to which the employed sector of the labor force is less than fully occupied. Some have also made the point that a similar calculation ought to be made of the impact of overtime as well as undertime work, and an analysis of this also has been done.(4)

In a sense, we could say that we have a spectrum that includes unemployment and zero hours of work; part-time employment that can involve anywhere from one hour of work to just short of a full-time scheduled workweek; employment at full-time hours; and employment where work hours go beyond the normal or scheduled amount with overtime pay.

There is another dimension: a growing number of persons work part time voluntarily. In May 1963, for example, about 7.6 million persons in nonfarm industries worked part time for "noneconomic" reasons: either they did not want to work full time or they could not work full time, because of family responsibilities. In May 1950 the corresponding figure was 3.8 million Thus, voluntary part-time workers doubled in the period 1950–63 and now account for about one out of every eight at work in nonfarm industries.

Looking for Part-Time Work

Side by side with the growth in part-time employment has been a very substantial rise in the number seeking part-time work only. Witness the following figures:

Year (May)	*Percent of Unemployed Looking for Part-Time Work*
1963	15.5
1961	11.6
1958	8.6
1957	10.3
1956	14.2
1955	8.8
1954	7.7
1952	11.5
1951	7.1
1950	5.4

Source: Bureau of Labor Statistics.

While the figures have fluctuated from year to year, the trend since 1950 seems clearly upward. The 1963 proportion of jobless looking for part-time work was triple the corresponding rate for 1950.

It was only in January 1963 that data on part-time work seekers began to be collected monthly (the preceding years' data are based on special surveys). Enough have come in already to indicate that this is a group in which the young and old predominate.

In May 1963 about 42 percent of the fourteen- to seventeen-year-old unemployed and 40 percent of the unemployed men aged sixty-five and over were looking for part-time work only. The corresponding rate for men twenty-five to sixty-four years of age was only 3 percent.

Information from Work-Experience Studies

Among the various measures that aim at some indication of the magnitude of involuntary part-time work, there are three which have emerged and are used with some regularity; annual work-experience studies, current monthly data on involuntary part-time work, and current data on the jobless plus data on involuntary part-time workers.

The first was mentioned in Chapter 13 in our discussion of work-experience studies. We noted the fact that some proportion of the workers in any given year show up as part-year workers, those who worked less than fifty weeks. We noted that it was possible to discover from the data what effect unemployment had in causing some labor force members to be part-year rather than year-round workers.

In 1961 just a little under one out of every two (48 percent) of all the men with work experience as part-year workers gave unemployment as the reason for not working the year round. Other reasons varied from illness to unpaid absences from work; for example, because of a strike, going to school, retirement, or entering the armed forces. Even among women, of whom about half cited "taking care of the home" as the reason for being part-year workers, a fifth pointed to unemployment as the factor that caused them to fall out of the year-round category of workers.

Actually, unemployment as a factor in causing lost time during a year's period of time is much more important than these overall figures show.

For example, here is how unemployment ranked as the causative agent in part-year work, when arrayed by age in 1961:

	Percent in Part-Year Work Because of Unemployment	
Age	*Male*	*Female*
Total	48	20
14–19	19	14
20–24	53	24
25–64	80	22
65 and over	16	8

Source: Bureau of Labor Statistics.

Among women, as we noted, the big reason for part-year work is their family responsibilities; actually, in the major working ages unemployment is a more important factor. But for the bulk of the male adult working population, 80 percent assign unemployment as the factor responsible for their part-year work status. It turns out, therefore, that sheer joblessness is a formidable factor in generating loss of annual working time for a large proportion of the male labor force. During 1961 the number of men with work experience as part-year workers was 15.8 million, and 7.5 million of them were in that category because of unemployment.

Current Monthly Data

Moving to a current monthly basis, we find data regularly available since the spring of 1955 on the number of persons classified as employed but involuntarily working part time for economic reasons. These persons fall into two groups: (1) those who say they usually work full time but are employed part time because of economic reasons such as lack of work, material shortages, or repairs in their plants, and (2) those who say they usually work part time but because they could find only part-time work. The tabulation on this page shows the way that the figures for this sector have been running during the past half dozen years or so:

NONFARM WORKERS EMPLOYED PART TIME FOR ECONOMIC REASONS*
(In Thousands)

Year	*Total*	*Usually Work Full Time*	*Usually Work Part Time*
1956	1,967	1,067	900
1957	2,169	1,183	986
1958	2,953	1,638	1,315
1959	2,336	1,032	1,304
1960	2,550	1,243	1,317
1961	2,813	1,297	1,516
1962	2,336	1,049	1,287

Source: U.S. Department of Labor.
*Annual averages.

These yearly figures, as well as the available monthly data, indicate that this phenomenon is associated with changes in business conditions. The number working involuntarily part time came close to the three million mark in both 1958 and 1961, each of which contained the trough of a recession.

Over the years this group of involuntary part-time workers has accounted for approximately 4 percent of all of the persons in non-agricultural employment.

Data on Jobless plus Involuntary Part-Time Workers

Opinion to this date in the labor force field has held that those who are unemployed and those who work, but do so only on a part-time basis involuntarily, are two quite distinct categories and should in no way be lumped together.

It is held that the employed do have a job, an employer-employee relationship, they get paid, they and their employer pay social security taxes, their employers are paying unemployment-insurance premiums on their wages, and so forth. The unemployed are completely out of a job, are in a competitive position in the labor market in their active effort to secure employment, do not have the employer attachment and the benefits that go with it, and so forth.

In present circumstances these two groups are reported separately each month—one as employed, the other as unemployed—although the information is there for anyone who would like to put them together to show the joint effect of total joblessness and involuntary part-time employment.

There has been considerable demand for some such calculation, especially in recent years from the Joint Economic Committee of the Congress, and the Bureau of Labor Statistics has made available a series that portrays the labor force time lost through unemployment and part-time work.

The way this is done is relatively simple: All unemployed persons are assumed to have lost 37.5 hours a week;(5) multiplying the number of unemployed by this figure gives the total number of man-hours lost through joblessness. The difference between 37.5 hours and the actual hours worked by employed persons involuntarily working part time, multiplied by the number of these persons, gives an estimate of the man-hours lost through part-time work for economic reasons. Added together, we have the total number of man-hours lost by both groups. This serves as the numerator of a fraction, the denominator of which is total man-hours provided by the economy to its fully employed, plus total man-hours lost. Dividing one by the other gives a percent of labor force time lost through unemployment and part-time work, which has run as follows during the past several years for which data have been available:

Year	*Percent of Labor Force Time Lost*
1956	5.1
1957	5.3
1958	8.1
1959	6.6
1960	6.7
1961	8.0
1962	6.7

Source: Bureau of Labor Statistics.

Fig. 14-5 portrays how some of the different measures we have described have moved since 1955. They respond similarly to changing economic conditions. The unemployment rate for married men is at the lower end of the scale for reasons already mentioned; the series on the standard unemployment rate for all civilian workers and that for experienced wage and salary workers have been very close indeed; and the labor force time-lost curve is, as expected, at the higher part of the scale, since it adds an estimate of time lost by involuntary part-time workers.

International Comparisons

One of the most difficult exercises in any field such as this is to engage in a comparison of some phenomenon like unemployment on an international basis. Not only are data collected under different conceptual and technical rules, but the problem is compounded by the different historical backgrounds, attitudes, institutional arrangements, and economic development of the countries involved. In recent years, however, there has been great interest in how we compare with other countries in terms of unemployment. The Bureau of Labor Statistics has made an analytical survey of this problem that we will now review briefly. This survey undertook to compare the

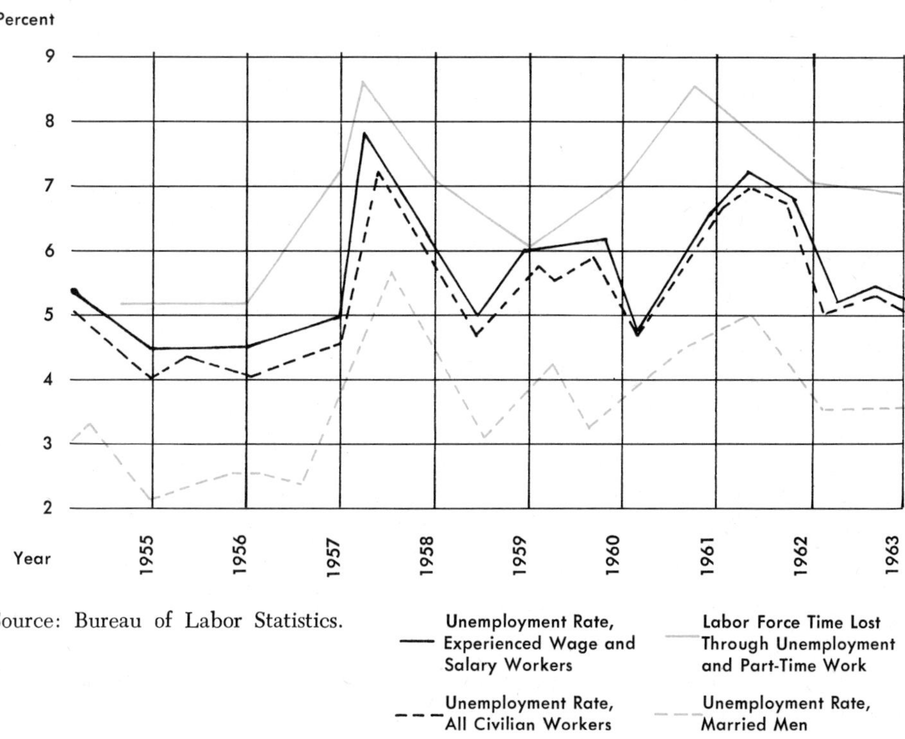

Source: Bureau of Labor Statistics.

FIG. *14-5 Selected measures of unemployment and part-time employment, 1955 to 1963 (seasonally adjusted).*

unemployment rate for 1960 in the United States with that in seven other countries. This necessarily involved a painstaking review of the concepts, methodology, and survey results of each country and making corresponding adjustments to get maximum comparability.

Labor Force Surveys of Other Nations

It is of some interest to note that *Canada* has a labor force survey very similar to ours that has been run on a monthly basis since

November 1952. Its concepts are consistent with ours, and its sample of 35,000 households is the same in size as ours, even though Canada's population is only one-tenth that of the United States. *Japan,* too, runs a labor force survey (in existence since 1946 and set up with U.S. help) with concepts and techniques quite similar to ours. Some differences do exist: for example, they include some members of the armed forces and certain segments of the institutional population; they start with age fifteen rather than fourteen as we do; they count persons on temporary layoff as employed while we put them in the unemployed category.

Both Italy and Germany depend in good part for unemployment information on registrations with their employment exchanges, but both have recently also produced official labor force statistics. Collected quarterly in *Italy* since 1959, the Italian data include regularly employed children ten to fourteen years of age, workers employed abroad, and career military personnel, while they exclude occasional workers employed during the survey week. In addition, new entrants into the labor force and temporarily laid-off workers are excluded from the unemployment count. Each of these categories is estimated separately, so that adjustments to our definitions can be made. In *West Germany,* a 1 percent sample household survey conducted in October of each year yields results generally consistent with ours. Adjustments are necessary, however, not only for the fact that the German results refer to the seasonally low unemployment month of October, but also because they include among the employed military personnel and unpaid family workers who worked less than fifteen hours.

In *Sweden,* the basic unemployment statistics come mainly from the trade unions, but since 1956 monthly statistics on registrations of unemployed at local employment exchanges have been available. Data are also available on unemployment among members of unemployment-insurance funds, covering a substantial proportion of wage and salary workers. In 1959 Sweden began to try sample labor force surveys, and it expects to conduct quarterly surveys from now on. Its concepts and definitions used are very similar to ours, although its sample is one of individuals rather than households and most of its interviews are conducted by telephone rather than in person.

In *France,* the official statistics are predicated on a count of registrants for jobs and are quite incomplete. The French have been experimenting with labor force surveys for some time, and the more recent ones are very similar to ours in concept and technique. There is no evidence at this point, however, to indicate that they intend to make these surveys a permanent part of their system.

In *Great Britain,* we have an example of a country that has excellent data based entirely on a count of registrants at the employment exchange; it has never conducted a labor force survey such as ours. The result is that its definitions and techniques are quite different from ours. The British figures relate to wage and salary workers only; their registration is as of a day, and everyone registering that day is counted as unemployed—in this country such a person with even one hour of work during the week would be enumerated as employed. The British also exclude unemployed who are temporarily ill, and there seems to be a good deal of underregistration among certain groups, such as teen-agers, retired workers, and married women.

Results of the 1960 Comparison

After adjustment for all of these factors for these countries, the comparable-as-possible results for the year 1960 came out as presented in Table 14-8.

From this table it appears that the U.S. rate of unemployment

TABLE 14-8
Adjusted Unemployment Rates, United States and Seven Foreign Countries, 1960

Country	Unemployment Rate
United States	5.6%
Canada	7.0
France	1.9
West Germany	1.0
Great Britain	2.4
Italy	4.3
Japan	1.1
Sweden (1961)	1.5

Source: R. J. Myers and J. H. Chandler, "Comparative Levels of Unemployment in Industrial Countries," Gordon Committee Report, Appendix A, pp. 233–270.

is significantly above the rates of the foreign nations for which comparable data could be obtained—with the exception of Canada. The seven nations (including Canada) had a combined labor force of about 143 million in 1960—double that of the United States; but their combined unemployment, at 3 million, was about 25 percent lower than the comparable figure for this country.

Behind these differences are, of course, a multitude of social, economic, demographic, legal, and institutional forces that make each country's situation unique. Thirty percent of Italy's workers are in agriculture—about four times the proportion in the United States. Germany was physically devastated during World War II and began from scratch in building up its economy; in many Japanese enterprises a worker customarily joins the company for life—and his employer customarily takes responsibility for him in good times and bad. These are factors that can be overwhelmingly more important than statistical incomparabilities and have to be weighed in making these international comparisons.

Unemployment has been higher in this country than in most industrial countries of western Europe, where recent economic growth has been more rapid. Many if not all of these countries, however, are beginning to experience the same occupational, industrial, and technological changes that have had an important bearing on our own employment situation.

In the meantime our own programs—for accelerating economic growth; for providing guidance, education, and training and retraining; for redeveloping areas of lower economic opportunity; for increasing employment opportunities for disadvantaged groups—can if consummated, enable us to achieve the goals of economic advance, stability, and minimum levels of unemployment.

Reference Notes

1. Subcommittee on Economic Statistics of the Joint Economic Committee, Eighty-seventh Congress, First Session, *Unemployment: Terminology, Measurement, and Analysis* (Washington, D.C.: Government Printing Office, 1961).
2. Joint Economic Committee, Eighty-sixth Congress, First Session, *The Extent and Nature of Frictional Unemployment* (Study Paper No. 6; Washington, D.C.: Government Printing Office, 1959).
3. See *Unemployment: Terminology, Measurement, and Analysis, supra,* pp. 35–48.
4. *Ibid.*, pp. 43–45.
5. The 37.5-hour standard was suggested by the Joint Economic Committee of the Congress.

Readings

A discussion and analysis of terminology and of recent developments in the employment and unemployment situation has been sponsored by the Joint Economic Committee of the Congress, which has had printed for its use two documents of particular value, cited in Reference Notes 1 and 2 of this chapter.

Background data on levels, rates, and characteristics of the labor force, employment, and unemployment are available from the Department of Labor, Bureau of Labor Statistics. Excellent up-to-date summary tables can be found particularly in the following report, which is the first of a series scheduled to be issued sixty days after Congress convenes each year:

Manpower Report of the President. Washington, D.C.: Government Printing Office, March 1963.

Tables also are found in the annual report that is prepared for the Joint Economic Committee:

Supplement to Economic Indicators. Washington, D.C.: Government Printing Office.

Analyses of the characteristics of the unemployed have received considerable attention in recent years. Monthly data are of course available from the ongoing current publications and releases of the U.S. Bureau of Labor Statistics. For a review and discussion of the various dimensions of unemployment in terms of people and places, see particularly

Manpower and Training: Trends, Outlook, Programs. U.S. Depart-

ment of Labor, Office of Manpower, Automation, and Training, February 1963. Chapters 1 and 2.
Who Are the Unemployed? U.S. Department of Labor, Spring 1961.

Special reference is made to the problem of school dropouts because of the current and expected social and economic problems they pose. For background, see

CONANT, J. B. *The American High School Today.* New York: McGraw-Hill, 1959.
____. *Slums and Suburbs.* New York: McGraw-Hill, 1961.
WOLFBEIN, S. L. "The Transition From School to Work," *Journal of the American Personnel and Guidance Association,* Vol. 38 (October 1959).

Data on the labor market experience of dropouts are reported annually from special October surveys of the MRLF, the latest being

SHIFFMAN, J. *Employment of High School Graduates and Dropouts in 1962.* (Special Labor Force Report No. 32.) Washington, D.C.: Department of Labor, Bureau of Labor Statistics, July 1963. (Prior findings are available in Special Labor Force Reports No. 5, May 1960; No. 15, May 1961; and No. 21, May 1962.)

The impact of unemployment on annual work time is reviewed in the annual work-experience studies conducted in connection with the MRLF, the latest being

ROSENFELD, C. "Work Experience of the Population in 1961" (Special Labor Force Report No. 25), *Monthly Labor Review,* December 1962. (Previous findings are in Special Labor Force Reports No. 19, December 1961; and No. 11, December 1960.)

Data on persons working part time for economic reasons are presented in monthly releases on the employment situation by the Department of Labor. Information on unemployed seeking part-time work has been published monthly since January 1963; for background, see

MEREDITH, J. L. "Persons Seeking Part-Time Jobs," *Employment and Earnings* (Bureau of Labor Statistics), June 1963.

International comparisons of unemployment were analyzed by

MYERS, R. J., and CHANDLER, John H. "Comparative Levels of Unemployment in Industrial Countries," Gordon Committee Report, Appendix A, pp. 233–70.

SUMMARY:

PROGRAMS AND POLICIES

IN THIS BOOK WE HAVE PAID PARTICULAR ATTENTION TO THE UNDERLYING FORCES that have constantly shaped and reshaped the manpower profile of the United States.

Changes in the length of our working lives; the upending of the industrial and occupational structure, which has altered the jobs at which people work and even where they work; the ebb and flow of population; automation and technological development; changing attitudes toward various groups in the work force; increasing levels of income and living—all have combined to change the size and composition of the American labor force.

The thrust of these changes has also brought about a substantial and persistent unemployment problem, which we described in the last chapter. As the returns come in for the first part of the 1960s, the evidence seems conclusive that this problem may continue to be of urgent concern for some time to come.

Our concern stems of course from the social and economic costs of unemployment, viewed against the standards of maximum employment and minimum unemployment that the Congress set in the Employment Act of 1946.

As President John F. Kennedy said in his first Manpower Report:

> "The ideal of full employment, in the large sense that each individual shall become all that he is capable of becoming, and shall contribute fully to the well-being of the nation even as he fully shares in that well-being, is at the heart of our democratic belief. If we have never achieved that ideal, neither have we ever for long been content to fall short of it. We have measured ourselves by the persistence of our effort to meet the standard of the full development and use of our human resources. As we still fall short of that standard, we are still not satisfied." (1)

Increasing Employment, Persisting Unemployment

What has underscored the unemployment problem in recent years has been its perseverance at high and even increasing levels in the face of substantial growth in employment.

For example, total employment in the United States went up by a full 10 million between 1947 and 1962—a 17 percent upturn in a decade and a half. But the labor force went up by 13 million, or 21 percent, during the same period, with a resulting increase in unemployment.

This is not just the story of the post–World War II period as a whole. Exactly the same kind of trend took place, for example, between mid-1962 and mid-1963. Employment went up by about 1.3 million persons between July 1962 and July 1963, rising above the 70-million mark for the first time in our history. This was a year during which every major industry division of nonfarm employment showed a job increase, except for mining (which went down by 4000 workers), and during which factory workers' weekly earnings averaged $100, again for the first time in our history.

Yet, in this same 1962–63 period, unemployment rose by 300,000 as the civilian labor force went up by 1.6 million over the year.

Behind this persistence of unemployment is the current moderate rather than rapid economic growth, as well as the inability of many unemployed persons to move into new jobs because of their lack of education and of skills required by technological development.

Technology and Manpower Growth in 1960s

The 1960s are in fact witnessing more and more a head-on collision between two major forces that have been coming together for some time. Both have been examined at some length in this book.

The *first* is advancing technology on and off the farm. Between 1947 and 1961, for example, there was an increase of about 60 percent in the total output of the private economy in the United States; but employment went up by only 11 percent. In fact, man-hours went up by only 3 percent, because the average hours of work put in by workers went down at the same time.

Thus, more than four-fifths of the increase in output since 1947 can be attributed to increasing productivity or output per man-hour. Only the remaining one-fifth is attributable to more people working.

There seems to be nothing in the offing to change the course of this development. In fact, with expenditures on research and development running at about $15 billion a year (triple what they were ten years ago), the likelihood is that productivity will increase at an accelerating rate.

In agriculture, advancing technology has helped decrease employment by 200,000 a year since the end of World War II; total agricultural employment is down by one-third, but total output is up one-third.

In mining, the amount of coal dug by 106 workers in 1947 is now dug by 46 miners; the railroads now employ about 40 percent fewer workers, but handle the same volume of traffic.

It is important to point out also that today's technology has a different kind of effect on jobs than that in earlier periods.

The key technical advance of the 1920s, for example, was large-scale mass production, which required semiskilled workers with limited education and training. The new automatic assembly and processing techniques require highly skilled manpower to develop, direct, and maintain the machines.

Much the same development can be demonstrated in retailing, merchandising, machine vending, and automatic data processing in the clerical fields.

All of this means a very substantial limit to the number and kinds of jobs that unskilled and semiskilled people can fill. It has also cut down the number of unskilled jobs that young people with little education, training, and skill can move into at the beginning of their work careers.

The *second* major force that the 1960s have witnessed is the volume of new job seekers already on the scene and expected for the rest of the decade: 26 million new workers looking for employment, 7.5 million scheduled to be school dropouts with minimal education and training.

Needed Job Growth

What does this all add up to?

If productivity continues to go up at no more than the annual rate it has averaged since World War II, about 24 million jobs will be affected by automation and technological change during the 1960s. This does not necessarily mean that the people holding these jobs will consequently become unemployed. It does mean that alternative employment opportunities have to be available for them.

In addition, a net labor force increase of about 12.5 million persons is expected to occur during the 1960s. This represents the anticipated increase in new workers and job seekers over the number exiting from the labor force for reasons of death, retirement, and marriage.

Thus, it is estimated that during the 1960s we will need an increase in the demand for goods and services, and consequently in production and new jobs, to provide employment opportunities for about 36.5 million workers. This amounts to about 3.7 million jobs a year, or 300,000 a month, to take care of labor force growth and technological change alone.

It has been estimated that an expansion in our gross national product of about $30 billion a year is needed just to keep unemployment from going up in the face of increasing productivity and labor force growth. For the period 1958–63, the total gap between actual gross national product and the amount needed for a 4 percent unemployment rate is estimated at $200 billion. (2)

Economic Growth and Manpower Policy

Practitioners in the field will disagree on the programs and policies to be followed in dealing with the problem that we have described. But there is a growing consensus that we need action both to step up our rate of economic growth and to pursue a more active labor market policy. (3)

The first essential step toward reduction in unemployment is acceleration of economic growth, based on increasing demands for goods and services. There is nothing more needful to reduce some of the classic differentials in unemployment, as well as the overall level of joblessness, than growing economic activity.

At the same time we must deal with the problems being experienced by the distressed industries, areas, and occupational and population groups, including the Negro, as described in this book. This calls for a wide range of concurrent manpower policies.

Included are a variety of recently enacted programs as well as older programs receiving new emphasis: training and retraining of workers; an educational system—vocational as well as academic—that will make young people responsive to upcoming manpower needs; improvement of the mobility of workers in the face of the changing geography of job opportunities that we have described; an effective employment service with good job information and placement services; meaningful career guidance and counseling at school; elimination of discrimination, particularly by age and race, in education, training, and employment.

These programs recognize that meaningful full employment policies call not only for a low overall rate of joblessness but also for a low jobless rate for the industrial, occupational, and population groups described in Chapter 14. In 1955, for instance, when the overall unemployment rate was 4 percent (the "interim" goal toward which the Council of Economic Advisors looks), one out of every ten nonwhites was jobless. A 10 percent unemployment rate also prevailed for unskilled workers and boys eighteen to nineteen years old.

Growing levels of economic activity provide the essential foundation for building programs to help disadvantaged groups. The reverse is also true. A manpower program that matches people with jobs helps economic growth; education, training, and retraining activities also involve investments in plant, equipment, and teachers' salaries, which, like other investments, contribute to growth.

Reference Notes

1. Manpower Report of the President, *op. cit.*, March 1963, p. 11.
2. See Gardner Ackley, "Our National Economy: Present Situation and Outlook," address before Vermont–New Hampshire School of Banking, September 8, 1963 (Council of Economic Advisors, Washington, D.C.).
3. The relevance and importance of economic growth are detailed in the *Economic Report of the President,* January 1962 and January 1963. The arguments for an active labor market policy and its relation to economic growth are presented in S. L. Wolfbein, "Retraining and Labor Market Policy" in *Proceedings of a Conference on Unemployment* (April 1963, University of California at Berkeley). Discussion of various programs to relieve unemployment, against the background of an excellent study of long-term joblessness, can be found in *Unwanted Workers,* by R. C. Wilcock and W. H. Franke (Free Press of Glencoe; New York: Macmillan Co., 1963).

INDEX

A

B

C

D

E

F

G

H

I

J

K

L

M

N

T

U

W

Y